WHEN
FEELING
BAD
IS GOOD

• • • • • • • •

ELLEN McGRATH, Ph.D.

WHEN FEELING BAD IS GOOD

HENRY HOLT AND COMPANY • NEW YORK

Published by Henry Holt and Company, Inc.,
115 West 18th Street, New York, New York 10011.
Published in Canada by Fitzhenry & Whiteside Limited,
91 Granton Drive, Richmond Hill, Ontario L4B 2N5.

Library of Congress Cataloging-in-Publication Data
McGrath, Ellen.
When feeling bad is good / Ellen McGrath.—1st ed.
    p.   cm.
Includes bibliographical references and index.
1. Depression, Mental—Social aspects.   2. Women—Mental Health.
3. Adjustment disorders.   4. Self-help techniques.   I. Title.
RC537.M397   1992   92-14573
616.85′27′0082—dc20   CIP

ISBN 0-8050-1474-8

Henry Holt books are available at special discounts
for bulk purchases for sales promotions, premiums,
fund-raising, or educational use. Special editions
or book excerpts can also be created to specification.
For details contact: Special Sales Director,
Henry Holt and Company, Inc., 115 West 18th Street,
New York, New York 10011.

First Edition—1992

Designed by Victoria Hartman
Printed in the United States of America
Recognizing the importance of preserving the written word,
Henry Holt and Company, Inc., by policy, prints all of its
first editions on acid-free paper.∞

10 9 8 7 6 5 4 3 2

*This book is dedicated with love and appreciation
to my family of origin—
Harry, Joshua, Jordan, Bernadette, and Paul—
and to each member of my family of choice*

CONTENTS

PART III

Putting It All Together

ACKNOWLEDGMENTS

My family of origin and my family of choice have made this book possible.

Without the birth of my two sons, Joshua and Jordan, I would not have felt able to give birth to the next miracle, *When Feeling Bad Is Good*. And without my husband, Harry, this book would undoubtedly not have been written for another twenty years. His willingness to shoulder so much added responsibility made it possible for me to do this project at this time. Only with his support could I justify spending so much time away from the family to do the enormous amount of work this project entailed. The quality of our partnership and love deepened through this process. I feel very grateful for his support, humor, strength, and clinical wisdom, and the fact that he shared my vision of trying to give something of value back to the world. His two children, my stepchildren, Dr. Karen Wexler and Danniel Wexler, could not have been more loving as a brother and a sister to Joshua and Jordan, nor more supportive friends to me.

Our two boys, now 6 and 3, learned very early lessons about the price and value of working passionately on projects and for principles in which you believe. They learned about how to make acceptable compromises to respond to the needs of loved ones and that the work women do is just as valuable as the work men do. It is my strong hope that this experience planted the seeds in them to be leaders of a new generation of men who value equality, diversity, creativity, personal growth, and women.

My family of choice was also critical in the completion of this effort. Dr. Alice Rubenstein, one of my closest friends since my earliest professional days, read every draft of this work. She is one of the most gifted clinicians I know. Her genius has enriched every page of this manuscript and the theory on which it is based. Her emotional support for me and for "the boys" was also a mainstay throughout the three years of the project. Her effort, commitment, and love will never be forgotten and will always be felt.

My adopted sister and office partner, Lynne Deane Barbaro, was the other emotional anchor for me during this process. It was an amazing experience to have so much wisdom and warmth available right next door. I am constantly in awe of Lynne's unusually keen insight about what is critical but often invisible to the eye, as well as her skill at connecting to people on the deepest levels. She was also a superb substitute mother to my kids when intimidating deadlines loomed on the horizon. Her husband and another of my dearest friends for many years, Frank Barbaro, has often been one of my wisest advisors. He has inspired me by making his own dreams come true and is a consistent supporter of my reaching for the stars.

Another vital member of my family of choice is Jerry Holderman. A very talented journalist for the *Los Angeles Times,* he is a trusted friend who rescued me from my intellectualizing and occasionally obscure writing style. When it became clear that I needed help to more clearly translate what I know, Jerry helped me rewrite and edit the book.

For ten months, we labored intensely together. Again and again, I watched him take the best writing I could possibly do and shape it into something better, sometimes a work of verbal translucence. His gift for writing has given this book its quality and clarity. I am enormously grateful for his level of commitment, tenacity, and good spirit, as well as his deep wells of creative talent, his black humor, and the special friendship and partnership we share and continue to enrich.

Others have made essential contributions to the book as well. A pioneer in the project was my agent, Faith Hamlin, who nurtured me through many setbacks in developing the proposal and the book. She combined patience, encouragement, and insight with a keen business savvy to successfully navigate the shoals of the publishing world, not to mention my own fear of success.

Anita Weill used her sensitivity, integrity, and impressive writing skills to help me organize and write the proposal for this book.

Janice Rotchstein and Barbara Winkler, also excellent writers and editors, served as consultants, providing moral support and helping me reorganize and rewrite the initial ideas until they made sense.

Cynthia Vartan, my editor at Henry Holt, deserves special acknowledgment. From the earliest stages of this project, Cynthia shared my vision of what it could be and what this book could mean to women, although her vision was based on much more maturity and wisdom than mine. She excelled at crafting a workable structure for this book from the chaos I sometimes delivered to her desk. My admiration and respect for her abilities and who she is as a person steadily grew as we worked together. I feel privileged to have enjoyed her consistent, stabilizing support, and I hope to work together again on a future project.

T George Harris, founding editor of *Psychology Today* and *American Health* magazines, is not only one of the most engaging people I know, he's also one of the most inspiring. His drive, creativity, and vision with regard to the utility and meaning of psychology is unparalleled. He is one of the strongest and most positive forces in American psychology today. The fact that he took an active interest in this project and in supporting me during its development was one of my greatest rewards for this arduous labor. His warm voice echoes throughout these pages in one way or another. His wife, Anne Roberts, was also an inspirational force who served as a role model for how to write and how to live.

Several other close friends have emerged as guardian angels for me and for the book. Mary and Blair Brewster were instrumental in developing several key concepts and offering a gem for each section they read. They were and are there for me and our children in every way. Lora Piazza, with her brilliant mind and warm heart, is another person who consistently comes through. Only a true friend would sit for days researching endless footnotes for the book and still make jokes and offer even more help.

My clients in both New York and California have been wonderful teachers. They demonstrated remarkable courage and commitment in their willingness to take risks as we developed and refined the action strategy techniques, and I thank them for sharing their inner journeys with me.

The American Psychological Association (APA) National Task Force on Women and Depression provided another foundation for this work. Special thanks to my buddies and coauthors of the Task Force book: Drs. Gwen Keita, Bonnie Strickland, and Nancy Russo. I also want to recognize Drs. Laura Brown, Lillian Comas Dias, Jean Hamilton, Margaret Jensvold, and Susan Nolen-Hoeksema for their contributions to the task force. Through the example of their own lives and their knowledge of the psychology of women, they taught me priceless lessons about women, depression, and myself.

Several other special women have also been especially supportive. Pamela Armstrong and Lisa Wyatt of the Public Affairs Office of the APA have been instrumental in teaching me how to be more effective in the media and throwing me life preservers when I begin drowning in insecurity and performance anxiety. Deborah Szekely, owner of the Golden Door and Rancho La Puerta Health Spas, taught me key lessons about mind ↔ body potential, as did Lu Blecher, who has converted physical handicaps into emotional wisdom that she has graciously shared with me.

Lillian Smith, a senior producer at *Donahue,* deserves warm recognition for her diligent efforts in presenting the findings of the APA Task Force, including a taped sample of group Action Therapy. The show provided hope to millions of depressed women. And special thanks to Oprah Winfrey, Joan Lunden, Sally Jessy Raphael, and Phil Donahue for tackling such important topics in psychology in such a sensitive and caring way.

Many other people made various contributions that are deeply appreciated: Brett Barbaro, Casey Barbaro, Patricia Bellucci, Sally Besco, Dr. Karen Blaker, Dr. Matty Canter, Linda Chapin, Gary Costa, Andre Covell, Annie Diablo, Marge Doering, Harold Dolph, Zelma Dolph, Janet Eastman, Ali Fadakar, Dr. Ray Fowler, Dr. Don Freidheim, Dr. Herb Freudenberger, Ellen Golden, Dr. Leonard Goodstein, Dr. Stanley Graham, Dr. Sandy Haber, Jack Herzberg, Jan Hoagland, Greg Hamlin, Lee Handy, Angela Hernandez, Sheila Holder, Jim Holderman, Judy Holderman, Kathy Holderman, Christine Jones, Neil Korlekar, Roseanne Kotzer, Susan Kraber, Ruth Lawrence, Laurel Best Linton, Peter Liu, Ginny Lowe, Chris and Lee McGrath, Anne Mello, Tim Miller, Judy Neeve, Gary Parks, Joyce Pederson, Anne Roberts, Gregg Schwenk, Dorothy Sebell, Gail Sheehy, Lottchen Shivers, Carolyn Smith, Dr. Charles Spielberger, Javier Villalobos, Pauline Wampler, Dr. Jack Wiggins, Marya Yee, and Dr. Karen Zager.

Finally, I want to thank my mother, Bernadette, and my grandmother, Muriel, for continually reminding me how strong and how smart women can be. They have consistently reinforced the fact that we all can choose to dance rather than shuffle through our lives, no matter what our age.

WHEN
FEELING
BAD
IS GOOD

· · · · · · ·

INTRODUCTION

To the outsider looking in, my life twelve years ago seemed too good to be true. And it was. At 34, I held a prestigious faculty position in the Department of Psychiatry and Human Behavior at the University of California, Irvine Medical School. I had a thriving private practice and had just begun working in the media, doing psychology commentaries for a Southern California all-news radio station. I had good friends. I drove a red sports car and lived in a little white house with a sweeping view of the ocean and hills in the beautiful seaside community of Laguna Beach.

On clear days, I loved sitting on my deck and gazing at Catalina Island on the horizon some twenty-six miles out to sea. But closer to home, my vision was blurred. I couldn't see a future for myself that held any real promise or purpose. I had lost hope and control over my life. I was divorced, forty pounds overweight, miserably lonely, and totally frustrated in my search for a supportive, secure partner to share my life. The more successful I became in my career, the more trouble I seemed to have in my relationships. Often I sank into a recurrent depression and overate. It wasn't unusual for me to devour an entire bag of Pepperidge Farm cookies at one sitting during those dark times.

The cookies, of course, rarely helped anything. In fact, those sugar binges only made matters worse. The next morning I not only felt depressed but fat, too. More than once I seriously considered driving into the garage, closing the garage door behind me, and leaving the engine running. I was haunted by an ache that had no name. I saw no other way out.

There was only one reason I didn't commit suicide during those moments of total despair. I couldn't justify the damage it would do to my best friend, Alice, and to others who loved me. At that point, it

3

was my love for them that saved my life. I knew deep in my soul that they didn't deserve to carry the burden of lifelong wounds and pain inflicted by me just because I was unable to handle my own depression.

You would think that since I was trained to identify and help heal depression in others and had achieved measurable success in doing so, I could have done a better job with myself. Yet like a number of health and mental health professionals, I found it impossible to "heal thyself." I was totally unaware just how severe my own depression was and how badly I needed help. Worse, I didn't even identify my bad feelings as "depression." All I knew was that I felt bad far more often than I felt good.

When I could no longer deny that something was terribly wrong, I went for professional help. At first, acknowledging the grim reality that I was clinically depressed made me feel much worse. I felt helpless, vulnerable, inadequate, and alone. But I wasn't alone at all. In fact, female professionals have a rate of depression three times higher than the general female population, and we commit suicide more frequently than men and nonprofessional women.[1]

Even though some women are more culturally or genetically vulnerable than others, depression is an equal-opportunity illness. It cuts across all socioeconomic and racial lines and affects women in all walks of life. It's estimated that at least one of every four women in America will suffer from a serious depression in her lifetime. There are currently more than 7 million American women with diagnosable depressions that won't be resolved without professional help.[2] The sad reality is that only one in five of these women will receive the help she needs.[3] The rest will continue to suffer, even though there are increasingly effective treatments available for depression, if women will only seek them out.

I know how hard it can be to take that first step. It took me many years to accept that I had been periodically depressed since the age of 10, when my mother asked my warm but weak Irish Catholic father to leave our home. Three years later, my parents divorced. My father was devastated. He fled our hometown of Portland and moved to eastern Oregon to escape the pain and start over again. I saw him only every other weekend for the next four years. And even though my mother and I lived under the same roof, I rarely saw much more of her. Burdened with the relentless pressure of being a single parent, she had too much responsibility and too little time and money. Not surprisingly, she became angry, overwhelmed, and depressed. She developed and taught us solid survival skills, but she rarely had anything left emotionally to give me and my two brothers.

When I was 17, my father and my 14-year-old brother were killed one rainy Sunday afternoon in a violent head-on collision. I felt indescribably alone. Even though my weekend visits with my father had been brief, they had been consistent and were very nurturing. They provided me with the sense of balance I needed so much at that time in my life. Grief-stricken, my mother became even more withdrawn and less emotionally available than she had been before.

The trauma and loss was too much for me to absorb. I needed help, but there was no one for me to turn to. In Portland, in the fifties, it was considered a humiliating sign of weakness to go into therapy. Even if I'd thought of it, neither I nor any of the adults in my life would have had a clue where to turn for professional help. Unable to confront and resolve the pain on my own, I denied my feelings and buried them deep inside. Effective therapy could have saved me years of pain and suffering. Instead, depression became a way of life for me from that point forward.

I began overeating, cultivating fat as insulation between myself and what I saw as an uncaring, insensitive world. Later, I overworked, frantically striving to be the "high achiever good girl" who could justify being loved because of how much I *did* rather than who I *was*. If someone who mattered to me didn't show me the attention I craved, I blamed myself and tried harder. I became an Oregon state debate champion in high school, striving to communicate more and more effectively. I'd become addicted to recognition and validation since my parents' divorce. I mistakenly thought this kind of attention would somehow fill the emptiness that continued to grow inside me. After my father died, my attention addiction grew worse.

Depression remained a constant companion during my years at University of California, Berkeley, where I somehow managed to graduate *magna cum laude* with my degree in psychology. It later traveled east with me to Washington, D.C., where I earned a Ph.D. in clinical psychology at George Washington University.

I was independent and outwardly successful all right, but I still wasn't getting the love and support I wanted more than anything in the world. It took me twenty years and a great deal of self-help and therapy to realize that my overeating, overachievement, relationship failures, and recurrent "bad moods" were largely the result of a lifetime of denying and avoiding my anger and pain.

I'd be lying if I didn't tell you there were many moments when the growth process was terrifying. Sometimes I wondered whether I would survive. There were times when I drove straight from my therapy session to the local market, where I would buy all the cookies, candy, bread, and jam I needed for an evening of emotional eating.

But I knew intellectually that self-exploration was my only chance to repair the childhood damage I'd left unresolved for so many years and learn to manage current stress that often felt unmanageable. I discovered firsthand that by confronting my bad feelings, I was finally able to resolve my pain and leave the baggage of the past behind. For me, this process of feeling the pain and acting to resolve it has led to a freedom from depression I never thought possible.

Today I have what I need to make my life work. The media stereotypes had insisted that due to my "advanced age," my chances for marriage were doomed. However, at 37, I met another psychologist at an American Psychological Association national convention and married him two and a half years later. He's a growth partner and a wonderful father to our two healthy sons, who were born when I was 40 and 43. To be with him, I relocated to a loft in the SoHo section of Manhattan and started my life all over again.

Starting over meant building another private practice and a new network of friends. I joined the faculty of New York University. Maintaining my California connection, I began conducting workshops and therapy groups on both coasts, as well as in other cities across the country. These experiences taught me how similar the patterns of female depression are, no matter where women live, and sometimes no matter what women do. Based in New York, I also had an opportunity to do considerably more media work, which I'd begun in California but had been too insecure to pursue. I sometimes still feel insecure when I see myself on television, but the opportunity to learn and grow by sharing experiences and information is too rewarding to allow my fears to silence me.

I sometimes still reach for a cookie or two when I'm feeling stressed or when I'm burning the midnight oil on a work project. Food, however, is no longer the crutch it once was. Today I do what I do because I'm genuinely excited by learning, living, and loving more fully, and by supporting others to live as powerfully as they possibly can. Depression is no longer a lifestyle. Best of all, I have people to love and who love me. My husband and I survived enormous battles early in our relationship and went on to build a strong marriage. I also feel supported by my "family of choice," a circle of carefully selected friends who are as close, if not closer, than my own family.

I'm certainly not alone in overcoming my past and breaking free from depression. There are many inspiring stories of healing to be shared. Some can be found in biographies and psychology books. Others can be heard in classes and in self-help groups and are passed on person-to-person by women and men who have quietly and effectively done this personal growth without professional or group support.

How did we do it? The same way you can. We acknowledged that there are times when it's perfectly healthy and normal to be depressed, especially if you're a woman living in this culture. To not feel angry or victimized by some of our typical female experiences would be to live in a fantasy world of denial. Yet until now we haven't had a name for this depressing aspect of contemporary female experience. Because we couldn't name it, we couldn't understand or resolve it. As a result, we women have remained far more depressed, repressed, and less powerful and creative than we need to be.

So what do we call it when our feelings are healthy, "good," and appropriate reactions to unhealthy, "bad" realities? After many years of researching and treating depression, I've developed the term "Healthy Depression" to describe this aspect of our female experience. I became increasingly convinced that many female depressions are not the result of medical conditions, nor are they as unique to each individual as existing theory and practice would have us believe. We needed a category to account for realistic bad feelings.

At first, the notion of feeling bad being good may seem like a contradiction in terms. Isn't that like saying something right can be wrong or something black can be white? Not really. Bad feelings can be good because they can teach us the most important life lessons and inspire and motivate us to grow.

We've all heard the expression "No pain, no gain" in relation to physical fitness. The same holds true for mental health. Seeing reality accurately—painful as it may sometimes be—motivates us to change. Experiencing pain and depression and making difficult changes are often necessary steps on the path to growth and true satisfaction. I don't know anyone who has achieved a psychological success who hasn't felt worse before feeling better, who hasn't wanted to quit before she achieved a breakthrough.

Our bad feelings serve as a springboard toward growth and power. We can reclaim and transform the negative energy we had devoted to suppressing and denying these bad feelings and use it instead to set our lives moving in a healthy new direction. Once we accept that there are times when feeling bad is good, we've taken an important step toward living more fulfilling lives, because we're finally free to use our bad feelings positively and creatively rather than letting them anchor us in depression.

To help you understand and accept this process—and learn to use it to empower you in breaking free from your own depressions—is why I wrote this book. My clients and students have been encouraging me to write it for many years. They've been very enthusiastic about sharing with other women the strategies that have worked for them, and they've been remarkably supportive in contributing their ideas and suggestions throughout its development. Every one of the action strategies you'll read in this book has evolved through our work together and has been used in my workshops, therapy and support groups, and private practice. Many of my clients and students, in fact, have allowed me to share their stories in this book, though their names, occupations, and other identifying details have been changed to ensure their privacy.

I finally realized just how powerful these action strategies had been in my own life when I stood on stage at the American Psychological Association (APA) national convention last summer and received a Presidential Citation for mobilizing psychologists during the Gulf War, and later when I delivered my presidential address to the APA's Division of Psychotherapy. I was also in the middle of writing this book, which my depression would have sabotaged if I'd attempted it even a few years earlier. I could not have imagined such experiences even ten years before.

Most important, I had loving family and friends around me and available to me. Considering how riddled my background had been with loss and dysfunctional relationships and how depressed I had been as a result, these achievements speak more clearly than words about how much we can change our lives when we free our energy from depression. This growing realization was the driving force to complete this book.

The other inspiration for this book was a National Task Force I chaired for the APA. In 1986, a close friend and colleague, Dr. Bonnie Strickland, a professor of psychology at the University of Massachusetts, was elected president of the 100,000-member professional organization. While discussing possible agendas for her presidency, we agreed that one of the most compelling problems in America was the amount of undiagnosed and untreated depression, particularly among women. Are women more vulnerable to depression, we wondered, or do we just talk about our feelings more openly? What could be done to address the problem, effect real change on a national level, and improve the quality of women's lives?

To explore and answer these questions, we developed a multidisciplinary group of twenty-five of the top experts in the country to study the issue of women and depression. Women and men representing all mental health disciplines, as well as several mental health consumer groups and government agencies, joined forces to assess state-of-the-art research and clinical information on the causes and most effective treatment methods for depressed women. Colorado Congresswoman Pat Schroeder served on our advisory board and was instrumental in organizing a congressional briefing for presenting our findings and helping us define and develop agendas for the new Office of Women's Health at the National Institutes of Health.

Several years and many meetings later, the APA National Task Force on Women and Depression published its comprehensive final report, *Women and Depression: Risk Factors and Treatment Issues,* in December 1990. The report, which is available to the public through the publications office of the APA, detailed the major risk factors and causes of women's vulnerability to depression and offered an overview of the latest treatment technologies. The report also examined how depression specifically affected "special populations," such as women in poverty, the elderly, women of color, lesbians, substance abusers, and professional women. Although the report was written mainly for mental health professionals, it included a number of new and important findings that turned out to be of great value to the general population. Many of those findings are included in this book.

To our surprise, our work generated a great deal of national media attention. Articles about our findings appeared in more than three hundred newspapers and our results were covered extensively on television news shows throughout the country. We were delighted with the degree of media interest in the subject, because of our strong commitment to educating the public on the issues and needs of depressed women. We were also enthusiastic to discover how receptive the public was, not only to understanding why women are more depressed than men, but to learning what can be done about it. As one reporter observed, it seemed as though depression could finally come out of the closet and be acknowledged not as a failure or weakness but as an illness or a deficit in life skills.

I've written this book with the hope and vision of helping women become more powerful and more aware of how to put depression in its place, to acknowledge that it's often a healthy reaction to an unhealthy culture.

When Feeling Bad Is Good is for the many wonderful women and men who have inspired and supported me in writing it. It's for the young woman who finds herself feeling depressed and confused by the many choices she faces in a rapidly changing world. It's for the housewife who feels trapped and is convinced that her quality of life will never improve. It's for the struggling single mother overwhelmed by her responsibilities. It's for the professional woman who's exhausted from juggling her career, home, and family in her quest to have it all. It's for the single woman trying to carve out her niche in a couples-oriented culture. It's for women of color who are served a double helping of discrimination and depression by our culture. It's for lesbians faced with the challenge of building loving relationships in a society that pays lip service to freedom of choice and expression but is often threatened by people who exercise either. It's for the older woman who can't escape sometimes feeling ignored, inadequate, and devalued as she ages.

We're living in a unique, exciting era in which millions of women are taking the first steps toward having the freedom and power they need. Women today are part of a transitional generation, caught in an extraordinary moment in time between a traditional past and a "liberated" present and future. As a result, there have never been such enormous psychological demands on us. But at the same time, there have never been more choices and opportunities for women to achieve so much in so many arenas. We've accepted the challenge, begun to clarify our goals, and faced the process of enormous change in both ourselves and the world. But that change is often intimidating, and each of us needs and deserves quality support along the way. This book offers such support in its practical, innovative strategies for resolving many of the old and new problems we all face.

To use the book most effectively, take your time with the first chapter to make sure you understand the concepts of Healthy and Unhealthy Depression. It's important to appreciate fully the distinction between the two and to recognize how significant a role depression has played in your life. While Healthy Depression is normal and even predictable at various stages in women's lives, Unhealthy Depression is not. It's a frightening, draining condition that can be life threatening. If it's not resolved, Healthy Depression can easily evolve into Unhealthy Depression. That's exactly what happened to me. My first depression, which was a healthy and appropriate reaction to so much loss so early in life, remained unresolved for too many years. Because I ignored it and had also inherited a vulnerability to depression, my depression grew and became increasingly unhealthy as the years passed. Only through professional help and a concentrated effort using a number of the self-help strategies in this book was I able to overcome it.

In Part I of this book, you'll also learn more about the destructive power of Inherited Depression. We'll explore how vulnerable you may be to it, and why. You'll learn, too, about the Traditional Core, a woman's cultural conscience, which lives deep within every woman and can be both a blessing and a curse.

In Part II, we'll examine the new designations for each of the six Healthy Depressions. The first three are the major Healthy Depressions, those that virtually every woman will face during some phase of her life. In fact, many of us carry the vulnerability to these depressions from cradle to grave. They are: Victimization Depression, the most difficult and dangerous because it is generated by the emotional, economic, physical, and sexual abuse targeted at women in our culture, and it can most easily move into Unhealthy Depression;

Relationship Depression, which stems from a lack of relationships or conflicts and losses within the relationships we do have; and Age Rage Depression, the anger and bad feelings women have from being culturally devalued, isolated, and restricted as we grow older.

The remaining Healthy Depressions are more episodic and less potentially destructive, but they are common enough to cause millions of women significant discomfort at various times in their lives. Depletion Depression is the drain of energy that comes from role overload or role conflict between traditional and nontraditional roles; Body Image Depression results from the feeling that our bodies are inadequate or defective unless they meet the impossible standards of physical perfection our culture imposes on women; and Mind ↔ Body Depression is caused by hormonal and biochemical imbalances interacting with psychological and social factors to make us feel ill.

If the Healthy Depressions add up and you find yourself slipping into Unhealthy Depression, Chapter 10, "Beyond Self-help," will acquaint you with the symptoms and varieties of Unhealthy Depression and the most effective therapeutic approaches being used today. Chapter 11, "Putting It All Together," summarizes the best information available to date on how to use action strategies to better manage any type of depression, especially the Healthy Depressions.

Each of the chapters on the six Healthy Depressions features a quiz or exercise to help you evaluate how vulnerable you are to that particular depression. The quizzes are not formal or standardized professional tests developed in a research laboratory. They've evolved from practical, firsthand experience and, in fact, many of the questions have been suggested, reviewed, and refined by women who have attended the Healthy Depression classes and workshops.

Even if the quiz tells you that the particular depression is not relevant for you at this time, it may be helpful to read the action strategies at the end of each chapter, since they include many ideas and approaches that are valuable in managing other kinds of depression and anxiety.

There's certainly no right answer or approach in the evolving theory and treatment of depression. In deciding which of these coping strategies to use, trust your instincts. Think of them as a menu of choices, and select the techniques that best fit your style and personality. Some women prefer more intellectual approaches and like to make lists and practice imagery exercises. Others prefer a more active, intuitive approach. They need emotional release and favor action strategies that tend to evoke and express intense feeling. Some women do better interacting and supporting each other in doing the exercises, while there are those who need to be alone in order to focus, concentrate, and pursue their own individual growth.

All of the exercises, techniques, and strategies in this book have been refined through research, clinical practice, and personal experience. I've done every one of the action strategies myself and appreciate the challenges that some of them may present for you. I encourage you to take risks. Be open-minded and flexible enough to experiment with exercises and techniques that may at first glance seem foolish or irrelevant. For example, exercises involving the making of dolls or hitting symbolic objects are typically done in a workshop with group support. My clients urged me to include these exercises, however, because it is these very action strategies, which are often the most challenging and uncomfortable, that are often the most productive and liberating in reducing or alleviating depression.

For several years I've urged other professionals to consider that if all they're doing in treating depressed women is listening and talking, they're not doing enough. Those of us developing alternative techniques to the traditional depression therapies have found that active processes—such as safe expressions of anger; creative expression of pain through art, movement, and letters; and making complex internal states more real through the use of symbols and rituals —are extremely effective approaches in overcoming depression.

In fact, a number of my colleagues and I are so enthusiastic about the potential of this work that we're developing a new theory called Action Therapy. We've begun developing a textbook of theory and exercises for other professionals describing how to use these action techniques in treating depression. We are also conducting research on which techniques are most effective and why. You don't need to wait for research results or a textbook to try these strategies, however. The ones in this book are designed for self-help and they work very well without professional assistance.

It is my hope and goal that the ideas and strategies in this book will enable you to find strength in your vulnerabilities, convert your depression into new energy sources, and examine and clarify your life priorities. You'll then be empowered to live your life more consciously, creatively, honestly, and depression-free than ever before.

PART I

. . . .

A New Understanding of Female Depression

·1·

"HEALTHY DEPRESSION":
A NEW MODEL FOR WOMEN

Women truly are more depressed than men, primarily due to their experience of being female in our contemporary culture.
American Psychological Association National
Task Force on Women and Depression, 1990

Does it really matter whether my depression is Healthy or Unhealthy?" wondered Jamie, one of the students in my Psychology of Women class at New York University. "When I feel this bad, I couldn't care less *what* kind of depression I have. That's sort of like getting hit by a truck and wondering whether it was a Ford or a Chevy. To tell you the truth, I'm not even sure if what I'm feeling lately *is* depression. All I know is that I'm feeling bad a lot more than I'm feeling good."

At 21, Jamie was living away from home for the first time and found her new independence intimidating and stressful. She was attending college in the heart of Manhattan after growing up in a quiet Connecticut village. Two years of community college in her hometown hadn't prepared Jamie academically or emotionally for the challenge that awaited her at NYU.

An unannounced visit from Jamie's parents a month after her move to New York certainly didn't help. They wanted to tell her face to face that they had finally decided to divorce and were selling the home in which Jamie was raised. She knew her mother and father had been unhappy for many years, but the news still devastated her. Even though Jamie had been relieved to escape the mounting tension between her parents, she found a certain comfort and security in knowing that she could go home for a visit whenever she wanted.

17

During the months that followed, Jamie felt increasingly melancholy. The adjustment to a new school and life in the big city was tougher than she had ever imagined. She was having trouble making friends, rarely dated, and was struggling to maintain the grades that had come so easily in junior college.

Jamie felt embarrassed and ashamed that things weren't going exactly as she planned. She often wondered how everything had gone so wrong. For two years, she had counted the weeks until she could leave the monotony of her hometown and move to New York City. But the Big Apple had soured. Now that she was living there, she felt short-tempered, agitated, and frustrated.

No matter how old you are, where you live, or what you do for a living, it's a safe bet that you can identify with some of Jamie's feelings of depression. How many times in the past few weeks do you recall feeling "moody," "blue," "down in the dumps," irritable, or so tired that you just wanted to withdraw and do nothing? Once? Twice? Every day?

Chances are you've experienced some degree of depression over the past week. It goes with the cultural territory and the reality of being female in the nineties. And, if you're like Jamie and most other women, it's also very likely that you deny your depressed feelings, because you've grown up believing there's something wrong with you if you feel sad instead of happy. Many of us refuse to slow down long enough to take a closer look at our lives because we're terrified of what we might see. Some of us put our bad feelings on the emotional back burner and allow them to simmer because we either don't know how to overcome them or we lack the desire and drive to take responsibility for our lives.

Many of us convince ourselves that if we just ignore our depression and suffer silently, it'll magically disappear. And sometimes it does, for a while anyway. But inevitably it returns until we resolve the problems that stirred up the bad feelings in the first place. Others think acknowledging that they're depressed is a sign of weakness, rather than a positive first step toward growth. In fact, while half of those interviewed in a 1991 survey said they or a family member had suffered the pain of depression, 43 percent of the same group saw depression as "a sign of personal or emotional weakness."[1] If only I were stronger, many believe, I wouldn't feel this way.

But the reality is that sometimes we do feel bad for some very good reasons—as do an increasing number of American women. Depression has become the emotional equivalent of the common cold. And according to the report of the American Psychological Association (APA) National Task Force on Women and Depression, depression has become a mental health epidemic among women today. We're living in an era in which women have a unique vulnerability to depression. Physical and sexual abuse is on the rise, economic discrimination against women seems more resistant to change, and marriage and sex roles are more confusing and in flux than ever before.[2]

In addition, because of culturally conditioned negative thinking, fear of success, the increasing likelihood of becoming a single mother, our vulnerability to relationship disappointments, and role overload from trying to be everything to everybody, it's not surprising that twice as many women as men suffer from depression. Some experts would double that number, depending on the kind of depression we're talking about.

According to Dr. Marty Seligman, a leading depression expert at the University of Pennsylvania, we are estimated to suffer from depression ten times more often than our grandmothers.[3] In response, we take two-thirds of the antidepressant or antianxiety drugs consumed in this country, and our numbers continue to climb. And as Jamie's story reminds us, younger women are more at risk for depression than ever before. Their suicide rate has skyrocketed 300 percent in the past twenty years, and it's now estimated that nearly one out of every three women 18 to 24 is significantly depressed.[4]

As shocking and unsettling as these statistics can be, considering the multiple daily pressures and the depressing realities of so many women's lives, we need to be congratulated for not being even more depressed than we are.

What exactly is this state of mind we call depression, anyway? One of the least complicated definitions is in Webster's Ninth New Collegiate Dictionary:

> a state of feeling sad . . . marked especially by sadness, inactivity, difficulty in thinking or concentration, a significant increase or decrease in appetite and time spent sleeping,

feelings of dejection and hopelessness, and sometimes suicidal
tendencies; a lowering of vitality or functional activity.

When we're depressed, we usually suffer silently with the ache we
feel deep inside, unaware of just why we're feeling moody or having
such a bad day. We may believe there's something wrong with us,
which gives us a built-in excuse for why things aren't going well in
our lives. We manage to cope, but often not very well. We either see
our problems as insignificant or so overwhelming that we feel defeated before we even begin to resolve them. We "get by with a little
help from our friends," until our friends get discouraged or even
disgusted at offering so much support and seeing so little change in
our behavior.

Having discussed depression with thousands of women in the
classes, therapy groups, and workshops I've conducted since 1975,
I've heard women of all ages and from all walks of life describe their
depression. Their comments and descriptions paint a vivid and re-
vealing picture of what depression is and how it feels. They say,
among other things, that depression is "feeling bad and sad," "feeling lost, alone, and scared," "when I feel aggressive and have a very
short fuse," "feeling totally overwhelmed, like I'm falling into a bottomless black pit," "feeling disgusted and disappointed with myself
and just wanting to be left alone," "a physical pain, usually in the pit
of my stomach," "when I have no energy and can't remember or
concentrate," "when I make a secret run to the store and gorge on
Hostess Ho-Hos."

Each description is accurate, because each of us experiences depression differently. Unlike a physical illness, which often has a
more distinct pattern of symptoms, depression rarely runs on a predictable continuum. You don't automatically climb the staircase
from everyday blues to suicidal tendencies one step at a time. Depression can ebb and flow. You can feel up one day, down the next.
For some of us, depression is an occasional visitor who arrives quietly and vanishes without warning. For others, it's an invisible, aggressive intruder that seizes control of our bodies and our minds.

Depression can encompass a range of emotions that stem from
real or perceived losses, as well as from feeling helpless or out of
control or from engaging in negative, pessimistic thinking. Because
depression wears many disguises, it can be difficult to identify and

even more challenging to treat. But however you experience depression, the most important thing to remember is that it isn't necessarily a bad condition.

The notion that certain kinds of depression can be healthy and "good" is new, but after my years teaching and in private practice, I've become more and more convinced this is true. In fact, our current models of depression are inaccurate and incomplete in describing the female experience. Women are often defined in extremes: we're either "well" or "sick." True, we are permitted to experience the occasional, everyday "blues" (perhaps they're considered more acceptable because men also experience and acknowledge them). But what about our bad feelings, those that are more than "a bad day" but less than being sick or neurotic? What about the bad feelings women uniquely experience as the result of economic discrimination, emotional and sexual abuse, and being treated as second-class citizens in a society in which men continue to control most of the resources? There *is* a vague term, "Adjustment Disorder,"[5] but typically it is used to placate nervous clients who don't want a "damaging" diagnosis on their insurance forms. There is simply no psychiatric or psychological diagnosis currently available to describe the degree and depth of women's appropriate bad feelings toward a fundamentally sexist culture that devalues its female members. Consequently, we are shamed and blamed for too many of our depressed feelings.

To attempt to bridge this gap and begin a dialogue about an appropriate name and model for this aspect of female experience, I've developed a new model of depression: "Healthy Depression." It's not a term you'll find in textbooks. And, it's a concept that may make some of my mental health colleagues uneasy, because it seems to simplify a complex experience like depression into a simple dichotomy of "healthy" and "unhealthy."

In reality, feelings are too fluid, dynamic, and subjective in their meaning and experience to be so easily classified. But we need more practical, accessible terms that allow us quickly and simply to identify and describe women's predictable encounters with depression. "Healthy" and "Unhealthy" Depression and feeling "good" and "bad" are useful concepts because we currently have no way in our culture to efficiently identify and validate this aspect of our internal reality. Our current mental health terminology is still too dry and inaccessible for most people to really understand and apply. In a disturbing number of cases, even the doctors themselves don't fully understand what they're talking about when they use the term "depression." In fact, it wasn't until 1980 that "the experts" generally agreed on clinical definitions of the different kinds of Unhealthy Depressions.

So instead of relying solely on professionals and clinical jargon such as "atypical depression" or "clinical depression," we need a shorthand way to label our experience of bad feelings. Quick, accurate self-diagnosis is one of the most important steps to keeping Healthy Depression from developing into potentially life-threatening Unhealthy Depression.

Introducing the concept of Healthy Depression doesn't deny that depression, like a cold or a headache, is a symptom that something is wrong, that you need to take care of yourself. But it doesn't mean that you're inadequate, immature, incompetent, hysterical, weak, or headed for a nervous breakdown. That's why it's important to distinguish between depressions that are "healthy" and those that are "unhealthy."

Healthy Depression is defined as realistic feelings of pain, sadness, and disappointment (accompanied at times by guilt, anger, and/or anxiety) from negative experiences such as traumas, losses, discrimination, unfair treatment, and unresolved past damage. Women experiencing Healthy Depression can still function, although usually not as well as they would otherwise.

Unhealthy Depression is defined as an inability to function in one or more basic life areas (such as work, relationships, body functions, etc.) due to the depth of bad feelings. These bad feelings can be caused by changes in body chemistry, genetic vulnerability, and/or too many painful psychological experiences that we are unable to resolve.

As you can see, the main difference between Healthy and Unhealthy Depression is the ability to function. With an Unhealthy Depression, we're unable to function adequately in at least one important area of our lives, no matter how hard we try. With Healthy Depression, however, we manage to interact with other people and tend to the daily details of our lives, even though we may feel like one of the "walking wounded."

Unlike many Unhealthy Depressions, Healthy Depressions are not typically biologically rooted. They are cultural in origin, and are feelings, however troubling, that are reasonably based on the events contributing to them. Healthy Depressions also stem from struggles with our Traditional Core, the internal conflicts that result from centuries of female conditioning and cultural punishment. The Traditional Core makes feelings of inadequacy and self-hatred seem like a natural, normal part of being female.

Healthy Depressions are less severe than Unhealthy Depressions because they can be resolved through awareness and action and without professional help. They require attention, but with effort and determination, the bad feelings that cause them can be converted into new sources of energy, growth, creativity, and power.

What kind of bad feelings are we talking about? Kate, 39, knows all too well. A happily married homemaker, she's been living with a growing feeling of discontentment and restlessness for the past year. She and her husband, Bill, are both highly committed to raising their two children. Kate helps out part-time with Bill's manufacturing business and is his greatest source of support and creative advice. Kate's real passion, however, is her music. Over the years, she's become an accomplished classical pianist.

As much as she enjoys her music and working at the company, it is no longer enough. Their youngest child is about to start kindergarten and Kate feels the time has come to decide what to do with the rest of her life. The problem is that she has absolutely no idea what she wants to do. She's begun waking up at night, worrying about her future, the small wrinkles around her eyes, and the ten pounds that have crept on over the past year. These vulnerabilities bother her so much that she avoids looking at herself in the mirror. As Kate's insecurities grow, so does her irritability with those she loves. She's been so edgy and short-tempered recently that her exasperated son recently snapped back: "Get a grip, Mom!"

Christine, on the other hand, has an iron grip on her life, yet she's begun to wonder if everything she's worked for is slipping through her fingers. A labor relations attorney for a large Washington, D.C., law firm, she's been working twelve to fourteen hours a day, six days a week since joining the firm two years ago. Even though she often feels more weary than she ever has, slowing down isn't an option. She's competing with a large pool of attorneys for a permanent spot with the firm. Every morning, as she trudges into the office before seven, she reminds herself that in her profession, the rule of thumb is "up or out" within seven years. She's determined to move up and figures she can do anything for a few more years if it means such big financial and status rewards later.

But recently Christine has begun to question whether the rewards are worth the price. Her back has been "killing her" for the last few months, especially when her stress level skyrockets before project deadlines. She has virtually no free time to pursue relationships and is growing tired of eating takeout food alone every night in front of the television set before falling into bed. To make matters worse, a secretary recently confided that two of the men on Christine's legal team had received significantly larger year-end bonuses than she had. One of the men has less experience than Christine and the other spends considerably less time at the office. She's frustrated, exhausted, physically uncomfortable, and feeling victimized by economic discrimination and the subtle sexism that permeates the firm.

Although Kate and Christine live very different lives, both are struggling with Healthy Depressions. Kate has the Healthy Depressions often generated by the Traditional Core, with some Body Image Depression and Age Rage Depression thrown in for good measure. Christine is more comfortable being nontraditional, but is swamped with Depletion Depression, Mind ↔ Body Depression from her back problems, and Victimization Depression from her experiences with traditional male systems.

In contrast to Kate's and Christine's Healthy Depressions, which are uncomfortable but allow them to continue to interact with others and tend to daily details, Unhealthy Depression prevents us from functioning in at least one basic area of our life: work, relationships, ability to eat or sleep, capacity to enjoy activities, concentrate, or remember. Unhealthy Depression is an inappropriate exaggeration of bad feelings, making things much worse than they really are. Unhealthy Depressions can also be appropriate reactions to a bombardment of losses and/or traumas. With an Unhealthy Depression, we feel unusually tired—like we've hit a brick wall—and often withdraw, staying mostly in bed or on the couch for days or even weeks. We may feel burned out at work, avoid people who care about us, lack a sense of excitement about anyone or anything, and become increasingly irritated over the smallest things. We literally shut down and shut out the world.

Unhealthy Depression can also result from a chemical process with a life of its own. Even if you didn't have a chemical imbalance to begin with, you may develop one over time if your Unhealthy Depression is not resolved, because prolonged depression drains biochemicals you need to feel good. The diagram below summarizes the relationship between Healthy and Unhealthy Depression so that you can quickly see the difference.

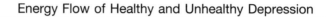

Energy Flow of Healthy and Unhealthy Depression

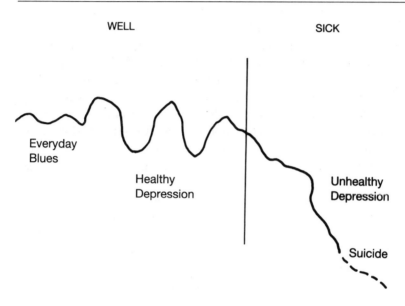

As you can see, "the blues" and Healthy Depression cause fluctuations in our energy and mood, but with effort we can return to positive energy and an even keel. Unhealthy Depression, on the other hand, drains our energy, makes us sick, and sends us on such a downward slide that no self-help program can resolve it. Unhealthy Depression is a progressive illness, and while it can lift and seem to go away on its own, it inevitably returns with greater intensity and frequency if we don't get professional help.

Paula knows the painful realities of Unhealthy Depression all too well. She watched both her mother and father battle with it, and then ended up following in their footsteps. Paula was in her late 30s when she was referred to me. Bright, personable, and ambitious, she had been a court stenographer for more than fifteen years when she decided to go back to school to earn a master's degree in counseling. During the day, she worked in juvenile court. At night, she was either in school or at a neighborhood crisis center, where she volunteered as an assistant in support groups for incest victims.

Paula was good at her volunteer work but often questioned whether she was really helping anyone, especially herself. The group often reminded her of her many unresolved relationship issues, especially with her mother. When Paula was told that her mother, a longtime smoker, was dying of lung cancer, the deep-seated pain, anger, and frustration exploded within her and pushed her over the edge into a deep Unhealthy Depression. She had watched her mother smoke cigarettes her entire life to medicate herself and numb her unresolved depression. "How could someone be so stupid?" she fumed. Her mother was the only person in the world with whom she'd maintained any real connection, and even the thought that she could be dead by Christmas made her physically ill.

Over the next several months, Paula completely withdrew. She started calling in sick to work, stopped doing her volunteer counseling work, and let her friends' phone calls go unreturned. She slept more than she ever had, and ate and drank whatever and whenever she wanted. The longer she stayed in bed, the more paralyzed and miserable she felt. Candy wrappers flooded the floor around her bed as she read magazines and watched old movies on TV. She felt too fat and tired to go to work, so she stayed home as often as possible. There were many days that she didn't even bother to shower or dress.

But even on her bleakest days, Paula kept her therapy appointments. It became increasingly clear, however, that Paula's depression had deteriorated to a point where therapy wasn't enough. Paula was so seriously depressed that she needed medication to replenish the brain chemicals depleted by her depression. After a consultation, a female psychiatrist agreed that Paula was biochemically out of balance and needed an antidepressant.

The psychiatrist and I worked together, testing three different medications before we zeroed in on one that was the right match for Paula's particular physiology. Within three weeks, Paula began to improve substantially. For the first time in months, she could concentrate and felt optimistic. Her therapy sessions became productive again. Paula finally had enough energy to begin exploring her feelings toward her mother. The more actively she expressed her anger, the more her depression receded.

It was a long, hard climb for Paula to pull herself out of her Unhealthy Depression, but she made it. Today, she's taking better care of herself than ever before. She has her weight under control and made peace with her mother, deciding to use her as a role model for how not to take care of herself. She took a six-month leave of absence from work to jump-start her education and is determined to earn her Ph.D. in psychology.

While she's still vulnerable to depression—and always will be— Paula uses the techniques she's learned to keep her bad feelings within a healthy range. Her work at the clinic has also measurably improved. Having lived through and resolved her own Unhealthy Depression, she's uniquely equipped to help other women survive theirs.

To better understand the difference between Kate's and Christine's experience with Healthy Depression and Paula's experience with Unhealthy Depression, the following comparison chart may help:

HEALTHY VS. UNHEALTHY DEPRESSION

HEALTHY: Based on real life experience.

UNHEALTHY: Based on distortion (exaggeration, delusion, fantasy, misunderstanding), denial of real life experience or facing too much negative experience to absorb.

HEALTHY: Able basically to function, although one feels bad and is less effective than usual.

UNHEALTHY: Unable to function effectively at work, in relationships, physically or other important areas of living; either sleep too little or too much; loss or increase in appetite; loss of interest in people, activities, and sex; little energy; loss of memory or ability to concentrate.

HEALTHY: Appropriate feelings of sadness, anger, guilt, or anxiety from a current loss, trauma, or unresolved past damage and losses.

UNHEALTHY: Distorted reaction to a current or past loss or trauma; experiencing past or present loss as permanent or greater than it was or is, and seeing current circumstance as a predictor of future losses.

HEALTHY: Feelings of temporary helplessness, but not suicidal.

UNHEALTHY: Feelings of hopelessness, despair; serious thoughts of suicide as an alternative to the pain.

HEALTHY: Withdrawn, isolated behavior lasting for hours or a day or two.

UNHEALTHY: Withdrawn, emotionally unresponsive behavior lasting for days, weeks, or months at a time.

HEALTHY: Feelings of being hurt or damaged, but hope and realistic expectation that healing is possible.

UNHEALTHY: Feelings of being defective and damaged beyond repair.

HEALTHY: Feeling bad about self, but self-blame comes and goes.

UNHEALTHY: Chronic, consistent low self-esteem, even self-hatred.

HEALTHY: Productive: leads to wisdom, creativity, and maturity.

UNHEALTHY: Unproductive: leads to paralysis; physical and mental deterioration, illness, and possibly even death.

This chart can be a useful tool in helping you evaluate your feelings and degree of depression. Make a copy of it and highlight the descriptions that apply to you and how you're feeling at the moment. It's important to understand that you may identify with feelings from both sides of the chart. That's not at all uncommon, because feelings are fluid and sometimes irrational. We can feel opposing feelings about the same issue at the same time. Occasionally, we move in and out of feelings or episodes of both Healthy and

Unhealthy Depression during times of extreme stress. But if this kind of movement continues for a prolonged period of time, it's very likely a signal that you may be heading for trouble and would benefit from professional counseling to keep your feelings from evolving into a full-blown Unhealthy Depression.

The following quiz will give you a clearer idea of the kind of depression you may be experiencing or have experienced in the past.

DO YOU HAVE A HEALTHY OR UNHEALTHY DEPRESSION?

Answer the following questions YES or NO.

1. I am sleeping more than eight hours many nights, or I find it difficult to sleep at all. I'm often waking up very early in the morning and typically can't go back to sleep. _____

2. I often feel lonely and isolated, and find myself withdrawing from relationships. I have no relationships I would consider successful. _____

3. I often think about how I would kill myself or I have attempted suicide. _____

4. I often use drugs, alcohol, cigarettes, and/or food to numb my feelings and escape reality, and have experienced destructive consequences, such as health problems or endangering myself or others. _____

5. I truly believe something is wrong with me and it can't be fixed. _____

6. I sometimes feel totally overextended and get very frustrated and edgy when asked to do more than I'm already doing. _____

7. I often feel that I'm giving more than I get in my relationships. I have too few quality relationships to feel satisfied, or too many to maintain without feeling depleted. _____

8. I have been sick quite often (colds, headaches, stomachaches, etc.) over the last year with illnesses that are stress related. _____

9. I often feel I'm a victim; I keep struggling to overcome feeling victimized although I haven't been particularly successful.   _____

10. I am still depressed over having been treated badly as a child. I blame my parents, but we tolerate each other and/or I've grown to accept what has happened.   _____

Total Number of Questions Answered YES: _____

If you answered Yes to two or more of the first five questions, you may be experiencing an Unhealthy Depression. If you answered Yes to two or more of the last five, you're likely to have a Healthy Depression. If you answered Yes to one or more of the questions from both the first and second part of the quiz, you may be moving in and out of Healthy and Unhealthy Depression—a situation that means you should be on "red flag alert."

Just because Healthy Depression is an inescapable reality of our lives doesn't mean there is nothing we can—or should—do about it. We can begin by acknowledging that some of our pain is inevitable, especially for women. While we can't avoid life's pain, we can decide how we'll respond at critical choice points in our lives. _We can either transform pain into gain or allow it to be pain in vain._ If we convert pain into gain, then feeling bad is good and we have a Healthy Depression. If we experience our pain in vain, then feeling bad is simply bad, and eventually creates an Unhealthy Depression.

While you may now be in the healthy range of depression, it's important to regularly evaluate your state of mind and quality of life to determine whether you're beginning to move toward Unhealthy Depression. Paula, for example, had been able to maintain a Healthy Depression until the stress of her mother's illness and death became more than she could handle and gradually left her feeling empty and unable to rebound.

If you think you have an Unhealthy Depression, first accept that it's not the result of your being too weak, too naïve, too stupid, too damaged, too inadequate, or too anything. It's simply an indication that you need help to break out of a complex cycle of biological, genetic, cultural, and psychological factors that are keeping you from having and being all that you want in your life.

Don't be tempted to treat Unhealthy Depression on your own.

Just as you wouldn't try to perform your own root canal or appendectomy, you don't have the necessary skills to deal with this degree of damage and/or chemical imbalance. A mental health professional who specializes in the treatment of depression does. For information on how to find such a person, see Chapter 10, "Beyond Self-help."

In assessing what kind of depression you may have, you've already taken the first step toward using your bad feelings in a positive way. The following two chapters provide you with the rest of the essential information you need in order to understand the six Healthy Depressions and what you can do to resolve them.

·2·

INHERITED DEPRESSIONS: HOW VULNERABLE ARE YOU?

She fell into a ghastly depression that went on for three years—until her death. Periodically she would call me on the phone in Florida and cry, "Mommy— Mommy— tell me the story of your depression and how you got over it." And although I had no real answer—no solution—I would repeat my story and that seemed to reassure her. That if I had gotten well, so could she.

Gertrude Nemerov on her daughter, photographer
Diane Arbus, who later committed suicide

I'll never forget the April afternoon I came home from school and discovered my father's bloodstained white shirt in a heap on the counter waiting to be washed. I was only 8, and except for an occasional skinned knee or paper cut, I had never seen real blood before. I was repelled and fascinated at the same time. But more than anything, I was worried. I didn't have a clue what had happened or what to think. All I knew was that something was very wrong.

I immediately yelled for my mother. When she came downstairs, she explained that my father had been involved in a car accident. She told me that he'd suffered serious head injuries and would be in the hospital for at least several weeks. When I was finally allowed to visit my father six days later, he was still wrapped in bandages. I'll always remember how helpless and vulnerable he looked. He eventually recovered, physically if not emotionally, only to have two heart attacks before he was killed in another car accident nine years later at the age of 50.

It wasn't until thirty years later that I realized my father's acci-

32

dents and heart problems were symptoms of a disguised depression. He had exhibited many of the typical symptoms of depression frequently seen in males: alcohol abuse, violent behavior toward oneself and sometimes others, preventable accidents, workaholism, psychosomatic problems, abuse of mind and body contributing to an early death, and chronic denial of any vulnerability or sad/bad feelings. Depression also ran in the family. My uncle—my father's identical twin brother—killed himself the day I was born, although his suicide was a dark family secret for many years.

Because his symptoms masked his depression so well, I had no idea that my father was significantly depressed for most of his adult life. After finding myself burdened with my own struggles with depression, I desperately searched for the cause of my vulnerability. It was only then that I began to uncover and understand the demons that haunted him—in order to understand the ones that haunted me.

It became clear that his depression had contributed to a lifestyle and a way of thinking that caused and perpetuated a great deal of pain and suffering. He refused to take his heart medication even though he knew he had serious heart disease. He would often drink and drive, and he refused to wear seat belts even after he had been thrown from a car twice. The older he got, the more often he traveled down a lonely road of self-destruction with labels for all his problems but little capacity to resolve them.

Martha also had names for her grandmother's disguised depression but, sadly, no name for her own. Her bouts of bad feelings and low energy had an anonymous identity until she discovered their roots. In her family, Grandma Wanda's bad feelings were euphemistically referred to as a "nervous breakdown." Martha had heard the family myths a hundred times about how Grandma Wanda would "go off her rocker" every five years or so and take to her bed, muttering dark thoughts that no one could understand. The neighbors dismissed her as "crazy"; at least twice, Grandma Wanda ended up in a hospital after refusing to get out of bed for weeks at a time. While she was out of commission, her eight children and the farmhands pitched in to cover her chores. They maintained the house and garden and handled the overwhelming task of preparing three meals a day for twelve people.

After completing a women's studies course in college that analyzed women's work roles throughout history, it occurred to Martha that if her grandmother had been crazy, she had been crazy like a fox. Grandma Wanda had adopted a sly survival strategy that served her well. Her "spells" provided her a necessary "time out" and rest from the unending demands and labor heaped upon farm women. Her mind and body desperately needed occasional breaks, but in those days and in that culture, vacations were a luxury few could afford.

The men, however, always managed to find some time for rest breaks, standing and gabbing around the machinery, going into town for supplies, or stopping for a drink at the local bar. The only way Grandma Wanda and many other farm women could find temporary respite from their unrelenting labor was to get sick and take to their beds.

Martha's grandmother had a Healthy Depression. She was reacting to a depressing reality in which she worked too hard and played too little. Grandma Wanda had always been a little eccentric, but Martha has only respect for her grandmother's nonconformist method of self-preservation that undoubtedly extended her life decades beyond the lives of those who considered her so unstable. Grandma Wanda is now 96. She has lived the last twenty-five years taking care only of herself and manages quite nicely on the retirement income she banked after selling the farm and moving to Phoenix.

Martha and I have both experienced Inherited Depression. **Inherited Depression is defined as the sad and bad feelings that result when biological, genetic, cultural, or psychological depressions grow in our families and are passed down to us as an increased vulnerability to both Healthy and Unhealthy Depression.** Both of us experienced a depression that was disguised as some other ailment or unnamed affliction, such as Wanda's nervous breakdowns or my father's refusal to take care of himself. You may very well have inherited a vulnerability to depression, too. To identify it, however, you will need to become a mental health detective in order to sort through the maze of clues that most families try to hide or forget.

Sometimes the depressions we inherit are biological or genetic, or both. These are the worst because they are difficult to identify as depression and are most likely to lead to Unhealthy Depressions. These kinds of Inherited Depressions are often disguised as alcoholism, addictions, eating disorders, or psychosomatic complaints such as chronic fatigue, headaches, constipation, insomnia, and the all-encompassing "nervous breakdown." Whatever their name, these depressions can become life-threatening if left untreated.

But more often, what women inherit is prolonged exposure to negative or restricted thinking patterns, attitudes, and victim behavior. It is passed down to us through example by our grandmothers, mothers, aunts, and other female role models who lived during inherently depressing times and who felt devalued and restricted in their choices. We learn a great deal through observing our elders; unfortunately, what we often learn are habits of negative thinking and self-defeating behavior.

Indeed, generations of women in the same family can be touched by the same kind of depression simply by learning and conforming to the "female role" within that given family. While we're highly vulnerable to this kind of learning and modeling, it's critical to remember that Inherited Depression doesn't guarantee that we will become depressed, but it definitely increases the likelihood, especially when we are highly stressed.

It's essential, then, that you take a closer look at your family history so that you can accurately assess your own inherited vulnerability to depression and then, if necessary, take steps to reduce that vulnerability. Don't expect your mother to be very helpful in your explorations. Mothers cannot give us what they do not have. Many of us futilely search for depression wisdom from our mothers, as did Diane Arbus, the noted photographer whose mother was quoted at the beginning of this chapter, when they never even had a name for their bad feelings, much less any idea of what to do to resolve them.

You can begin by taking the following quiz. Remember that Inherited Depression is often disguised. You're more likely to see symptoms that suggest an underlying depressive condition rather than a clinical syndrome of sad feelings and low energy that today would routinely be recognized as depression. So begin to explore your family tree and evaluate whether any of your relatives were chronically depressed. If so, what may have caused or contributed to that depression? Be careful not to overinterpret what you find. One depression clue or symptom is not enough to indicate an Inherited Depression. You need to establish a pattern of depressed symptoms or dysfunctional behavior that continued for at least a few weeks or occurred periodically before you can accurately label a relative "depressed."

INHERITED DEPRESSION INVENTORY

Answer the following questions YES or NO.

1. Do you have any close relatives who often experienced nonspecific illnesses that may have been symptoms of disguised depression (such as weakness, chronic fatigue, headaches, painful menstruation, constipation, sexual problems, obesity or appetite loss, sleep problems)?   _____

2. Do you have any close relatives who suffered "nervous breakdowns," attempted suicide, or were unable to function in some basic area of their work, family, or social life?   _____

3. Were any of your close relatives given shock treatments, antidepressants, or antianxiety drugs?   _____

4. Is there a history of alcohol or drug abuse (including prescription drugs) in your family that may have been caused by or contributed to depression?   _____

5. Did any of the women in your family consistently abuse food or have what would today be recognized as an eating disorder?   _____

6. Did your mother, grandmother, or other close female relatives often seem visibly unhappy or discontented with their limited choices? Did they experience multiple traumas such as loss of children, accidents, natural disasters, or major financial setbacks?   _____

7. Did your mother, grandmother, or other close female relatives work all or nearly all the time, caring for children, ill relatives, and/or working outside the home, so that they always seemed tired and rarely had any time for themselves?   _____

8. Is there a history of physical or sexual abuse in your family?   _____

9. Did any of your close male relatives exhibit the typical symptoms of male depression previously described in

this chapter (such as alcohol and substance abuse, violent behavior, preventable car accidents, being a workaholic, chronic physical health problems, denial of all sad, bad feelings)? Did many of them die prematurely? _____

10. Did your close male or female relatives smoke enough to cause them disabling health problems or premature death from smoking? _____

Total Number of Questions Answered YES: _____

SCORING

(0–1) Your vulnerability to Inherited Depression is nonexistent or very low.

If you find yourself scoring in this range, take a closer look at the quiz questions and carefully reevaluate them. It's unusual for women to be this immune to depression, if for no other reason than the fact that we've grown up female in a culture that so frequently devalues and consequently depresses women.

Consider asking more questions about your relatives' lives. Depression often runs deeper in families than anyone cares to admit. If, after further exploration, you still don't find any depression, then congratulate yourself: you're one of a lucky minority.

(2–4) You're definitely vulnerable.

You have a definite vulnerability to developing depression from inherited causes, especially during high stress points in your life. You're also prone to developing physical illnesses caused by unresolved depression. When bad things happen, don't blame yourself or your family. Take responsibility for solving the problem. You may have more "down days" than others do, but you can usually convert the depression into energy when you set your mind to it.

(5–7) You probably have an Inherited Depression.

We've learned that depression runs in families and yours is no exception. You're especially susceptible to Healthy Depressions and you're likely to develop an Unhealthy Depression at least once, if not several times, during your life. Until you resolve them, your depressions will probably deepen over time into clinical conditions needing professional help.

If this happens, be sure to get the help you need. If you respond early enough, you may not need long-term therapy. Learn all you can about your family dynamics so that you have a better understanding of how Inherited Depression has affected you. The guidelines in Chapter 10, "Beyond Self-help," and techniques in Chapter 11, "Putting It All Together," can also be useful to you in controlling your inherited vulnerability to depression.

**(8–10)   You very likely have an Unhealthy
              Inherited Depression.**
If you've scored in this range, Unhealthy Depression runs like blood through the veins of your family and has, in all likelihood, affected you and other family members. There is just too much depression in your family for you to escape its effects.

It's highly probable that you will have an Unhealthy Depression. If you've suffered periodic episodes of depression, as your score would indicate, seek professional help and plan to continue with it for a while. Depression vulnerability runs deep within you. It will take time, effort, and an investment in therapy to break free from depression and learn how to convert your vulnerability into a strength.

If your score on this quiz has helped you discover or confirm your vulnerability to Inherited Depression, the first thing you need to know is that you're not alone. To better understand why Inherited Depression is so common, we must focus on its sources. Only then can we more effectively learn and practice strategies that will enable us to cope with and resolve it.

Sources of Inherited Depression

We inherit far more from our ancestors than physical characteristics and a family name. The biological or genetic link is only part of what they pass down to us. We also inherit a vulnerability to attitudes, beliefs, and ways of thinking, which is why it's so important that we understand the wide variety of psychological and social factors that may have made the women in our families depressed.

With rare exceptions, the opportunities of the women who came before us were severely limited by social expectations and traditional conditioning, which placed them in passive roles that rendered them economically, emotionally, and sexually vulnerable. Women internalized these traditional expectations and roles as the "right" way to be female, and then suffered the stifling, depressing consequences.

Their way of thinking became a part of our cultural conscience, the Traditional Core of our being, which we experience as every bit as vital and real as our heart or soul. It lives within every woman and is fueled by centuries of cultural conditioning and expectations that dictate what a woman "should" be and how we "should" act. The Traditional Core is such a primary source of women's Healthy and Unhealthy Depressions that the entire next chapter is devoted to exploring its contribution to our collective depressions. Only when we understand the extent of the influence of our cultural conditioning and how debilitating traditional expectations can be can we fully understand the sources of our depression.

With little if any awareness of what they were doing, our parents and other relatives passed down to us depressive ways of feeling, thinking, and behaving. And many of us have learned our depression lessons all too well. Even if our mothers were psychologically protected from depression by truly healthy parents, they were still socially and culturally vulnerable because of the depressing times in which they lived.

If, for example, our fathers, mothers, or other close relatives were economically threatened during the Great Depression, you can be sure they were depressed. If they witnessed relatives being sent to slaughter in World War II or felt their sons or daughters were senselessly sacrificed in the rice paddies of Korea or Vietnam, you can be sure they were depressed. If they quietly grew up being physically and sexually abused, or lived with a parent who was alcoholic or addicted, you can be sure they were depressed.

We learn by observation and example, and most of us model our behavior, attitudes, and thought patterns after our closest relatives. We intuitively experience their unspoken sad feelings and sometimes even unconsciously absorb their depressions as a way to be closer to them.

These social, cultural, and psychological factors are so complex and individual, however, that it's very difficult to identify which particular factors led you and your family members to become depressed. We'll be exploring these social and psychological factors more fully as we look at the sources for each of the six Healthy Depressions. But before we do, there's one underlying source of Inherited Depression that deserves our attention and requires our understanding: our genes.

If a close relative suffered from a major depression or manic depression (if you're not sure exactly what these terms mean, see the definitions in Chapter 10), you're more vulnerable to developing the same kind of depression or mood disorder. According to current genetic research, this occurs because there seems to be a depression gene, or genes (there may be more than one), which can be inherited from either of our parents.[1]

Genes can be either recessive or dominant. The genes that cause depression and manic depression are dominant. So if one of your parents experienced significant depression or other mood disorders, you have a vulnerability to the same disease and are likely to pass that vulnerability on to your children. If both your parents had Inherited Depressions, your vulnerability to depression is considerably higher.

The research doesn't yet distinguish between Healthy and Unhealthy Depression, but scientific evidence and clinical practice suggest we can probably inherit a vulnerability to both. We'll know soon. By the end of the eighties, scientists had isolated only 1,500 to 2,000 genes.[2] But the American Medical Association predicts that by the year 2004, all of the 50,000 to 100,000 genes in the body will have been identified.[3]

By then, we'll probably know which genes contribute or predispose us to which illnesses. It's likely scientists will have isolated the gene that contributes to our Inherited Depression. Until then, the following facts and statistics will at least help you begin to assess your own genetic sources of Inherited Depression and how much you may be at risk.

YOUR ODDS OF INHERITED DEPRESSION

- If you're female, you have at least a one-in-four chance of experiencing major Unhealthy Depression among your close female relatives. The odds for men are one in eight.[4]
- If your relatives—especially the women in your family— suffered neurotic depressions or manic depression, you are two to three times more likely to have them, too.[5]
- The chances are nine in ten of finding milder depressions among your close female relatives.[6]
- Genetic predisposition to depression is so strong that if you're an identical twin, even if raised in separate households, you're 67 percent more likely to be depressed if your twin becomes depressed. On the other hand, depression genes aren't everything. Of identical twins raised in the same house, 25 percent did not become depressed even though their twin developed depression.[7]
- If you find depression symptoms such as alcoholism, sociopathy (operating without a conscience), or drug abuse among your close relatives, you're eight to ten times more likely to develop similar symptoms.[8]
- If a close relative committed suicide, you're much more vulnerable to suicide if you become very depressed. Studies by Dr. Janice Egeland of the University of Miami School of Medicine found that even among the ultraconservative religious sect of the Old Order Amish, in which suicide is strictly forbidden, evidence of Inherited Depression is compelling. Of the twenty-six suicides that occurred among the Amish during the past century, 73 percent happened within only four families.[9]

With an understanding of the vital role that genetics plays in Inherited Depression, you can better assess your degree of risk and begin to overcome it. The following strategies and exercises will help you build upon your awareness and decrease your vulnerability to this very common kind of depression. If you scored 2 or less on the Inherited Depression quiz, there's no need for you to spend time on the strategies in this chapter. If you scored 3 or more, however, these strategies can be enlightening and very useful.

As you search for clues to Inherited Depression, remember that it's natural to feel uncomfortable, embarrassed, and afraid of this process. The challenge is to do it anyway. Knowledge is power. It's also empowering. Nothing you discover will be worse than the consequences of not knowing the breadth and depth of your Inherited Depression.

Action Strategies to Protect Yourself Against Inherited Depression

The purpose of the following strategies and exercises is to help you learn more about your depressions so you can begin to better manage them. They also remind you that you do have a choice as to how to think and behave, even if you can't always choose how you feel.

1. Take an Inherited Depression Family Inventory.

To gain precious information regarding your depression roots, you'll need to become a persistent, patient mental health detective and ask as many questions as necessary to learn how deeply depression runs in your family. As we've seen, depression is like an elusive gray ghost. It haunts inner spaces that few of us are eager to visit. Talking about depression can often stir up painful memories, so be prepared to encounter resistance or even rejection from some of the people you'll want to interview. Expect that some of them will be deep in denial and won't even want to entertain the thought that anyone in their family had trouble coping with life. Depression wasn't a word the members of your mother's or grandmother's generation would have typically used to describe their sad or bad feelings. Even if they do use the term today, many won't feel the emotional freedom to talk openly about their feelings without risking ridicule and shame.

Begin by creating your own personalized version of the Inherited Depression Inventory on page 36. Many of the questions you may want to ask relatives or close family friends can be found there. Alter those questions as needed so that they apply to your family. Think of other issues you'd like to explore so that it feels thorough, complete, and personal. Among the more useful may be:

1. Your parent or relative was often immobilized and unable to get out of bed or off the couch, frequently irritable and/or withdrawn, and often emotionally unresponsive and self-absorbed. He or she frequently blamed everyone but himself or herself for bad feelings.
2. Your parent or relative was often "ill" with vaguely defined symptoms that kept him or her from meeting basic responsibilities.
3. Severe economic deprivation was a way of life.
4. Accidents, falls, and injuries were common.
5. The behavior and/or condition of your parent or relative was often described as "bad nerves," "the jitters," "consumption," a "drinking problem," a "weak constitution," a "nervous condition," etc.

When you've completed your version of the Inherited Depression Family Inventory, use it as a road map. Begin your historical journey by talking with members of at least two generations of your family if you can—your parents, their brothers and sisters, your grandparents, and any great-aunts or uncles. Ask about the cause of death of their parents, their ages when they died, and any chronic health problems they or others in the family may have had. Who do they think was most depressed in the family? Why? What did they do to cope with their depression? Write down or tape-record all the information you gather for later consideration.

Understand that this exploration will require time and tact. Do it in person, or by phone if face-to-face communication is impossible. You need to be as warm, gentle, and reassuring as possible when asking relatives for such sensitive information. Sending letters isn't recommended unless it's your only option. Such correspondence is often too distancing and rarely produces much useful information. It can also backfire on you by stirring anger among relatives who may see you as presumptuous or exploitative.

Some clients, especially those who have no living relatives, have found it useful to order copies of family members' death certificates from state health departments. You can find out how to do this by ordering a government publication called *Where to Write for Birth, Death and Marriage Records* from the Government Printing Office. Write to the Superintendent of Documents, Government Printing Office, Washington, D.C. 20402, or call (202) 783-3238. Death certificates usually cost $6 to $10 and nearly always list the cause of death. This may be the only way to get important information if you have no living relatives to interview. Even if you do, you can use the death certificates to ask them more about the listed cause of death and if or how it might have been related to depression or even suicide, if you suspect that might be the case.

Some doctors or hospitals will release medical records of deceased patients to close relatives. Such records may contain valuable clues about depressions that were expressed in physical symptoms. They can also provide insight as to how well a given relative may or may not have taken care of him- or herself. If you're not sure what questions to ask, you can obtain relative medical history forms by writing: The March of Dimes, 1275 Mamaroneck Avenue, White Plains, NY 10605. You can also obtain information on how to track hereditary diseases from the Hereditary Disease Foundation, 1427 Seventh Street, Suite 2, Santa Monica, CA 90401.

Another factor for depression is the incidence of divorce in your family. Divorce virtually always guarantees a certain degree of depression for parents and children, even when the divorce is highly desirable and is the healthiest alternative. So knowing who divorced, when, and why may be helpful in identifying family depression. You can learn more about obtaining copies of divorce records by ordering the pamphlet *Where to Write for Birth, Death and Marriage Records* from the Government Printing Office (see above for ordering information).

During this process, you may discover a great deal about your family that you didn't know. Martha, whom we met earlier in this chapter, grew up believing that Wanda's husband, her grandfather, had died in a hunting accident. What really happened was that her grandfather shot himself the day the bank foreclosed on the family farm during the Great Depression. To compound the tragedy, the bank was too overwhelmed with properties to take possession of the land and eventually Wanda and the family climbed out of the crushing debt and regained ownership of the farm. They were so ashamed of the suicide that it was never mentioned again until Martha uncovered it nearly sixty years later.

If you have no relatives who are willing or able to talk with you about these issues, rely on your best memory. Close your eyes and visualize your childhood. Try to remember your grandparents or great-grandparents as vividly and clearly as possible. Look at them from an adult point of view. Examine what depression symptoms, if any, they may have displayed. Do the same for aunts, uncles, and of course, your parents.

If you find this exercise too difficult to do on your own, feel you just don't have enough information, or can't even imagine talking with your family about such issues, consider doing what several of my clients have done: consult a genetic counselor. They are specialists trained to take a detailed family history and spot your genetic vulnerabilities for various medical and mental disorders.

Genetic counseling typically takes just one session. You can usually locate a geneticist at larger hospitals or medical centers in your community, or you can write to the following group for help in finding appropriate geneticists in your area: National Society of Genetic Counselors, 233 Canterbury Drive, Wallingford, PA 19086.

We've talked about how your relatives may respond to your questions, but it's also important that you consider how you may respond to their answers. Often I've found that clients initially feel worse instead of better after completing this exercise. Discovering family skeletons, confronting vulnerabilities, and acknowledging serious depressions can be risky business, and it's not uncommon to feel resentment, anger, or a need to withdraw temporarily from the family member(s) who "made" us vulnerable in the first place.

But these feelings are usually transitory and are a great example of when feeling bad is good. The next phase in the exploration process is a sense of relief: at least you now know where you stand and can better understand how your past affects your present. The action you take to uncover the truth and the knowledge you gain generate new energy and dissipate self-blame. You can then strengthen your commitment to preventing the same depressing experiences from happening to you.

After you've gathered information from your Inherited Depression Family Inventory, analyze the patterns you see. What depression symptoms have been passed down, especially among the women in your family? Note your feelings and observations in the margin of the lists and information sheets you've collected. When this step is completed, move on to summarizing this knowledge by making a Depression Family Tree and learn how to use your emotional inheritance to your advantage.

2. Make a Depression Family Tree.

Drawing a Depression Family Tree may sound silly at first, but we've found in our workshops that this exercise gives participants a clearer sense of their depression roots than words ever could. To begin, draw a big trunk with a brown crayon or felt tip marker on a large piece of paper. Then draw the branches, starting with your great-grandparents on both sides, your grandparents, your parents, and your brothers and sisters. Be sure to include any other important relatives such as aunts and uncles. Unlike other family trees, which are limited exclusively to blood relatives, there's also room on this tree for other people who may have influenced the behavior and attitudes of primary family members. They might include a stepparent or a close family friend.

On each branch representing a relative or extended family member, draw a red or black apple. Black apples represent relatives who were significantly depressed. Red apples represent those who were basically depression free and led (or lead) active, productive lives. On the red and black apples, assign a numerical rating from 1 to 10, with the scores representing the following:

> 1   Relative had minimal or no depression
> 2–5   Increasing degrees of Healthy Depression
> 6–10 Increasing degrees of Unhealthy Depression

If, for any reason, you find yourself unable to assign a numerical rating for a particular person, ask other family members for their impressions and ratings. Even though this can be a challenging process, it's important that you don't give up or avoid steps along the way. Once you've created your Depression Family Tree, study it carefully. The higher the numbers and the closer those black apples hang to your branch of the family tree, the more cause for concern you have. The more black apples you count, the more vulnerable and likely you are to have Inherited Depression. Those apples are potential poison and can be every bit as potent as the one Snow White naïvely accepted from the witch.

3. Inventory Your Current Depression Vulnerability.

Now do a personal inventory to see how your depression heritage impacts you today. One way to do this is to ask several close friends and family members to tell you honestly how emotionally happy and content you appear to them. Do they see you as depressed? Are you so chronically tired or so frequently irritable that they've often felt concerned or worried about you? Do they see you as either socially withdrawn or too socially active, yet lacking meaningful relationships? Ask them to rate from 1 to 10 how depressed they believe you are, with 10 being very depressed.

Write down, tape-record, or videotape their feedback. Ask questions to clarify anything you don't understand. If you feel a need to respond to their observations, wait. Let some time pass and give it more thought first. Write about your reactions to become more objective. Responding with a simple "thank you" will help protect both you and them from any negative feelings their honesty may stir up within you. If you become defensive, they may withdraw and be less open to you the next time you ask for help. An angry or defensive response on your part could also provoke a disagreement, which will distract you from absorbing the information they give you. Be open-minded—if you find what they say disturbing, there's probably some truth in it, or you wouldn't have had such a strong reaction to it.

Assess how much change, stress, loss, disappointment, sickness, and trauma you've experienced in the past six months. It's critical that you periodically check in with yourself to do this kind of stress assessment. Too much stress is sure to trigger your vulnerability to Inherited Depression. By keeping track of your stress levels, you'll have a better idea how high your degree of depression risk is at any given time. You can then compensate and protect yourself by taking especially good care of yourself whenever you're aware that your risk levels are higher than usual.

To assess your depression risk levels, begin by writing down events or situations that typically generate depressed feelings for you. The following list, based on clinical theory, my experiences, and those of my clients and students, includes the kinds of events most likely to make women depressed. The left column represents depression-producing events. The right column is the depression rating for each event, ranging from 1, which means these events are unlikely to produce depression, to 10, which means they are major contributors to female depression (and, in many cases, depression among men as well). Assigning a number helps place these events in perspective in terms of how much they contribute to your feelings of depression.

DEPRESSION VULNERABILITY SURVEY

In the past six months I've experienced:	Rating
• Death of someone I loved	10
• Significant physical or sexual abuse	10
• Major loss or disappointment in a close relationship (including separation or divorce)	9–10
• Other significant trauma: physical injuries from accidents, robbery, natural or man-made disasters, becoming very ill, etc.	9–10
• Significant economic setback or deprivation (including being fired)	8–10
• Failure to meet an important goal	7–8
• Moving (even if desired)	6–7
• Having birthdays or events that made me feel too old	5–6
• Sexual harassment from someone in authority	5–6
• Gaining more than ten unwanted pounds	4–5
• Working too hard for too long	3–4

Add any other similar stressful events or situations of your own to the list, and rate them for their contribution to your depression. If you have Inherited Depression and have recently experienced two or more events with a score of 5 or higher, you're currently vulnerable to depression. You're probably depressed at this moment and have good reason to be. Even if you have only one score of 7 or more, you're very vulnerable to depression and would benefit from doing something about it now.

If taking this inventory made you uncomfortable, that's a good sign. Not only did you have the courage to face your truth, but you're more ready to deal with it than you have been, which is why you may be feeling anxious. You've learned your degree of vulnerability and can now learn how to better protect yourself. Recommit to studying and practicing the rest of the strategies and techniques in this book. Focus your attention on the necessity of taking better care of your physical and emotional self. Attend workshops and classes in stress and emotional management. Learn the Dos and Don'ts of coping with depression by studying your family's successes and failures in dealing effectively with bad feelings.

4. Create Family "Depression Dolls."

How do you convert your knowledge about Inherited Depression into action to improve the quality of your life? One strategy that a number of my clients and students have found very useful is making family depression dolls. If, after reading about this exercise, you think you would feel uncomfortable or even foolish doing it, then move on. You'll find other strategies in other chapters that will feel more comfortable and useful. As I've said, not every exercise in this book will appeal to everyone. But if you are willing to at least try this and other action exercises, you may be surprised and pleased at how well they pay off.

To begin creating your family depression dolls, think of the one family member, living or dead, from whom you believe you inherited the most depression. Make a small doll out of cloth or cardboard to represent that depressed relative. You may wish to choose a dark-colored or gray material, or whatever color you associate with depression. Customize the doll so it visibly reminds you of that depressed family member. Martha made a grandfather doll carrying a gun in one hand and a mortgage document in the other. I made a father doll and hung a car on a cord from his gut, drenching the car and splashing the doll in red paint to represent my father's spilled blood.

Then make a second doll out of a bright, life-affirming color to symbolize the family member who was least depressed or who coped most powerfully and effectively with his or her depression and problems. Again, decorate it with whatever best reminds you of that person. Martha made a white silk doll of her Grandma Wanda and bought a small toy bed, which she sewed into Wanda's hand as a symbol of her survival tool. She covered Grandma Wanda in a brown burlap smock to represent her harsh farm heritage. As a final triumphant gesture, Martha made her Grandma Wanda doll a tiny red sun visor out of cardboard to symbolize her last years of freedom in the warm Phoenix sunshine.

Once you've made your positive and negative depression dolls, prop them up on your pillow every morning as you make your bed. Carry them with you in your backpack, purse, briefcase, or car for several weeks. Touch them. Think about what they mean and who they represent. Remember the feelings the dolls stirred within you while you were making them. Let them be a constant reminder that you have choices about whom you imitate and how you behave and think. Do you choose to identify with the dark, depressed doll, or the one who is bright and vibrant? Are you repeating the depressive patterns of family members?

Your depression dolls are visual reminders you can also touch, feel, and carry with you when you're feeling vulnerable. Let the dolls remind you that you have options and alternatives as to how you choose to deal with your depression. Keep the positive doll handy as a reminder that others before you have succeeded in living positive, productive lives. With effort and practice, you can, too.

The most important thing to remember from reading this chapter is that just because you have a vulnerability to Inherited Depression, you don't have to become or stay depressed. Many in your family may have taught you what doesn't work, and at least a few, I hope, have taught you what does. Uncovering Inherited Depression can be depressing at first, but it's essential that you not lose sight of the positive. You're learning how to manage depression in ways your family could never know or teach you, because this information about emotional management was simply unavailable until recently. You have tools they never had. By using them, you can break the generational chains of depression forever.

·3·

THE TRADITIONAL CORE:
OUR CULTURAL CONSCIENCE

You can't overestimate the power of the Traditional Core. It impacts and influences the identities and lives of even the most accomplished women. British novelist Agatha Christie, for example, was always reluctant to call herself a writer. She considered her work more of a hobby than a career. Here's a woman who wrote sixty-seven novels, sixteen plays and sixteen collections of short stories. How do you think she listed her occupation? Two words: "married woman."

Dr. Alice Rubenstein
psychologist and author

As Caroline prepared dinner, she and Roy, her husband of forty-one years, chatted about the day's events. Suddenly, the color drained from Roy's face as he slumped to the floor. Caroline screamed but quickly composed herself and attempted to revive him. When Roy failed to respond, she called 911 and rocked him in her arms until the paramedics arrived. All the way to the hospital, Caroline quietly murmured her litany, "Please, God, no." Roy was immediately admitted into the coronary intensive care unit, but efforts to revive his heart failed.

It took Caroline, 60, more than two years to accept that while Roy's life had ended, the time had come for hers to move on. She had often talked about going back to college—she had quit when she and Roy married—and decided it was finally time to fulfill her dream.

Making the decision was easy. Making it happen proved quite difficult. After Caroline enrolled at a local state university, she procrastinated and came up with all kinds of excuses not to meet with her counselor and take the proficiency tests at the campus career development center. She worried that she wasn't smart enough to make it and was also acutely age conscious, embarrassed at the likelihood of being the only grandmother in her classes.

The fact that both of Caroline's sons were unsupportive added to her dilemma. They planted seeds of doubt that made Caroline question whether her desire for personal growth and achievement was really as important as being there for her family. They were annoyed that she wouldn't just "leave well enough alone" and that she might not be available enough to fulfill her role as the apron-wearing, cookie-baking Grandma to their children. Their lack of support stirred mixed emotions in Caroline. She loved feeling needed but resented their selfish determination to relegate her to the nurturing role all over again.

Ruth, 43, was thankful she didn't have to deal with the kind of family ties that left Caroline in knots. Divorced and extremely independent, Ruth had been a freelance video producer for ten years. During the good times, she produced videos for sales promotions and a West Coast tourist board. When business slumped, she recorded weddings and bar and bat mitzvahs to pay the rent. She worked alone and had developed a fine reputation in her field, yet she found it increasingly difficult to muster the energy to market herself constantly and search for work. Ruth often felt burned-out and resented working so hard for so little.

Ruth wasn't interested in marrying again. She loved her freedom too much to compromise and limit her options, but there were times when she felt lonely and would ask herself whether something was wrong with her for wanting to stay single. After all, most of her friends were married and seemed happy. What, she wondered, was she missing?

Angela, 32, was also single, but not by choice. In fact, finding a husband was her obsession. She was a weekend regular at local nightclubs, where she cruised for a man who would help make her life better. Even at work Angela was on the prowl. She did everything she could to attract attention. She wore skirts that were too short and sweaters that were too tight. But all she seemed to attract was the ridicule of her female coworkers at the construction company where she was a typist.

Angela was lonely and it hurt. Her only reliable companion in the world was her cat, Tinkerbell. When Tinkerbell got caught in a neighbor's automatic garage door and broke her leg, the operation and its complications cost Angela nearly $600. She was flat broke and simply couldn't afford to spend two weeks' take-home pay on her cat.

To make matters worse, Angela's landlord was threatening to raise the rent on her studio apartment. There had also been rumors circulating around work that the ongoing recession might result in job layoffs. Even though she'd been with the company for five years, she wasn't sure whether she would have a job from one week to the next. For the first time in her life, Angela could understand how working women can become homeless and why she never should have listened to her father when he told her not to bother going to college because she would "just quit to get married anyway."

Caroline, Ruth, and Angela are each experiencing a Healthy Depression. And as different as their depressions may seem at first glance, they're all rooted in what I've come to call the Traditional Core (TC). **The Traditional Core is a woman's cultural conscience, a core of traditional values and thinking that exists deep within every woman and dictates how we must behave and what roles are "right" and "wrong" for us to fulfill.** It has been formed through centuries of cultural conditioning. Like a conscience, the Traditional Core is a guiding force that evolves over time from parental and societal messages we receive as females.

Our Traditional Core is formed very early, even before we can talk, because our parents respond to their cultural heritage and typically teach us the commandments of proper sex role behavior that they were taught. Some women, especially those who have been raised in strongly traditional households, have powerful, dominant TCs. Others, including those who were raised in more nontraditional, less conservative homes, have TCs that are less influential.

Like our conscience, our Traditional Core is a guide that seems to speak to us, telling us what is right, wrong, feminine, masculine, appropriate, and inappropriate for us as women. It communicates as powerfully and effectively as if it were Jiminy Cricket perched on our shoulder. Every woman has her own notion of what her Traditional Core looks and feels like.

One client envisioned her TC as resembling the great and mighty

Wizard of Oz before he was exposed as a mere mortal in a little booth. Another is sure her Traditional Core looks just like Harriet Nelson. Others see their Traditional Core as a healing angel in the mist, as a Wonder Woman who tries to do and be all things for all people, or as a whimsical fairy tale character whose words and actions are rooted in fantasy rather than reality.

No matter how we visualize our Traditional Core, the messages of "traditional values" are consistent because we all listened to similar cultural messages. These ancient voices stem from cultural deposits fossilized by centuries of conditioning about the proper roles for men and women. They are quite difficult to ignore even when they carry messages that are no longer realistic or appropriate considering the realities of contemporary life. When we speak of "roles," we're talking about socially expected behavior patterns, usually determined by an individual's status in society. The lower the status, typically the more rigid and prescribed the roles. Since women have occupied the lower rungs of the social ladder for centuries, our roles have had a great deal of time to become very well defined and well prescribed. The roles are so strong, in fact, that they've taken on a life of their own, like a force living deep inside us.

Even if we're quite modern and think we're independent of our Traditional Core, we need only violate its commandments and we're sure to feel its wrath. That's when the TC becomes a negative force, because it robs us of our freedom to make choices and requires a rigid code of behavior built on unhealthy and erroneous assumptions. Just like the Ten Commandments, the commandments of the TC also seem etched in stone and seem to reflect the directives of a higher power. While the specifics vary from woman to woman, the general commandments for women seem to stay basically the same, year after year, and sometimes even century after century.

TEN COMMANDMENTS OF THE NEGATIVE TRADITIONAL CORE

I. Thou shalt take care of thyself only after taking care of all others.

II. Thou shalt not take the name of men in vain.

III. Thou shalt not threaten abandonment no matter how bad it gets.

IV. Thou shalt be seen (and thou better look good!) and not heard.

V. Thou shalt be economically and emotionally dependent on men.

VI. Thou shalt always be thin.

VII. Thou shalt never grow old.

VIII. Thou shalt service men sexually whenever they wish.

IX. Thou shalt never consider thy work more important than a man's.

X. Thou shalt not assume any rights beyond what men have bestowed on thee.

As I made this list, I felt sad. What kind of feelings do you have while reading it? My sadness stems from being reminded how unhealthy these commandments have made our society for both men and women. They are so rigid and suffocating that they keep people of both sexes from growing and realizing their potential. They snuff out our freedom and drive to explore new behaviors and healthier relationships between men and women.

If blindly followed, the commandments of the Traditional Core cause major depression because they clash so strongly with the demands and realities of modern life. If we choose not to conform and decide to branch out beyond what the TC considers proper or feminine, we're sure to feel guilty and insecure. Just like our conscience, the TC has the power to haunt and control us.

It's no wonder the Traditional Core has such power. Since the beginning of recorded history, women have been treated as possessions, first by their fathers and then by their husbands. A woman's role was to serve as an extension of men. We were the emotional and physical heart of the home, expected to love, service, and obey. And in that capacity, we also learned many strengths from the TC.

It's important to remember that while the TC has a strong negative side, it has an equally well-developed positive side that can be a real source of strength. These strengths provide a natural resource for us to draw from if we stay aware of their presence and how and when to use them.

The Positive Side of the Traditional Core

1. The TC makes us good communicators.

Because women have historically been discouraged from speaking openly and directly, we've become much better at reading expressions, body language, and other nonverbal cues than men. Indeed, our "female intuition," our instinctive ability to understand and communicate feelings and talk openly and honestly about relationship and personal issues, is one of the greatest gifts our Traditional Core gives us. We can express the nuances of feelings in great detail, when many men don't even know if they're having a feeling. Ironically, these more developed communication skills are proving increasingly important in the business world as managers recognize the value and necessity of good communication and are turning to women as leaders and teachers of communication skills.

2. In empowering others, we empower ourselves.

Our Traditional Core is a source of enormous power in encouraging and empowering others. When we do, it's a win/win proposition that's satisfying and rewarding for everyone involved. When we foster growth and power in others by supporting them to excel, we build our self-esteem in the process. We feel effective and valuable because we are. It also strengthens our connection with others because we feel invested in them as people. As long as we maintain a sense of balance and don't forget our own needs in the process, the TC's emphasis on nurturing and support is one of the quickest pathways to intimacy and feeling appreciated and connected.

3. The TC reminds us of the value of home, family, and our history.

The Traditional Core serves as an anchor and reminds us that no matter how much we achieve, we're likely to feel incomplete if we don't also invest time and energy in building intimate relationships and maintaining a safe, pleasing home for ourselves. The TC helps us slow down from the frenetic pace of an increasingly nontraditional world and reconnect to our values, our traditions, our family history, and what's really meaningful to us. The TC is the warm, calm side of ourselves that perpetuates rituals and creates memories of connection for those we love.

The holiday season, for example, is an annual festival for the TC. The TC encourages us to decorate a Christmas tree or bake cookies, even when we're feeling overextended and too busy to bother. It's why we cook dinner for close friends instead of ordering takeout. It's why we take that extra minute to put a quick drawing in our kids' lunchboxes, even if it means rushing to get dressed for work. It's why we make time to share dinner with our intimate partner, even if it means eating frozen dinners zapped in the microwave. It's why we attend religious services and feel fulfilled. Through these kinds of activities, the TC keeps us in touch with our cultural heritage and constantly reminds us of the value of traditions.

4. The TC builds community.

The TC thrives on a strong sense of community and connection with other people—everyone from intimate partners, relatives, and kids to friends, coworkers, and the people who work at the bank or dry cleaners. It's the TC that helps us notice how people are feeling and encourages us to reach out and offer help, whether it is volunteering to work a booth one afternoon for a community charity, circulating a birthday card at the office, or putting everything on hold to support a friend who really needs us. These community connections—a direct by-product of our Traditional Core—enrich our lives and keep us healthier.

5. The TC encourages trust, patience, consideration, and forgiveness.

The TC encourages values that can easily be forgotten in an increasingly competitive, frantic society. We sometimes get so caught up in our own world of projects and priorities that we forget to be kind, patient, and forgiving—not only with others, but with ourselves. When we're operating in overdrive and constantly racing to accomplish certain goals, these qualities seem more like nuisances than necessities. But they're really the foundation of any successful communication or relationship. A balanced Traditional Core trains and encourages us to treat others and ourselves well.

The TC has thrived for centuries because it was convenient for both men and women. It was so deeply ingrained and women and men were so unaware of their cultural conditioning that they couldn't choose to change it. The TC worked because it matched the economic and cultural needs of a patriarchal system where men controlled the power and resources and women supported the men in return for protection, provisions, and, occasionally, status.

But in the 1960s, the system began to change and the Traditional Core became more unstable. For the first time since World War II, women were actually needed in the work force to maintain production levels and meet service demands. As the economy escalated, so did the need for secretaries, waitresses, word processors, clerks, and other lower level positions.

And women were ready, even if these weren't exactly the jobs of their dreams. Many of them had grown weary of washing, vacuuming, and cooking their way through the post–World War II years. When Betty Friedan wrote *The Feminine Mystique* in 1963, millions listened and related to her message of discovery: traditional feminine roles leave women emotionally bankrupt and bored.

Women began challenging the traditional role in ways that hadn't occurred since women demanded and won the right to vote in 1920. Not until recently, however, has the TC been so directly threatened. The nontraditional role of working outside the home has become an economic necessity for the majority of American women, and many women who don't have to work *choose* to work because of the financial and emotional rewards it provides.

Caroline, Ruth, and Angela have each violated their Traditional Cores in their own ways. Caroline challenged her TC by returning to college and pursuing her need to develop a new source of power and purpose. Her negative TC made her feel guilty and also planted seeds of self-doubt. Because it had been so long since Caroline had studied or competed academically, she had very little confidence in her intellectual abilities.

Caroline had also never learned to set realistic goals and take small, measured steps to achieve them. Rather than easing gradually back into school, she felt compelled to either stay anchored in her traditional role or to move totally into a nontraditional world for which she was completely unprepared. This kind of either/or thinking favored by the TC gave her no way out of her dilemma, so she became angry and depressed.

Ruth's conflict with her TC resulted from her choice to remain single in a couples-oriented society. The Traditional Core would have us believe that no one is single by choice, yet being single was the only way Ruth could have what she really wanted in life: the freedom to live creatively.

Angela, on the other hand, experienced firsthand the depression that results from maintaining peace with both traditional fathers and our TCs by taking the "easy way" out. Since puberty, she pursued the male attention she had been taught to crave, rather than attending college or a trade school. For generations, Angela's family believed a man could make a woman happier than a job ever could. Angela's TC absorbed the message and took it quite seriously, which is why today she's without marketable job skills. And because no man has yet materialized to take care of her as her TC promised, she is economically and emotionally vulnerable.

As you can see, the negative side of the Traditional Core produces and contributes to a variety of Healthy Depressions because it clashes head-on with our increasingly nontraditional world. We're given the classic double message: you must be a traditional woman, but be prepared to be poor, unimportant, unappreciated, and/or abandoned if you are.

If we fulfill the destiny of our Traditional Core, we're in the minority, even though the media and popular culture would have us believe we're part of an enduring and endearing majority. In 1970 40 percent of the nation's households were run by traditional homemakers. Today less than one in four women are full-time homemakers.[1] As the statistics have changed, so have our attitudes. Despite the Traditional Core's party line, society increasingly sees full-time homemakers as underachievers or even victims.

The TC tells us to be mothers to be truly fulfilled. But if we listen to that voice, many of us will find ourselves raising our children alone. The number of single parents in America has increased 41 percent in the past ten years, hitting a record 9.7 million in 1990. It's no surprise that the vast majority of these new single parents are women.[2] Forty percent of women in their twenties can expect to be single parents at some point in their lives.[3]

The TC tells us to depend on men for emotional and economic

security. After all, that's how it has always been. But when men leave, where does that leave us? One-half to two-thirds of women married in the 1980s will divorce;[4] women over 60 are at risk for divorce at numbers beginning to approach those of younger women.[5] Just like Caroline, who found herself suddenly single after forty-one years of marriage, we can expect to be widowed for at least fifteen years of our lives.[6] By age 65 over half of us will be widowed, and by 75 two-thirds of us will be.[7]

Even women who have lasting marriages may not be as satisfied and fulfilled as our Traditional Core would have us believe. As Susan Faludi reported in her best-selling book *Backlash: The Undeclared War Against American Women*, studies show that being married creates about "20 percent more depression than being single and three times the rate of severe neurosis. Married women have more nervous breakdowns, nervousness, heart palpitations, and inertia. . . . A twenty-five-year longitudinal study of college-educated women found that wives had the lowest self-esteem, felt the least attractive, reported the most loneliness, and considered themselves the least competent at almost every task—even child care."[8]

On the other hand, being employed outside the home and having multiple roles for multiple sources of self-esteem helps insulate us from depression. Employment outranks marriage and children as "by far the most consistent tie to women's health," according to a twenty-year study by the Institute for Social Research and the National Center for Health Statistics.[9] So it wasn't only marriage or children that kept us healthy, as the TC would have us believe. It is having multiple sources of self-esteem and achievement. In fact, the higher the level of the job, the better the physical and mental health ratings of the women who held them. Women who have never worked outside the home have the highest levels of depression and lowest levels of health.

To help visualize how central the Traditional Core is for most of us, review the following diagram. The farther we stray from the Traditional Core into nontraditional territories such as single parenthood, nontraditional relationships, or career success in formerly all-male terrain, the more vulnerable, anxious, and depressed we can expect to feel. We may feel enthusiastic about taking a stand and risking alternative lifestyles, but most of us still feel uneasy or anxious about violating our Traditional Core.

Our Traditional Core

Mind ↔ Body	The	Body Image
Depletion	Healthy	Age Rage
Victimization	Depressions	Relationship

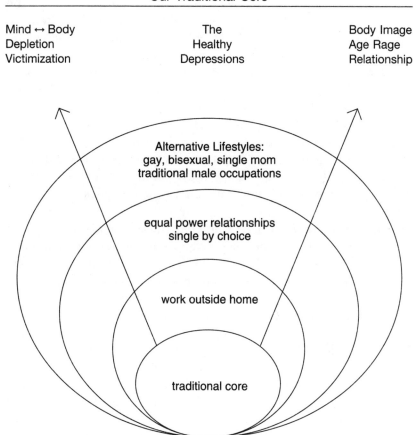

Alternative Lifestyles:
gay, bisexual, single mom
traditional male occupations

equal power relationships
single by choice

work outside home

traditional core

As you can see, the Traditional Core is fertile ground for all kinds of depression. The conflict between the Traditional Core and the realities of modern life plants seeds of anger, resentment, low self-esteem, even self-hatred as women struggle to find the "right" answer during a time of such cultural collision. There is, of course, no such answer. All of us compromise in ways we wish we didn't have to, and many of us feel we're selling out to either the traditional or nontraditional worlds no matter what we do. It's clear how easily the six Healthy Depressions can sprout from the Traditional Core:

Victimization Depression results from the TC's emphasis on being accommodating and nurturing. When confronted with conflict, the TC has not been trained to respond with assertion, so we tend to respond quietly and carefully or become aggressive and defensive. Either approach invites further victimization.

Relationship Depression happens when our TC's innate desire to manage all our relationships perfectly collides with the real world, where nothing is perfect. We feel depressed when we discover unending intimacy is the Impossible Dream.

Age Rage Depression hits home as we realize we're growing older in a society that places an extraordinary premium on youth. The TC tells us to be the impossible: forever young. Young women are prized possessions for men, but older women quickly lose their value.

Depletion Depression occurs when our traditional need to nurture clashes with our nontraditional drive to achieve. Rather than make choices and simply say no, many women attempt to placate the TC and be all things to all people. "Having it all" puts us on a treadmill; we run in place until we drop into depression.

Body Image Depression materializes when we try to achieve impossible physical standards of perfection promoted by our culture and upheld by the TC's underlying message that women must create bodies that fit men's ideal of female beauty.

Mind ↔ Body Depression emerges from the TC's denial of how often our mind creates physical problems and the belief that we are weaker, more fragile, and more in need of medicine and doctors than we really are. The TC cannot imagine us being responsible for our own health care and encourages a "patient identity" that promotes development of physical problems.

You can see how important it is to discover and understand the positive and negative qualities of this powerful force inside us. To evaluate how well developed and influential your Traditional Core may be and begin thinking about its constructive and destructive energy, take the following quiz.

The TRADITIONAL CORE QUIZ

Answer the following questions YES or NO.

1. Do you generally become passive or withdrawn during conflict? _____
2. Are you economically dependent on someone else (i.e., parents, partners, relatives, or friends) for your survival? _____
3. Do you feel significantly anxious and/or depressed about losing your looks and getting older? _____
4. Do most of the compliments you receive focus on your abilities and skills to perform traditional roles such as homemaker, hostess, volunteer work, etc.? _____
5. Are you hesitant to express anger directly, especially toward those close to you, or do you explode inappropriately with accumulated anger you were unable to express as you felt it? _____
6. Do others often tell you that by being a homemaker, you're not living up to your potential or doing enough with your life? _____
7. Do you spend most of your time nurturing and caring for others and not enough time on your own personal growth and achievements? _____
8. Do you see your job as a burden that gets in the way of your marriage or raising your children? _____
9. Are most of your relationships unequal in power, with you in the one-down position? _____
10. Do you consistently put your partner's sexual pleasure ahead of your own? _____

Total Number of Questions Answered YES: _____

SCORING

(0–2) Your Traditional Core is a source of strength.
Your Traditional Core is much less dominant than most and is a source of strength rather than depression. You have either resolved

the weaknesses in the TC or you weren't taught them in the first place. You have a wonderful natural resource to tap into if you only stay aware of its presence and positive power.

(3–5) Your negative Traditional Core has average strength.
Most women in this range experience some Healthy Depression from the TC, but they are also able to utilize its strengths. This score indicates an average number of childhood and adult problems related to the negative side of the TC.

(6–8) Your Traditional Core can be threatening for you.
Beware! With scores in this range, it's quite likely that the TC is causing you a great deal of inner conflict that you experience as feelings of depression and inadequacy rather than as a violation of your cultural conscience. The TC is strong enough to restrict your choices and keep you in a vulnerable, dependent position. You're highly vulnerable to Healthy Depression.

(9–10) You're dominated by your negative Traditional Core.
You're at significant risk for Healthy and Unhealthy Depression because you're dominated by your Traditional Core in ways that are bound to make you feel inadequate and miserable. This score is a red flag for depression and nearly guarantees its appearance at various times of your life. Do the exercises in this book and others like it or see a mental health professional to protect you from or help you manage depression.

No matter what your score, you can benefit from becoming more conscious as to how and why the Traditional Core is such a powerful, compelling force. Beware, however, of a typical problem that often occurs in this stage of exploration of the TC. The more women come to know about the power and influence of their Traditional Core, the more they want to deny its existence. But doing so is a mistake, because denying the TC is denying who we are. This denial causes depression because we underestimate how much of ourselves is still traditional, regardless of how radical or "alternative" our current lifestyle may be. Denying our Traditional Core makes us impatient with how slowly role change occurs, and lowers our self-esteem as we struggle with inevitable role overload and confusion. In short, denying the Traditional Core denies our choices and a source of positive life energy, and only makes the negative TC more powerful because we remain unaware of how deeply rooted it is in ourselves.

Another common mistake women make is to overprotect and defend the Traditional Core. In some ways, it's the opposite of denial, but it can be equally damaging. In the process of defending the TC, women often strive to become more traditional than ever, especially if they have misgivings about their nontraditional behavior. Unlike most men, women don't see their jobs as justification for doing less at home. Instead, we try to do even more so that our Traditional Core and our families aren't too threatened. There are many signs of overprotection of the Traditional Core. Only 57 percent of women who can afford household help, for example, actually have it.[10] Indeed, many women still buy into the notion that we must clean and manage the house in order to be real women. Many of us also put a self-imposed ceiling on our career advancement, advancing just fast enough to feel valuable without threatening any egos or upsetting any balance in our work and personal lives.

Understanding Your Traditional Core

There are countless examples of how our negative Traditional Core creates self-sabotage and our positive Traditional Core creates love. The following exercises will help you better understand your Traditional Core and the powerful role it plays in determining how you live and think. If we can't name, recognize, and understand how these cultural teachings influence our daily lives, we're missing a significant part of our experience and are therefore out of touch with a major part of ourselves. Knowing the signs of the TC gives us more choices about whether the old traditions are valuable to us or whether we would do better to develop new ones.

1. Make a List of Your Traditional Core's Strengths.

Start by reviewing the Traditional Core's typical strengths discussed on pages 56–58. Now personalize this list by adding other positive qualities your own Traditional Core provides. It may help to think of women in your family or environment who had strong, healthy Traditional Cores.

After you've completed your TC strength list, hang it up in a conspicuous place so you can think about it and memorize it. When your self-esteem dives, it's helpful to remember you have positive qualities that are so deep within you that no one can take them away. If you keep the TC balanced and in perspective with the demands of the real world, it can serve as a consistent source of strength. Rather than serve it, allow it to serve you.

2. Make a Traditional–Nontraditional Role Line.

To see where you stand on the continuum between traditional and nontraditional roles, draw a Traditional–Nontraditional Role Line from 1 to 10. This is a graphic way to measure how traditional or nontraditional you are in various situations or roles. The Role Line looks like this:

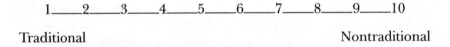

1____2____3____4____5____6____7____8____9____10

Traditional   Nontraditional

Which end of the spectrum do you typically live and operate in? If you're in the role of nurturing mother, where do you fall? How about when you're supervising a staff of employees on an important deadline project? Think of all the roles you fulfill over a one-month period. Are they predominantly traditional? Nontraditional? Is there a comfortable balance between the two? If you find you're consistently operating at either extreme of the spectrum, then you are at greater risk for conflict with the TC. You're probably either too traditional for the world in which we live, or so nontraditional that you experience life as a general anxiety attack and a constant struggle against conservative forces. Either extreme makes us vulnerable to feeling bad if we can't maintain balance by moving back and forth comfortably within the middle range (3–7) when more moderate, "middle of the road" behavior is appropriate in given situations.

It can also be enlightening to see where you stand relative to other women close to you. Considering all the roles you fulfill, circle an overall score on the scale. Then rate your mother, grandmother, close female relatives, friends, and colleagues. It is very helpful to have close friends and relatives rate *you* on the Role Line and discuss any discrepancies between your scores and theirs. Also, note in which direction your roles are evolving over time. This quick overview will enable you to see how traditional your heritage is and how your roles clash with or complement the women around you. You can begin to better understand how and why they may see things differently from you. If you choose, you can then adapt your own behavior to connect more intimately with them. In the chapter on Relationship Depression, we'll explore guidelines for more effective communication and behavior when you're dealing with staunchly traditional or nontraditional people. A better understanding of who they are—and who you are—will make your communication and relationship more healthy and rewarding.

3. Make a Checklist of Your Typical Traditional Role Conflicts.

Make a list of the conflicts you feel when your Traditional Core collides with the realities and pressures of the modern world. By doing so, you'll be taking another step toward better understanding when and why you sometimes feel uncomfortable and depressed when pursuing and fulfilling nontraditional roles. By becoming more conscious of these feelings, you're actively diminishing their power to make you feel bad and increasing your ability to use them constructively.

Listed below to get you started are some examples that I've seen appear on many women's checklists. How closely do they mirror your own feelings and concerns? Add your own statements to the list.

"I'm never content with my choices."
Whether we choose to be a homemaker or a home builder, we never feel like we've made quite the right choice. Yet when we explore new roles that seem more appealing, we often feel uncomfortable and as though we've lost a part of ourselves. Conflicts with the TC can leave us feeling dissatisfied and incomplete. Even when we're

doing something we really want to do—like Caroline going back to school or Ruth remaining single—we often still feel like we may be making the wrong choice. These feelings have much more to do with the inadequacy of the culture in which we live than with ourselves or our choices being inadequate. Our culture is inadequate because it attempts to deny freedom of choice over the lives of more than half of its members: women.

"Nothing I do is ever good enough."
No matter what we do, we often feel like it's not good enough. We feel as though our "quality time" with the kids must always be magical, yet it rarely is. If we're successful at work, our personal lives often feel incomplete and in need of repair. Our TC tells us we're neglecting our relationships and role as nurturers for selfish pursuits like achievement and work interests. If our relationships are in good shape, we often wonder why we're not doing more professionally. Because we can't do and have it all—at least not all at once—we often find ourselves depressed and feeling as though we've failed to measure up to the cultural standard of perfection.

"I feel like I have to constantly justify my choices and actions, particularly compared to other women."
Women in conflict with their Traditional Core frequently feel defensive and need to justify their choices to themselves and others. When we defy our TC and do something nontraditional, we can't fully value the choice we've made because it doesn't feel quite "right." We also tend to devalue ourselves for not being able to excel in both traditional and nontraditional roles at the same time. Many of us have a continuous dialogue with our Traditional Core, rationalizing and justifying every choice we make. We often look to our family and friends as a Supreme Court, awaiting their praise or condemnation of our role choices. We frequently give away the power to evaluate our own decisions and choices, as though others somehow have a better idea what's "right" for us. Because we are so vulnerable, we often compete and compare ourselves with other women to assess how we're doing in our role choices.

**"I'm tired of fulfilling so many roles
at the same time."**

To balance the needs of the TC with the world's nontraditional demands, we often assume multiple roles. Mother, wife, homemaker, employee, friend, boss, neighbor, and mentor are just a few of the roles we might fill in a given day. For many of us, it feels natural and necessary to be all things to all people. To set limits, after all, is to run the risk of disappointing others and courting their disapproval. So we keep pushing, even though we rarely enjoy the feeling of being pulled in so many different directions at once. If you frequently find yourself performing multiple roles, you're probably controlled by your TC and are vulnerable to depression as a result of feeling drained, resentful, and angry.

If you've ever noticed yourself verbalizing these or similar feelings, pay attention. Think about which commandment of the Traditional Core you may be violating and where the cultural conditioning for that commandment comes from. Remind yourself that these ancient and modern cultural expectations no longer have to determine your behavior. Write down all the conflicts your TC causes you. Place your list in a linen handkerchief, an apron, a white glove, a basket, a frilly box, lacy lingerie that you no longer wear, or any symbol of tradition that appeals to you. Then take your first symbolic step toward breaking free from the grip of your negative by burying it or tossing it in the garbage. This action will effectively strengthen your commitment to staying aware of unhealthy cultural expectations and then assert your freedom and power to make role choices that really work for you.

Before we move into the next section of the book, which describes the six Healthy Depressions, it is helpful to summarize how all of these depressions and the Traditional Core are related to each other. The Healthy Depression pathways spawned by the Traditional Core and traveled by me and millions of other women are an inescapable part of being female in contemporary society. Women easily "grow" Healthy Depressions. Our culture seeds and fertilizes our Healthy Depression as a cost-effective, efficient mechanism to keep women "in our place." To better understand how this happens and how interrelated Healthy Depressions are, study the following diagram of the pathways of the Healthy Depressions.

Pathways of the
Healthy and Unhealthy Depressions

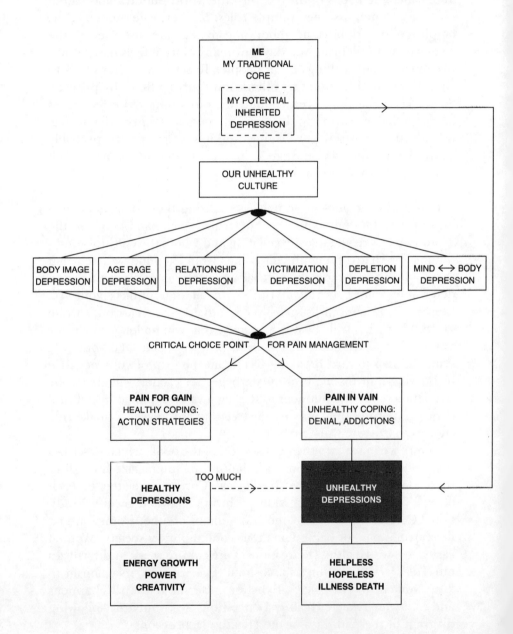

Note that in the top box, all of our Healthy Depressions begin with our Traditional Core and, for some of us, Inherited Depression. The Traditional Core is part of each of us because it is our cultural heritage. Inherited Depression may or may not be present, depending on our genetic makeup. Inherited Depression is the one depression that can lead to Unhealthy Depression without cultural influences, as probably occurs with manic depression.

The Healthy Depressions, on the other hand, all result from our cultural heritage and current cultural experience. We can't avoid the Healthy Depressions. Every woman has at least one or more in her lifetime, and often we experience several simultaneously. But we do have a choice about how we cope with them. If we use constructive coping mechanisms such as the action strategies in this book, our depressions stay healthy and manageable and become a source of growth and power because we have learned to convert our pain into gain.

If we use unhealthy coping strategies such as denial, addictions, blaming others, and feeling victimized to deal with our Healthy Depressions, we inevitably move into Unhealthy Depression. An accumulation of too many unresolved Healthy Depressions can also lead to Unhealthy Depression, which is precisely what happened in my own life. To keep this from happening to you, read the following chapters to become more aware of your own vulnerabilities to depression and experiment with the action strategies that appeal and apply most to you. When you come to your critical choice points in managing your depression, you'll be able to make more conscious choices regarding which path to take and what results you want to achieve.

PART II

• • • • • • • •

The Six
"Healthy Depressions"

·4·

VICTIMIZATION DEPRESSION

*Men still dominate; their critics still control; they and their
values are everywhere in command. To tell the truth about
women's lives involves courage, pain and commitment.*

Blanche Wiesen Cook

Ms. magazine

W hat I remember most about my childhood is a nagging feeling
that I wasn't quite good enough," says Sara, a round, effervescent
woman whose sense of humor was a welcome addition to our
women's group. "I always felt like I should try harder to please my
parents, especially my father. I can't remember him ever paying me
a compliment. What I remember are subtle threats and intimidation. He never hit me, but would sternly threaten to 'give me something I'd never forget' if I wasn't good."

The problem was that Sara never quite figured out what "good"
meant to her rigid, demanding father. His definition seemed vague
and ever-changing. What Sara learned instead was how to be quiet,
how to please and defer to men, how to play it safe and not take
risks, and how to use humor to neutralize aggression. She considers
men to be strange, unreliable creatures and typically keeps them at
a slight distance.

Considering her background and attitude, it's not surprising that
Sara has had little success in finding an intimate partner. She has
managed, however, to find a boss whose temperament and behavior
are remarkably similar to her father's. Without being consciously
aware of what she was doing, Sara re-created the unresolved relationship with her father by working for David, a notoriously stern,
unappreciative supervisor who believes the only way to manage a
staff of twenty-two women is with a scowl and an iron fist.

Whenever David is critical, which is more often than not, Sara swallows her pride and her pain and silently vows to try harder. But what has come to disturb Sara more than the treatment she receives from her boss is the fact that it doesn't bother her. When David threatened one afternoon that her job as a word processor was at stake if she made one more typing error that day, Sara felt anxious but not angry. The threat of abandonment, rejection, and loss from a male authority figure was so familiar that it seemed like a natural way to live. At 36, she continues to be a victim. The only thing that has really changed since the days when Sara's father threatened her is the identity of the perpetrator and the method of victimization.

By the time Sara received her third warning about her job performance in a matter of months, she was constantly worried about being fired and began experiencing stomach cramps, headaches, and fatigue. She was sure her physical symptoms were the result of working in a "bad building" with inadequate air circulation. In fact, the symptoms were rooted in a Healthy Depression, which was fueled by the chronic emotional victimization she faced every day on the job. Converting psychological stress and bad feelings into physical symptoms is a very common camouflage for Healthy Depression. Sara desperately wanted to believe she was physically ill. She felt more capable confronting a physical problem, but she had no idea what to do about feeling so bad emotionally.

Like Sara, Maria, 26, was unaware of how her past has led to her present vulnerability to Victimization Depression. Even though her husband, Joe, makes a decent living as a city fire inspector, Maria valued the sense of independence she got from working and contributing financially to the household. She was determined that the life she created for herself would never be like the one her mother led.

Maria wishes she could remember a time when she truly respected her mother. She grew up the youngest of three daughters in a traditional Italian household in which the roles were very clearly defined. Her father was a construction worker who brought home the bacon; her mother was a housewife who fried it up and served it. While there were times when happiness prevailed in the household, tempers often flared. Whenever her mother provoked her father or he had had one beer too many, it wasn't unusual for physical violence to erupt. Although they disagreed on many things,

Maria's mother and father seemed to agree that part of a man's duty was to discipline and put—and keep—his wife "in her place."

"My most vivid memory of my mother is watching her cower as my dad hit her," remembers Maria. "After slapping her around, he'd often storm off and disappear for the rest of the night. She was so frustrated that she would take it out on us kids. I blamed her for putting up with the abuse as much as I blamed my father for dishing it out. I vowed that I'd never let that happen to me or my kids."

Maria was stunned the first time her husband, Joe, slapped her several years ago. She had been working as a waitress at a busy neighborhood Italian restaurant and decided one day to open her own checking account. Maria was personable and good at her work, and it wasn't unusual for her to make $60 a night in tips.

In the five years they'd been married, Joe had never been violent before. But Maria's financial independence was beginning to threaten his ego. He backhanded her across the face one night while screaming that no wife of his was going to work outside the home if it meant she couldn't keep the house clean, too. Several hours later, when he cooled down, he apologized profusely and said he didn't know what had gotten into him. Maria told him that if he ever hit her again, she would leave. But what she ended up leaving was the job.

"The job just created too much tension at home," recalls Maria. "The hassle wasn't worth the money. We wanted to start a family anyway, so I guess it was all for the best."

Or so she thought. The next time Joe hit Maria, she left for an afternoon but was too scared and had nowhere else to go with a new baby. She returned and continued to be a victim of sporadic physical abuse. Maria thought it was futile to fight back because Joe was so much bigger and stronger. And he was often so loving and apologetic afterward, she remembers, that sometimes she felt the price she paid was worth the rare attention she received later.

Amy, a 28-year-old executive assistant in a large commercial real estate firm, would never tolerate being struck by a man.

"I'd kick the S.O.B. where it hurts," insists Amy. "As far as I'm concerned, any woman who puts up with that kind of treatment deserves exactly what she gets. You have to set limits and be very clear about what you will and won't accept."

Amy was as good at setting limits as she was at setting goals. She was extremely ambitious, good at her job, and always "dressed for success." She'd hoped to be placed in the company's management training program within the next six months. Her father had been a respected, successful real estate executive. She appreciated the good life it afforded her parents, and she wanted very much to win her father's approval by following in his footsteps.

Amy's personal life was as well planned as her career. She had been living with her boyfriend for nearly three years and was convinced they were right for each other. She wanted to be married before the end of the year. By 36, she planned to have two children and continue to work. She saw no reason she couldn't "have it all." Amy felt totally in control of her life and her future, and had little patience with women who weren't.

The only snag in Amy's master plan was Keith, a corporate vice president whose office was two doors down from hers. Keith was a major-league flirt, and he'd taken a shine to Amy. At first Amy good-naturedly laughed off his advances and jokingly told him to "save it for the Mrs." But as Keith became more persistent, she became more upset. For the first time in her career, she found herself without an answer.

She made every effort to avoid Keith, and her strategy seemed to be working. But at the office Christmas party, Keith cornered her as she came out of the ladies' room and held a sprig of mistletoe over his head as he tried to give her a kiss. The more Amy resisted, the more Keith insisted. As she pushed him away they were interrupted by a concerned coworker who had heard Amy's raised voice. Amy retreated back into the bathroom, just as she had years ago to escape a cousin's wandering hands. Keith angrily stalked off, embarrassed and humiliated in front of their coworker and concerned about the gossip that was sure to circulate around the office.

The next morning, Amy was called into a meeting by the company's vice president of human resources and informed that she was being terminated for releasing company secrets. No explanation. No proof. No hearing. Her belongings had been emptied out of her office and packed in a cardboard box. The locks to the executive suite had already been changed.

Amy's carefully planned future unraveled before her eyes. Her self-esteem, her reputation, and her future employment possibilities had all been compromised as a result of unfounded accusations and a wounded male ego. What made matters worse was her boyfriend's reaction when she explained what had happened. Although he tried his best to be supportive, he was clearly disturbed by Amy's corporate fall from grace.

In the days that followed, Amy's emotions ran the gamut from rage to disbelief. She considered filing a sexual harassment lawsuit, but her father convinced her it would be a costly and ultimately losing battle. Although she knew she'd been set up, she was still haunted by the nagging question: "What secrets?" She began to doubt her perceptions about everything, especially herself.

Like Sara, Maria, and Amy, most women have experienced some form of Victimization Depression. **Victimization Depression is defined as the bad feelings resulting from learned or real helplessness and a lack of coping skills to respond to the violence, negativity, and discrimination often directed against women living in this culture.** Many women gradually and quite naturally develop a victim mentality as a result of the pervasive sexism and cultural punishment we experience as the birthright of being female in our society. Feeling threatened, either vaguely or directly, wears us down and takes a toll. So does feeling helpless and out of control. And that lack of control is something women of all ages feel. Younger women are especially vulnerable to physical and sexual abuse. Older women are vulnerable to prescription drug abuse, poverty, abandonment, and isolation. Women in the middle are most prone to emotional and economic victimization and the victimization caused by excessive role demands.

Many of us are quick to deny our feelings of Victimization Depression because we often think there's something wrong with us rather than with the culture in which we live. Victimization has become so woven into the fabric of our lives, so familiar and so typical, that it's hard for us to step back and see that it's a major cause of our vulnerability to depression. It's also difficult to spot because it takes so many forms. In fact, there are four major varieties of Victimization Depression: Emotional Victimization, Economic Victimization, Physical Victimization, and Sexual Victimization.

Emotional Victimization

Emotional victimization is the result of being threatened with either abandonment or violence, feeling a consistent lack of emotional and/or physical safety, or being treated in a disrespectful or devaluing manner. Sara, who traded her threatening father for a threatening boss as the central male relationship in her life, suffered from chronic emotional victimization. Like Sara, we're likely to feel intimidated, insecure, and vulnerable when we're being consistently victimized emotionally. And, like Sara, we're often less effective at work and more likely to become physically ill as a result of the emotional drain.

Emotional victimization is the most common form of Victimization Depression among women. It often has the most devastating long-term effects because it robs us of our power and instills in us the identity of a victim. We learn to think and respond like victims in order to protect ourselves from direct or implied threats. According to experts, the consequences of living with the *threat* of physical or sexual abuse can be as damaging and debilitating to a woman as the actual experiences of battering, rape, and other sexual abuse.[1]

Women who identify with the role of emotional victim early in life often do exactly what Sara did. They populate their personal and professional lives with people who mirror and echo the emotional victimization they suffered as young girls and teenagers. As much as women hate it, victimization is familiar and sometimes even comfortable.

Economic Victimization

Economic victimization is the experience of inequality, devaluation, and oppression that occurs when a woman is not receiving equal or adequate pay for her work, or when she's threatened with living in or near poverty if she doesn't conform to society's or her partner's expectations of what a "good" woman is supposed to do.

Every woman has experienced this kind of discrimination at various points in her life, because society is set up to discriminate against us financially. Whether you're a woman who's earning big money in an established career or a woman who's suddenly faced with supporting herself in a work world that places little premium on the multiple skills of traditional women, you're a prime target for economic victimization. Divorced women are especially hard hit. Studies suggest that when a couple divorces, the wife's standard of living drops anywhere from 33 to 73 percent while the husband's increases approximately 42 percent.[2]

Things haven't changed much on the financial front for women over the past twenty years. Seventy-five percent of the people living below the poverty line in America—defined by our government as those living in households with earnings of less than $5,778 a year—are women and children.[3] A *Time* poll in 1988 found that 94 percent of working women reported significantly lower pay than men.[4]

Even though professional women are more insulated by money and status, they also feel the effects of economic victimization. Bigger gains are tempered by equally big losses, particularly psychologically and often economically. The fact that professional women are three times more likely to be depressed than nonprofessional women may very well reflect the economic and emotional victimization they experience.[5] Many professional women end up feeling helpless and hopeless as they try to advance in their careers, only to bump into "glass ceilings" and discover that the door to their future is locked from the inside. Over time, this frustration can lead to a Healthy Depression because feeling bad is the only healthy, appropriate response to such unfair conditions.

Physical Victimization

Physical victimization is more than being beaten. It's any kind of harmful or unwanted physical or sexual contact. How vulnerable are women? Probably more than you'd like to believe. And you're most vulnerable where you may believe you're safest—at home. Domestic battery is the single most significant cause of injury to women in America, according to former U.S. Surgeon General C. Everett Koop and the American College of Obstetrics and Gynecology.[6] A woman is physically abused in this country every fifteen seconds. Over half of all couples have had at least one incident of domestic violence in which the wife has been physically abused.[7] Physical victimization also occurs in lesbian partnerships, although it doesn't seem to be as common as in heterosexual relationships.

The devastating effects of this physical victimization live long after the bruises have faded. The depression some women experience, for example, may be partly related to undiagnosed head trauma that has resulted from being battered. Many women who have been physically victimized also suffer from a variation of posttraumatic stress disorder (PTSD), which comes from prolonged hyperalertness to danger and/or absorbing the actual effects of significant physical and emotional trauma. The chronic anxiety, physical withdrawal, frequent nightmares, deep mistrust, and emotional numbness experienced by women who have been physically, sexually, and emotionally abused may be part of a PTSD syndrome that has yet to be fully recognized as a consequence of the violence so many women face.[8]

Maria's mother was one of these women. She exhibited behavior consistent with PTSD as the result of the chronic physical abuse she took from Maria's alcoholic father. As the years passed, the abuse damaged her spirit as well as her body. Having seen how her mother's passive approach only fueled the fire of her unhappiness, Maria vowed to protect herself in the face of Joe's occasional physical abuse. But then one night, Joe smacked her and she lost her balance, hitting her head on the tile counter in the bathroom. For the next six weeks, she experienced periodic episodes of intense headaches and dizziness. Joe convinced her that the pain was "all in her head" and all but forbid her from "wasting money" on a neurological examination. It's entirely possible that Maria is suffering from an undiagnosed head trauma, a too frequently unrecognized consequence of battering. But she'll never know until she goes to the doctor. With this kind of physical victimization, she's also certain to develop a dark Unhealthy Depression that will only get worse until she takes a stand. She runs a high risk of becoming a chronic victim like her mother.

Sexual Victimization

One of the most damaging forms of physical victimization is sexual victimization. This includes any unwanted sexual contact, the threat of such contact, or exposure to unwanted sexual experiences or images. It can be as subtle as a stranger rubbing up against you in a crowded elevator or as violent as a brutal gang rape. It can include fondling, exhibitionism, voyeurism, oral sex, intercourse, and sodomy, as well as exposure to abusive sexual images in the media or in real life.

Understanding just how susceptible women are to sexual victimization is an eye-opening lesson in vulnerability and violence. A woman is raped in this country every six minutes.[9] At least one out of four of us will be raped or sexually assaulted in our lifetime.[10] Since only one in ten rapes are reported, according to the National Coalition Against Sexual Assault, the actual figures are certainly much higher. The same group has estimated that as many as one woman in three may become a rape victim.[11]

Sexual victimization of women is much more pervasive in America than in most other cultures. Women are twenty times more likely to be raped in the United States than women in Japan, and thirteen times more likely than women in England.[12] Rape reports surged 10 percent in the first six months of 1990, marking the sharpest six-month rise in ten years.[13] What's especially alarming is the decrease in the age of men who are victimizing women. There has been a 27 percent increase in rape arrests for boys under age 18, and a 200 percent increase in rape arrests for boys under 13.[14]

While rape is certainly one of the most violent physical acts committed against women, it's only one example of sexual victimization. Even though Amy never had any sexual contact with Keith, the vice president who attempted to steal a kiss beneath his traveling mistletoe, she ultimately lost her job as a result of sexual harassment and victimization. In their particular corporate climate, part of her unwritten job description as a "sweet young thing" was to service the boss's need for sexual validation, particularly in the "harmless" arena of a peck on the cheek or a playful pat on the rear. When she failed to meet this expectation, Keith felt entirely justified in having Amy unceremoniously fired.

Sexual victimization can be anything from obscene phone calls to men exposing themselves to us as we're driving down the street. It can be having a man secretly watch us undress from the window next door, or a husband or boyfriend who won't take no for an answer when we tell them we're not in the mood to be touched at the moment.

While none of these incidents is as emotionally devastating as rape, the variety and frequency of such sexual abuse adds up to create conditions in which Healthy Depression is a perfectly appropriate response. And more of us are vulnerable than you might suspect. A number of the experts have suggested that more than 50 percent of adult American women have had at least one significant incident of physical and/or sexual abuse before the age of 21.[15]

The implications of this statistic are quite disturbing. It means that in our society, it's normal for women to have been physically and/or sexually abused before becoming an adult. Unfortunately, what's also normal is that these kinds of victimization virtually guarantee a future depression. And when women experience those upset feelings, their depression is often fueled by the fact that they don't have a clue as to why they are feeling so bad.

This pain of victimization can be intense. If you're feeling hostile, detached, or depressed even while reading some of the material in this chapter, you know exactly what I'm talking about. It's probably hitting a little too close to home and tapping feelings of victimization from your own life. In individual therapy sessions, many of my clients become quite groggy or hungry at this point in our explorations. When I discuss Victimization Depression with women in my workshops or therapy groups, most of them simply slip into denial. The typical defense is to deny ever feeling victimized and to suggest that while they're sure the material is relevant to many *other* women, they've personally been spared.

Perhaps it's wishful thinking. Perhaps it's a desire to forget or leave the past behind. Perhaps some women think this is all an exaggeration or overstatement and believe things are changing for the better. Unfortunately, that's not the case. Violent crimes against women have jumped 50 percent in the past fifteen years, according to a recent U.S. Senate committee report. Over the same time period, violence against men *decreased* by 12 percent.[16]

Women who are deep in denial might dismiss such facts as mere statistics and consider them irrelevant to their lives. If you're one of those women, you may also think the word *victimization* is too strong a word for any of the bad things that may have happened to you. You may have done such a good job denying that you've had experiences similar to those of Sara, Maria, or Amy that you really can't reconnect to your bad feelings and therefore ultimately let go of the pain you felt.

Ironically, it's our very denial that makes us more vulnerable. That's why it's critical for you to appreciate how the statistics you've encountered in this chapter reflect reality—perhaps the reality of some or many of your own life experiences—and then invest the time and energy to explore how vulnerable you are to Victimization Depression and what you can do about it.

The following quiz will help you assess how at risk you may currently be to Victimization Depression.

VICTIMIZATION DEPRESSION QUIZ

Answer the following questions or statements YES or NO.

1. My parents, relatives, teachers, friends, or spouse called or call me names like "Idiot" or "Bitch," yell(ed) at me a lot, and/or abandon(ed) me, even temporarily. _____
2. They never hit me but many times threatened or still threaten to hurt me. _____
3. They often gave or give me the feeling I'm second rate simply because I'm female. _____
4. My mother wasn't allowed to work or was a single parent, so we struggled to have even the basics. _____
5. My brothers got money and support to go to college because they would "have to support a family"; I was left to fend for myself. I received no support for education or job training. _____
6. I am/was being paid less money than the men at my job, but I keep/kept quiet because I need(ed) the work. _____
7. My basic needs (proper clothes and food, medical care when I was sick, etc.) were neglected when I was a child. _____
8. I was spanked, slapped, kicked, pinched, bitten, burned, and/or shaken hard enough to leave bruises or marks or to feel pain. _____
9. I was forced to engage in oral sex, intercourse, or sodomy, and/or I was touched sexually or forced to touch another person when I didn't want to. _____
10. My husband or boyfriend threatens to leave me or withdraw his economic and emotional support unless I do what he wants me to do. _____

Total number of questions answered YES _____

SCORING

(0–2) Congratulations! You've escaped or been spared female victimization.

Many of us are unable to escape the victim mentality created by the cultural punishers because the sources of female victimization are pervasive and perpetual. You have either escaped or been spared the effects of this cultural punishment, and are in the wonderful position of being free from victim mentality. Savor and celebrate your freedom and use it to create and grow.

If, on the other hand, you suspect that you may be more vulnerable than you care to at first admit, then turn to the Denial Checklist on page 94 and fill it out. If you receive a high denial score, then come back and take the Victimization Depression Quiz again to get a better idea of where you really stand with this potentially debilitating form of depression.

(3–5) Caution: Proceed carefully.

You know what victimization feels like, but it doesn't rule your life. You have some Victimization Depression, but it's still within the healthy range. But proceed cautiously, because you are somewhat at risk for the depression to grow and deepen. The action strategies in this chapter may help you to contain and control your vulnerability to Victimization Depression.

(6–7) Beware: You have a Victimization Depression.

Your depression could become unhealthy if you don't make some changes immediately. This score indicates long-term potential damage that requires a great deal of direct attention and effort. If you still find yourself feeling victimized after finishing the exercises and strategies in this book, refuse to continue being anyone's victim and get the professional help you need. Even short-term therapy will be helpful and speed your healing process.

(8–10) You have an Unhealthy Victimization Depression.

While this book may help you understand what you're facing, it can't really help you heal it. No self-help book can, because the trauma you've experienced has been so great that you'll need professional help to resolve and heal it. There's just too much damage for you to fix alone. And if you don't get help, it's quite likely your Unhealthy Victimization Depression will get worse over time until you become mentally and/or physically ill.

Don't let this happen to you! You've already been victimized enough. Refuse to continue the cycle. One way to stop it is to turn now to Chapter 10, "Beyond Self-help," and read the section on page 297 on how to find a good depression specialist. Plan how you will go about finding that specialist and then *do it!* You can't afford not to.

With a better idea of what kind of Victimization Depression you may have and how severe it could be, you can begin to take steps to heal it—on your own if it isn't severe, or with a therapist if it is. There's a great deal you can do to resolve this kind of depression and decrease your vulnerability to it. The first step involves understanding the cultural and individual sources of the victimization.

Sources of Victimization Depression

1. Centuries of Male/Female Cultural Conditioning.

Centuries of cultural conditioning have trained men and women to play clearly defined roles. Men have been trained to be aggressors and to assert themselves. Women have been trained to be nurturers and victims. Men have been taught that their physical strength and size qualified them as the logical candidates to fill the role of provider. The implication, of course, was that this role made men inherently superior to women. Because of this conditioning, many men continue to believe they have certain exclusive rights and prerogatives, including the domination of women, ultimate sexual control, and even the right to become violent if women don't comply with their wishes.

Just as aggression is culturally perceived as "the male thing to do," women often tolerate the victimization because it's "the female thing to do." We receive training on how to be a victim from infancy. "From our earliest days, girls are trained to withdraw and

avoid conflict at all costs," says Shelley Neiderbach of Crime Counseling Services in Brooklyn, New York. Many developmental and
clinical psychologists would strongly agree with her statement.

Even the milder forms of victimization are silently endured by
most women. Emotional abuse is almost expected, as if it were our
due for being female. All of this deepens female patterns of passiv-
ity, dependence, and denial. It teaches us a kind of learned helplessness. These conditioned behavioral patterns guarantee a lifetime of
victimization for women if we accept them. If we don't learn how to
protect ourselves, it can also guarantee a lifetime of depression.

2. Women Are Culturally Punished for Wanting to Grow and Change.

The successes and failures of previous generations help establish the
social privileges and agenda for the generation that follows. Indeed,
the cultural punishment inflicted upon women in the 1990s is
deeply rooted in the past. The reality is that men have owned
women, both psychologically and legally, throughout many phases
of history. And many women—some consciously, many unconsciously—want to feel "owned." They see being the property of men
as a way to feel feminine and valued. In some respects, this behavior
may be self-preservation. After all, being or feeling owned and protected by men is still the safest, most rewarded role for women
in this society. One sure way to keep the peace is to maintain the
status quo.

The problem is that although these traditional roles may be comfortable for both sexes, they're healthy for neither. Women seem to
have recognized this fact sooner than many men. For the first time
in history, many women no longer want to be owned. We want,
need, and have begun to demand the right to make our own
choices, control our own bodies, and determine our own destinies.

Our motivations are both economic and emotional. Our culture's
economy increasingly needs women's power, resources, and skills
simply to remain competitive with other global economies and
maintain our standard of living. The June and Ward Cleaver sce-
nario of man as breadwinner is no longer realistic. Most women
today, whether married or single, work because they must. Others
work because they want to, for the same reasons men do: financial

security, self-esteem, personal challenge, peer contact, self-expression, and to make a contribution to society.

Profound economic and cultural changes have caused a collective anxiety attack for both men and women. Many of us find ourselves threatened by the rapid tide of change. No one is certain what is going on or where it's leading, and many women feel they can't win no matter what choice they make, which isn't surprising when you consider the mixed messages bombarding today's women. Those of us who choose to stay at home to raise a family are culturally revered for fulfilling a traditional role and then ignored at social events because what we do is "boring." We're encouraged to remain economically dependent and then often find ourselves with no money when we're widowed or divorced. Those of us who work outside the home are applauded for our determination, but we're often paid less than the man sitting at the desk next to ours.

For the first time, many men also feel fundamentally out of control. The traditional White Male power structure is crumbling. Our society is becoming so ethnically diverse that white male models of power are no longer automatically accepted. Territory that once was exclusively the white male's is now being invaded by women and ethnic minorities. Men are encountering women in the boardroom and sometimes even in the locker room, and many of them are outraged and depressed by what they perceive as an invasion. Men who never before worked with a woman are suddenly reporting to one. Some feel women are stealing their jobs. Rapidly shifting role changes are fundamentally challenging men's basic identities and their historically rooted superior position of power.

This fear and anger among both sexes has unleashed a phenomenal backlash of cultural punishment against women. While many men feel powerless to stop what they see as a steamroller of feminism, they can at least throw a wrench into the engine. By quietly or actively oppressing women emotionally, economically, even physically and sexually, many men subconsciously feel they're doing their part to maintain male superiority and protect their individual territory.

When you understand that female punishment is a cultural process, a legacy of the end of the twentieth century, you no longer have to experience your struggles, fears, and pain as a personal inadequacy or deserved punishment. You can appreciate your bad feelings as a healthy response to the unhealthy culture in which you live. With this insight, you'll feel empowered to move forward and refuse to be victimized by a process that's unjust, unfair, and unhealthy for both sexes.

3. The Media Continues to Perpetuate Images of Women as Victims.

According to the National Coalition on Television Violence, the typical child in America will have viewed 200,000 violent acts, including 40,000 murders, on television before the age of 18. And as anyone who watches movies or television knows, the great majority of this violence is directed toward women. An article in *Newsweek* reported: "In all of pop culture (as in most of society), women are the victims of choice. . . . An awful lot of hostility against women is being played out in popular culture these days, and it's not pretty."[17] This media violence may mirror society, but it also promotes and encourages the abuse and punishment of women by making it seem natural, and in some cases, even deserved.

Such victimization is more pervasive than ever before. Countless examples demonstrating the breadth and depth of the cultural punishment in the media can be found throughout the recording and advertising industries. The word "bitch," for example, is a common refrain in a number of popular songs. Female victimization is glamorized on album covers and music videos. Women are depicted being chained, tied up, and abused. Many times, the expressions on their faces suggest they're loving it. In 1987 the American Women in Radio and Television decided not to present its annual award honoring advertising that portrayed women positively. Why? Because they decided there were no worthy candidates.[18] In 1988 four of the five actresses nominated for the Academy Award for Best Actress were honored for their role as victims. The lone exception was Melanie Griffith, who played a victim turned victor in *Working Girl*.[19]

Ironically, even some self-help books do more to contribute to women's victimization than to resolve it. Despite the authors' good intentions, books like *Women Who Love Too Much, Being a Woman: Fulfilling Your Femininity and Finding Love*, and *Smart Women, Foolish Choices* explore a basic female inadequacy of thought or behavior, and then set forth a healing plan laid out by an expert who presents himself or herself as having The Answer.

Because the author is cast as the expert, whether or not he or she has the credentials or experience to support that position, it's implied that if you're smart, you'll listen as they explain The Answer to "fix" your inadequacy. This places the woman in a passive "patient" role in which she is viewed as sick or defective. Our review of the research on women and depression suggests that this expert/patient, superior/inferior model increases rather than reduces women's depression.[20] We've found that depressed women need to work in equal partnerships with their therapists, acknowledging that both have different roles but contribute equally to the success of the work.

There are a number of other problems with these types of self-help books. One of the biggest is that they begin with an assumption of individual inadequacy rather than cultural inadequacy. Susan Faludi articulates this problem eloquently in her book *Backlash:*

> Instead of assisting women to override the backlash, the advice experts helped to lock it in female minds and hearts by urging women to interpret all of the backlash's pressures as simply "their" problem. While of course many of the psychological problems that women (and men) struggle with are highly individualized and idiosyncratic . . . the counselors who dominated '80's bookshelves recognized *no* outside factors in their analysis and treatment of women. Backlash psychology turned a blind eye to all the social forces that had converged on women in the past decade—all the put-downs from mass media and Hollywood, all the verbal attacks from religious and political leaders, all the frightening reports from scholars and "experts," and all the rage, whether in the form of firebombings of women's clinics or sexual harassment or rape. These popular psychologists failed to factor in or even acknowledge the sort of psychic damage that a prolonged cultural onslaught was capable of inflicting on its targets.[21]

By wearing cultural blinders, the authors of some self-help books promote an expectation that by simply reading the book the reader should be able to change. If we cannot or do not, the failure is ours. After all, the expert *told* us what to do—why don't we just go do it?

The answer, of course, is that real, lasting change requires substantial determination and commitment. Most of us cower while standing at the gateway of growth. There are no easy answers, and shortcuts and quick solutions are typically what self-help books offer. Most oversimplify the complex in order to sell hope. At times, we have found that simplification is a necessary tool in this book, too. It's a way to communicate more efficiently about such a complex phenomenon as depression. However, a concerted effort has also been made to adopt simplified terms for women's experience without glorifying simple, quick-fix solutions. When experts advocate such solutions, we only broaden and deepen female depression.

4. Impossible Cultural Performance Expectations.

As Texas governor Ann Richards observed while addressing the 1988 Democratic National Convention, "Ginger Rogers did everything Fred Astaire did, only backward and in high heels." Increasingly, our society is demanding that we all perform as brilliantly as Ginger did. The pressure to perform in our multiple roles is overwhelming. Not only are we doing more, but we're expected to do it better. We're supposed to look beautiful. We're supposed to earn a living and still have energy to keep the house clean, the kids fed, the laundry done, the refrigerator full, and the lovemaking exciting.

The expectations our culture places on us are impossible. It's no wonder that depression results. It's not only understandable, it's healthy. We explore these performance depressions in detail in Chapter 7, "Depletion Depression" and Chapter 8, "Body Image Depression." Just remember: these impossible cultural performance standards not only create Healthy Depression, they are also one of the most consistent sources of victimization of women.

5. Women Reap Great Cultural Rewards for Remaining Victims.

"Nice girls" and "good women" are still rewarded in our culture for being victims. In fact, some women feel they have enjoyed so many rewards for being victims since early childhood that the role can be a very hard habit to break. A natural part of victim psychology is to victimize others when the opportunity arises, because we feel justified in treating others the same way we have been treated. The bottom line is that *victims victimize*. The person who is victimized reacts negatively, relationships become more problematic, and depression deepens.

Other women do the opposite and retreat to the traditional feminine victim role whenever they're stressed or victimized. Ironically, women who embrace this role either consistently or occasionally do so because they like being "protected" and "taken care of." They can be less responsible for their own behavior and choices. They can blame others for their pain and suffering. They can refuse to take responsibility for themselves and continue to express their rage through the passive-aggressive behavior loved so dearly by victims. All of these approaches, however, guarantee Healthy Depression and greatly increase the risk of Unhealthy Depression. By implementing and practicing the action strategies that follow, you will be better able to break free of Victimization Depression and lessen the risk of Unhealthy Depression.

Strategies for Overcoming Victimization Depression

1. Dissolve Denial.

Denial is a refusal to see or admit the truth. And many of us deny the truth of our painful experiences as much as possible. We often develop "selective amnesia" when it comes to remembering victimization experiences, especially things that happened to us as children. Experiencing the fears and pain of childhood makes us feel too vulnerable and out of control, so we simply try to forget as a way to protect ourselves.

Denial and selective amnesia are natural reactions to victimization and are often rooted in our Traditional Core, which makes us feel that we're to blame and that victimization is a natural part of being female. That cultural implication is so depressing that most of us need to deny or forget it in order to survive. It's very difficult to challenge these expectations and try to discover and tell the truth as we see it.

All things considered, denial may at first seem to make sense as a survival strategy for women. But while these self-defense strategies are natural and familiar, they're also quite dangerous and counter-productive. Denial creates blinders that keep us from seeing potential danger. Denial robs us of our feelings and drains our emotional energy. We find it difficult or even impossible to repair damage because we no longer have a true sense of what needs fixing.

Victimization amnesia is equally counterproductive, because it prevents full recovery. As author and counselor John Bradshaw has said, "We must feel to heal." We can't feel the pain if we choose to forget or pretend it never happened. The first step in resolving Victimization Depression is to confront your denial. By doing so, you'll begin to build the skills and confidence so that you can handle reality no matter how bad it gets. To dissolve denial, you must know what you are denying and that the payoffs for dissolving denial are enormous. Living openly and honestly allows us to be more focused, more alert, more aware, and more energized. Those who have confronted their denial and resolved the pain of their past find they experience a greater energy and vitality, which makes them feel more powerful and less vulnerable to further victimization.

To begin dissolving denial, review the following list of statements.

DENIAL CHECKLIST

Place a check next to the statements you have found yourself saying or thinking:

1. It happened to her, but it could never happen to me. ____
2. I'm as good or better than the men here; it's just a matter of time before they give me the credit I deserve. ____
3. I won't be intimidated. If I want to walk alone at night, I will. I'll kill those bastards if they bother me. ____
4. He would never leave me. He loves me too much. ____
5. I was never hurt as a kid; I had a great childhood. ____
6. I can "have it all"—a great relationship, kids, a good job, a beautiful body, etc. I just have to get organized. ____
7. I've never been treated differently just because I'm a woman. ____
8. I don't cry and I'm never depressed. What do I have to be depressed about? ____

If any of these classic denial statements sounds familiar, be careful! In virtually every instance, the reality is likely to be the opposite of what's being said. We are all vulnerable to victimization. "It" could happen to any of us. Many of us did experience abuse as kids, even if the rest of our childhood was "great." Few of us will ever be fully acknowledged for what we contribute on the job. All of us have suffered discrimination at some point simply because we're female.

It's becoming clear that although we may be able to "have it all," we can't realistically have it all *at the same time.* Women who deny the possibility of being abandoned are ignoring statistics that show the divorce rate for women over 60 has begun to approach the rate of divorce among younger people. And while most of us would love to believe we could kill a violent attacker, many women faced with the situation find they have difficulty being violent, even when under attack. Men have been conditioned to fight for their lives, but our Traditional Core has told us since childhood that violence toward another human being is wrong. When we have to protect ourselves, we often feel weak or even paralyzed.

Clearly, women have good reasons to feel depressed. But we also have some compelling motivations to do something about it. If you checked any of the statements above, go back and quickly rate how strongly you believe the statement applies to you on a scale of 1 to 10, with 10 meaning you believe the statement is true beyond any shadow of a doubt.

The higher your scores, the stronger your potential denial and the more you need to pay attention and be alert to actual or potential victimization. You're likely to be missing important cues around you and are probably forgetting or ignoring important information from your past. When you're more aware of your denial, taking the next steps in resolving Victimization Depression will be easier and you'll be more successful in using the strategies in this book.

2. Take a Victimization History.

A second important step toward dissolving denial and becoming free from victimization is taking a history of your previous and potential victimization experiences. The value of this process is that it will encourage you to examine these experiences more thoughtfully than ever before. You'll begin thinking about how things that happened to you as a child and adolescent affect the way you live your life as an adult.

Begin with a close examination of the four areas of potential victimization for women: emotional, economic, physical, and sexual. Utilizing some of the techniques in Chapter 2, become a mental health detective and search your family history for possible victimization experiences. Use the Victimization Quiz as a place to start asking questions of other family members and friends or to remind yourself of past experiences. Write down everything you can remember and are told, so that later you can put the pieces of the information puzzle together.

If you're sincere and others sense how much you want and need this information, they may be able to cooperate more fully than you think. Check with your family doctor or former pediatrician for information about potential victimization you may have experienced as a child. If you're in therapy, ask your therapist to cooperate with you in doing this project even if it's not a technique he or she might normally use. The information you may uncover will be invaluable for both of you.

If you find little or no evidence but still have a sense that victimization such as physical or sexual abuse occurred, you're not alone. This is a very common experience. Sometimes it truly means that nothing happened, but your feeling that something did occur is important and still needs to be explored. You're reacting to something meaningful even if it's not a specific traumatic event. Sometimes it means that victimization did happen, but it's just too hard to retrieve. The actual memory may or may not surface later. Sometimes it means that there were pervasive but indirect threats of harm that felt like abuse but were never directly expressed in a specific incident. What is important is the *feeling* of victimization. That's what must be explored and resolved.

3. Learn the Secret of Action Therapy: Action = Power.

In order to fully benefit from your feelings, memories, and reactions to your victimization, it's important that you recognize the enormous, energizing power of taking action. That's why we've developed Action Therapy as a supplement to existing therapy techniques for depression. It's based on a model of Action = Power, a model especially effective for women. We've discovered that it's not enough to simply ponder the past or talk about what happened. You need to directly express and release your feelings before you can heal the pain and repair the damage. As the following activities will remind you, words aren't the only way, or sometimes even the best way, to communicate.

A word of warning: As you prepare to begin this process, your negative Traditional Core may be sending messages remarkably similar to those you heard as a victim: "Just shut up, will you? There's nothing you can do anyway. It'll be over soon, dear." "It's not ladylike to be so angry. What's wrong with you, anyway?" "You have it so good—why are you complaining?"

But instead of choosing to listen to that ancient inner voice, you have a choice to communicate in a modern, action-oriented language. This means responding quickly and actively to memories of being victimized as well as to things that make you feel victimized today. It means expressing whatever feelings you experience when you feel them. It means rather than complaining to someone who can't correct a situation, communicating honestly and directly with the person who can. It means learning from past events so that you can prevent and avoid further victimization.

I know that the strategies in this chapter can help you become more powerful to reduce your victimization, because they've already helped many other women, including me. For you to get as much as possible from these activities and exercises, it's critical that you give yourself full permission to express *any feeling, any way you choose,* as long as you don't physically hurt yourself, hurt anyone else, or destroy others' property.

The following is a description of the Action Therapy program, which you can do on your own. The program involves two steps. The first is doing the exercises. If you express feelings directly through some kind of activity, you're less likely to deny the severity or impact of the feelings on you and others. The second is eventually talking about what you've experienced and what it means with a close friend, relative, partner, or even just out loud to yourself. A note of caution: if you try to talk about the feelings too soon, you're more likely to use denial, rationalize your feelings, and diminish the severity of your victimization.

What many of us who work in this field suspect is that no matter how mild or severe the victimization incidents, they are somehow registered in the brain, perhaps just as physical reactions to fear and/or abuse. Therefore, it would follow that if you don't use physical means to express these experiences, it's very likely you may not be able to release them completely. To date, little definitive research has been done on this front, so at this point we must continue to operate from instinct and clinical experience until these ideas can be clinically tested. Simone de Beauvoir in *The Second Sex* described the need for physical expression, which is the essence of Action Therapy, thirty years before the therapy was formally developed: "Anger or revolt that does not get into the muscles remains a figment of the imagination."[22]

At the Psychology Center, we do Action Therapy as well as "talk therapy," often combining talk and action exercises in working on nearly every aspect of victimization. The results our clients have experienced reaffirm my belief in this process. The action moves people more quickly and gets them in touch with emotions faster. The more people talk, the easier it is to drown in a sea of bad feelings and the harder it is to stay focused and connected. As Sara said after she beat up a pillow that symbolically represented her oppressive boss, "I get it now! Actions do speak louder than words —it releases my feelings more directly."

The following are the most effective Action = Power exercises we've developed to this point that can be done without professional guidance. There are exercises for each season, although you can do most of them throughout the year. At any time, there's always something you can do to cope with past, present, or future victimization. You just need to learn how.

When you first try the Action = Power exercises, you may find them embarrassingly primitive. In doing them, many women typically feel more physical and unfeminine than they're used to feeling. If you feel any of these things while doing the exercises, that's helpful. It's probably an indication you're doing them right. That's exactly what you want to feel so that you can break free from the conventions of the Traditional Core that would have you be delicate, shy, passive—and set up to be a victim.

Give yourself permission to roar, grunt, scream, kick, flail, moan, or hit. Do whatever you need to do to get it out. You won't feel unfeminine and awkward for long. A metamorphosis will occur. You'll feel increasingly powerful and effective as a woman and soon the Action = Power exercises will feel more natural and necessary. The Action = Power experience will become incorporated as part of you.

The Pumpkin Project

One of my favorite action exercises is the Pumpkin Project. It has taken years to develop and refine. By now it really works, thanks to the feedback of many women who have used it to help themselves become ex-victims. It works best to do the exercise with a friend, but it can be done alone. Buy a large pumpkin. If it's summer, a watermelon will do. In the winter or spring, you can always use the largest canteloupe you can find. Spread newspapers over and under your kitchen table, or do this project in the garage or outdoors where cleanup is easier.

Using a black felt-tipped pen, draw the face of a victimizer you're angry with on the pumpkin. The victimizer being symbolized in this or any other Action = Power exercise can be anyone from your past or present—a relative, friend, or stranger—who has hurt you and with whom you still have unresolved feelings. Make the face as ugly, abusive, and negative as you possibly can. As you draw and then study the face, pay close attention to how you feel. Give yourself permission to experience all the rage, sadness, regret, pain, and guilt you can muster as you stare into that ugly face.

Cut off the top of the pumpkin, as you would if you were making a jack-o'-lantern. But instead of neatly scooping out the seeds, pretend those are the guts of the person with whom you're enraged. Rip those guts out with your bare hands and throw them onto the floor. You can scream your rage, whisper your fear, or call him or her names. What's important is that you try to express verbally whatever you're feeling. Then use your bare hands to rip the pumpkin apart. Smash it, hit it, stomp it. Some women have used knives, but I strongly discourage it for one very practical reason— it's very easy to get caught up in this exercise and accidentally cut or stab yourself or damage your surroundings in ways you'll later regret.

Dealing with the remains of the destroyed pumpkin person is also very important. It's not enough merely to sweep them up and dump them in the trash. One client zapped her pumpkin boyfriend in the microwave. Another barbecued her pumpkin ex-husband on the grill. One woman who delivered wonderfully creative "last rites" put her abusive pumpkin mother in a plastic bag and ran her car over "her," gleefully driving back and forth at least forty times while listening to the loud heavy-metal music her mother always hated.

Another risk-taker smashed her ex-best friend on a fire hydrant and then dumped the remains in the garbage. An incest survivor buried her victimizer father at a remote beach and conducted a mock funeral for him though he continued to live nearby. During the service, she suddenly felt free from him for the first time in her life. It was dusk and the beach was deserted. She impulsively stripped off her clothes and dove into the water. As she swam in the sparkling white water and felt the warmth of the setting sun on her face, she cried tears of joy. She had never felt so free, so strong, or so clean.

When you're cleaning up after the Pumpkin Project, save some of the seeds. You can plant them to symbolize the growth and power that can spring from dealing directly with bad feelings and victimization. Later, if or when you feel ready, you can also broil the rest of the pumpkin seeds and eat them to symbolize forgiveness, letting go, and taking in the positive parts of the person or the experience. In the chain of human emotion, forgiveness often follows sadness and rage to complete the cycle and heal Victimization Depression. But be careful. Don't move to forgiveness until your anger is resolved or you'll abort the healing process and remain a victim.

Home Remedies: Ice and Phone Books

Action = Power exercises don't need to take as much time as the Pumpkin Project. Many items that are readily available can be converted into home remedies and quick responses to Victimization Depression. Ice is a great symbol of how we feel inside after being victimized. Many women experience their rage as having a cold, brittle, frozen quality. Our Traditional Core won't allow us to flare in the "heat of anger" as men sometimes do. We are expected to stash away our anger in an emotional deep freeze so it will never thaw. Angry women are just too dangerous, the negative Traditional

Core tells us. Women who have frozen their emotions are safer and less threatening.

To help thaw your rage, try the ice exercise. Take a bag of ice cubes and smash the ice against the wall of your house, on a nearby sidewalk, or on the roof of your apartment building. Better yet, try to go somewhere where you're alone and don't feel inhibited about disturbing your neighbors. You might go to a nearby park, playground, or beach. Throw the ice cubes with all the force you can muster and watch them explode as they hit the concrete or rocks. Pretend you are shattering your victimizer with each handful of ice you smash.

If ice is unavailable or unappealing, or if you're citybound and often stuck inside, you can achieve the same release of anger by tearing up old phone books. Hold the phone book, think about who you're angry at and rip that person apart, page by page. Crumple him (or her) up and throw him on the floor. Make a big mess around you. Relish your power to reduce your victimizer to trash. Push the remains into a garbage bag as you clean up and dispose of the garbage in the way you'd like to dispose of this person.

Spring Fling and the Spring Healing Garden

Spring is a time of growth, renewal, and expansion. Here are more Action = Power exercises that allow you to reverse roles and be the aggressor. Use an old doll or teddy bear or cut a body shape out of canvas to represent the victimizer and fling it to the ground from a second story window or from the top of a flight of stairs. Kick it, sock it, stomp it, smash it, rip it, tear it. Do damage, but only to your victimizer—never to yourself or your environment. Be creative in thinking up new punishments for the victimizer. When you're finished with this exercise, be sure to complete the process by "properly" disposing of the body as you did the pumpkin remains.

One of the most healing ways to dispose of victimizer remains is to plant a Spring Healing Garden, which can actually be planted any time of the year. Use your backyard, a garden box inside or outside your apartment, a special spot in the city park, the countryside, or the beach. Bury the remains of the victimizer you damaged. You can also make angry, ugly drawings of any of the other victimizers you've experienced and bury them in your new spring garden as well. Have a mock funeral. For example, make a coffin out of a shoebox and cover it with black construction paper. Burn candles, wear either black or life-affirming spring colors, and play special music (George Winston's "December" tape or CD has been a workshop favorite for victimizer funerals).

If you wish to share this experience with a trusted friend or relative, explain the context and meaning of the exercise and ask if he or she would like to join you. Amy asked her best friend to help her make a model of her office out of cardboard. They imprisoned a small doll representing Keith inside and buried it in the flower box. As she planted red geraniums over it, she vowed never again to be victimized so unfairly without fighting back. You can either plant your favorite flowers, as Amy did, or simply let nature take its course. Every time you look at your garden, you'll be reminded that your victimizer can no longer hurt you or stand in the way of your personal growth.

Summer Solace

Most of us have more energy and free time during the summer, so plan a summer retreat where you can go alone, take good care of yourself, and spend some time thinking, feeling, and writing about the victimization experiences you've had. Take a Feelings Journal (described in detail in Chapter 11 on page 305) with you to write down and/or draw your thoughts and feelings. It's a great way to keep track of your emotional life and the development of your problem-solving skills. During your retreat, be sure to write a letter to your victimizer telling him or her how you really feel about what they did to you, and what you would like to do to them in return. Spare no feelings of revenge. Anything is fine as long as you keep it symbolic. You may find at some point that you'll be at a loss for words. If that happens, don't stop writing. Just continue drawing lines or scribbling until you can tap back into your feelings. Keep writing until you've run out of anger and words, until you can write without intense feelings. This may take you one page, it may take thirty. Whatever you do, don't cut corners. Take your time.

When you're finished and have had time to absorb the experience, share your letter with a friend or relative who understands you and won't be judgmental. Ask your friend to help you bury or burn the letter to remind yourself how you're learning to let go of victimization and how you have support in doing it. Do not mail the letter to your victimizer, as it's likely only to invite further victimization.

Sharing the letter with someone you trust is important for two reasons. First, it will help you gain support at a time when you're vulnerable and can use it. But more important, it will release you from your role as a silent, compliant victim. You're a victim as long as you keep your victim experiences buried as dark secrets. By speaking the truth and acknowledging your pain, you will be taking a bold step toward freeing yourself from perhaps years of shame and anger.

Move with Power

To prevent victimization, there are times when we must see ourselves as powerful and learn how to move with power. It will serve you well, especially any time you find yourself feeling threatened.

Breathe deeply. Shallow breathing, which many of us unconsciously lapse into when we're feeling stressed or anxious, doesn't allow oxygen to flow as freely to the brain. As a result, our reaction time is slower. Muscles tighten and we don't think as clearly.

Stand Ten Feet Tall. When we feel potentially victimized we generally shrink. Researchers call it *somatic retraction*, which means we respond to a threat by slouching, tightening, or collapsing our chest, pulling our shoulders down and forward, and tensing our neck and back.

This body language invites victimization because we look like easy targets. We also begin to think like victims while in this stance, because that's the role we associate with such defensive body language. Not only are we draining our mental resources, but the muscle tension created from this position also drains valuable physical energy we may need to protect ourselves. When you're standing or walking as if you are ten feet tall, you're less likely to become a victim because you don't look or feel like one.

See Yourself as a Problem Solver. Whenever we're stressed, the familiar female response is to become the victim. Instead, use mental control to immediately replace your victim identity with a problem-solver identity. Rather than thinking, "I can't believe they did that to me," think in terms of "How can I correct this situation? What can I do to solve this problem?" Take a moment and write down these phrases as passwords to stimulate positive thinking. When stressed, think of your passwords and about solving the problem at hand. Put your feelings on hold. You'll have plenty of time to deal with them later, after you've resolved the stressful situation you're facing at that moment.

Acknowledge any stressful reality and see it as an opportunity to learn and grow. Quickly assess your alternatives and make the best decision based on the information you have. Then act. Even if you're feeling totally out of control, move with purpose and power as though you're completely in charge. This stance and strategy will prompt a potential victimizer to think twice before making his or her next move and will help you move more quickly out of victim identity.

4. Create an Anger Space.

Create a space in your home where you give yourself permission to get angry. This is the nineties' version of *A Room of One's Own*, which Virginia Woolf described many years ago as essential to a woman's mental health. The British novelist and critic believed that a woman's mental health depended on having her own room: a space for work, study, or relaxation, a space where she could go and not be interrupted by family or outside demands.

She was on to something. Not only do we need our own physical space, we also need a private emotional space to express and understand intense negative feelings. These days, we need a space both to nurture ourselves and tend to our mental health, as well as a space where we have the privacy and tools to deal fully with our anger. To help manage Victimization Depression, we need to create an Anger Space.

It might be a corner of the basement, where a punching bag substitutes for your victimizers. It might be a corner of the bedroom where you can pound on large throw pillows. Your Anger Space may not even be in your house. I have one client who goes for a short drive whenever she's angry. She pulls over on the side of the road and screams at the top of her lungs. She's usually back home within twenty minutes, feeling much better than when she left.

To insure that your Anger Space feels safe, it's important that you communicate your needs with those who share your living space. Explain that your Anger Space is your own private area, and ask them not to disturb you when you're in there. A Do Not Disturb sign may help to remind them. A Rogue's Gallery, a collection of pictures or drawings of people who have victimized you, is also a useful addition to any Anger Space. It helps make the victimizers visible and gives them an identity you can see and touch, so that you can deal more directly with your feelings about them. When you express your anger more actively, you'll begin to feel more in control.

You don't need to explain what you're doing or why. You do need to demand respect for your feelings and give those feelings the time, space, and attention they need. If you feel uncomfortable making noise or shouting because you can be overheard, learn the art of the silent scream and air kicks and air punches. Pretend that you're beating up an image of your victimizer and silently kick and hit him or her, screaming at least in your mind whatever he or she deserves to hear.

Even if you live alone, still designate a specific space so that you associate that area with permission to be angry and have all the tools you need in one place. The last thing you want when you're inspired to express your feelings is to be distracted searching for supplies. Supplies for your Anger Space might include large pieces of paper for life-size figures and feelings, red paint, colored markers, scissors, tape, darts, pins, foam rubber bats, pillows, cloth dolls, stuffed animals, piles of old telephone books, a punching bag—anything that will help you symbolically and actively express and release your anger.

If you give yourself the time necessary to express your anger fully, you won't need an Anger Space for long. But we all need a temporary sanctuary for a while in order to rid ourselves completely of the anger that so easily converts into depression.

5. Learn Nonvictim Thinking to Avoid Emotional Victimization.

How we think determines how we feel. If we think like victims, we're going to feel like victims. Changing how we think is one of the quickest ways to break out of our victim mentality. We can make that change by first understanding how often we cast ourselves in the role of victim, and then mastering the technique of non-victim thinking.

Begin by keeping a record of your victim thinking for three days. Jot down every time you find yourself feeling or thinking like a victim. Note where you were, why you felt that way, and how you responded. You don't need to make a big project out of it. The entries can be scribbled and brief. What's more important is that you write them down quickly so you don't forget.

You know you're engaging in victim thinking when you find yourself making the kinds of statements (to yourself or others) that fit into any of the following categories:

Category 1: It's a Cold, Cruel World

"This is so unfair! It shouldn't be happening to me."
"I shouldn't have to work so hard."
"I always help everyone else, but no one ever helps me."
"I try so hard to be a good mother. I should get love, but all I get from my kids is backtalk and headaches."

Note that "should" is a very popular word in this category. "Shoulds" are sure tip-offs that you're engaged in victim thinking, because "should" assumes that it's a fair, supportive world. Often it isn't, especially for women. To assume that it is only sets you up for disappointment and chronic feelings of victimization.

Category 2: It's Hopeless/I'm Helpless

"I'll never be able to lose weight."
"My wrinkles make me look so old and unattractive."
"No matter what I do, I never feel better."
"I've tried. I just can't do it."
"Things will never change. I just have to learn to live with it."

Absolute, extreme words like "never," "always," "can't," "everyone," "no one," and "impossible" are favorites in this category. We want to believe things can't be changed so that we don't have to make the effort to change them.

Category 3: The Angry Victim

"I hate my life and everything in it."
"Every time I trust men, I get hurt. I'm not about to give any more of them a chance to hurt me."
"She was so bad to me. I can never forgive her."
"They're to blame. I didn't do anything."

In this category, unresolved anger equals avoidance of responsibility for ourselves, which only keeps us stuck in our victim identity. If you can't let go of the anger and blame, you'll continue to feel and be victimized.

Whenever you catch yourself engaging in victim thinking, be sure to jot it down. Write down any thoughts you even suspect may be victim thinking. Then study what you've written when you have time to reflect on how you've been feeling. Write down some strategies and solutions to convert victim thinking into positive, problem-solving thinking.

If you think "This is unfair and shouldn't be happening to me," for example, you can convert that thought into "This is unfair and so typical of the way women are treated. What can I do to cope? I'm going to excuse myself, regain my composure, talk with friends later to learn how they've handled similar situations, and move with power until I feel more in control."

Instead of thinking "These wrinkles are so ugly!" think "Each wrinkle is a sign of my hard-earned wisdom. A woman my age doesn't look like she did at 18. Anyway, who would want to be 18 and go through all that again?"

"I hate him" can become "I'm so angry that I could really hurt him. But he's not going to drag me down and keep me stuck in all this hatred. I'm going to do some Action = Power exercises to release my anger so I can figure out what to do once I'm thinking more clearly." The key is to learn to identify when you're engaged in victim thinking and then convert these thoughts into more results-oriented, problem-solving thinking.

6. Develop Financial Power to Avoid Economic Victimization.

Women often feel powerless where money is concerned. Many of us were raised in households in which our father earned and controlled the money. Money is seen by many women as masculine, the ammunition of powerful men. As a result, we are often uncomfortable having financial power. Spending money is easy, especially if it was earned by a man or has male permission attached to it. But earning money is where many women run into psychological roadblocks. It's much more difficult for us to appease our Traditional Core, which tells us to pull back and be cared for. It's also harder for us to make realistic economic plans for our future because the Traditional Core doesn't value that kind of planning as relevant to our lives. These conditions make it all that much easier for us to be easy targets for economic victimization. To cope with this vulnerability, consider the following strategies.

Learn to be economically self-sufficient.
This is one of the most critical steps you must take to protect yourself from depression. Unless you're able to take care of yourself economically, you're vulnerable. Regardless of what our Traditional Core would like us to believe, it's virtually impossible to enjoy an equal, balanced relationship when we're dependent on another person for the basic necessities of life. Reduce your vulnerability by developing marketable skills. This must become a top priority, even if it means going back to school at 50, staying in school at 21, or working long enough in an industry to establish a level of expertise that will make you valuable to more than one employer. If you are not economically self-sufficient, you guarantee later bouts of serious depression.

Make a budget.
It's remarkable how many women don't keep a budget. They remain vulnerable to economic victimization because they never know how much they have or how much they need. More than 60 percent of my clients don't even balance their checkbooks. In some cases, their husband does it; for others, it never gets done. Tending to such monetary matters has never seemed like a necessary skill to

many women, unless they were asked by the man in their lives to help manage the family finances. While this is less true today than it used to be, many women are still fundamentally uncomfortable managing money.

It's important for women to gain a sense of financial awareness and power, no matter what their circumstances. If you're single and working but have never had a budget or financial plan, now is the time to change that. If you're married and working but your husband still handles the money, ask him to review the family finances with you. Since you contribute, it's not unreasonable to have a say in how that money is spent. If you're married, have never worked, and have never learned anything about finances, talk with your husband about your desire to know more about your financial status so that if you find yourself alone, you'll be better able to manage your affairs.

You can begin gaining a greater sense of financial power by simply balancing your checkbook if you don't already. If you're not sure how, ask the customer service representative at your bank to show you. I know some women who've gone so far as to close their existing account and start out fresh with a new account number that represents their new attitude of financial responsibility.

Once your checkbook is in order, make a budget. You can consult with an accountant, read a book on personal finance management, ask a friend or relative for help, or attend a workshop.

Update your budget once a month as you record what you spent the previous month. You'll soon have an accurate picture of how much you spend, where you spend it, and what you buy. You'll be able to examine your cash flow and evaluate whether the way you spend your money is compatible with your priorities.

By taking these first steps, you'll be reclaiming control of your finances. Not only will you be better prepared to build a more solid financial future, you'll be much less vulnerable to economic victimization. If you have a partner who is threatened by your desire for financial independence, reassure him and explain that it doesn't mean you're planning to leave. Explain that your goal is to feel safer and more secure in the relationship.

You can also point out that your efforts in this arena will relieve his pressure to always be the ultimate provider. You can share more of the burdens and benefits of that position. If you have a partner who still refuses to cooperate, keep negotiating. Be firm but as nonconfrontational as possible. You do have power because you have legal access to your shared financial records. You may need to exercise that right for your financial and emotional health, especially if your relationship is as unsupportive as this situation suggests. Knowledge of your financial resources is such an emotional and economic necessity that you can't allow anyone to interfere with your acquiring it.

Do short-term work to achieve long-term goals.
After you've made a budget and have established your financial priorities, look at your specific goals and make a list of what is most important to you. Do you want to attend your high school reunion? Do you want to send your daughter to camp? Do you want to enroll in school? Do you want to buy a new car?

If you're in a traditional role and want something you can't afford under your present budget, why not take on a part-time job with a specific goal in mind? If you work full time, you might consider looking for a part-time job one or two evenings a week. A number of my friends and clients have come up with creative, flexible ideas for part-time work. One offers Saturday day care. She loves children but doesn't want to have her own, so her weekend job satisfies multiple needs. Other women I know have part-time jobs word-processing at home, waitressing Sunday brunch, bookkeeping, teaching aerobics classes, and working as a salesperson in a department store some evenings and during holiday periods. Some volunteer for paid overtime at work.

All the jobs I've just described involve skills these women already had or could readily acquire. None of the jobs have to consume all your spare time, and all can be short-term until they provide enough money for you to achieve your specific goal. And unlike career opportunities, which are often hard to find, these part-time jobs are usually plentiful. Check out the job board at a nearby college and scan the classified ads. Put out feelers by letting your friends, coworkers, and neighbors know you're interested in part-time work. Read the ads on the supermarket bulletin board. If you look and are willing to work, you will earn the money and achieve your goal of feeling more powerful and less economically restricted.

7. Learn Self-defense to Prevent Physical and Sexual Victimization.

It's essential that we women learn to protect ourselves. To do that, we must learn to appreciate our strength and recognize that brains can overpower brawn. We must be willing to get in touch with our vulnerabilities and fears. By acknowledging how vulnerable we are to physical and sexual victimization, and by learning self-defense, we greatly reduce our odds of becoming victims. Recent statistics suggest that being properly trained in self-defense can stop about 75 percent of potential assaults.

There are some self-defense techniques you can learn without taking a class, such as trusting your instincts and being emotionally and physically prepared to defend yourself. But to combat vulnerability to Victimization Depression more effectively, women should seriously consider taking some type of self-defense course. Such courses are given through your local police department, YWCA, health clubs, or community colleges. Don't overlook the self-defense listings in the Yellow Pages. In the meantime, include these two common-sense strategies in your self-defense arsenal:

Trust your instincts.
Our Traditional Core provides great training in developing strong "women's intuition" and an inner sense to feel what we cannot see. It's one of the more positive qualities our Traditional Core affords us. Use it well! Many women second-guess their sixth sense and wonder, "What if I'm overreacting or I'm wrong?" We must learn to trust our gut instincts so that when we sense danger for any reason, rational or not, we respond with decisive action by moving away, saying or doing something to protect ourselves, and recognizing that it's always better to err on the side of safety.

If you have to defend yourself, be prepared.
Any prizefighter will tell you that the most grueling preparation for a fight is mental. That's just as true for you. You have to rehearse in your mind again and again how to protect yourself from battering or attack until your strategy of self-defense becomes second nature.

Only you know when and where you feel most vulnerable. Make a list of the articles you have around the house that could be safely used as weapons if an intruder surprised you, such as a fire extin-guisher you could keep under the bed. Decide on a potential non-lethal weapon, such as an umbrella, pin, or key, and be sure you always carry it with you. Mentally rehearse how you would use it if you were confronted on the street with a dangerous situation. Prac-tice in front of the mirror until you automatically know what to do and how to do it. It's important that you become comfortable with the notion of self-defense, even if it does mean responding to vio-lence with violence.

Adopt whatever mental images work in motivating you to protect yourself. One strategy that works for me is to imagine that I'm protecting my children from attack. The thought of anyone harm-ing them stirs such rage within me that I abandon my ambivalence about violence. I instantly shift emotional gears and find myself pre-pared to fight fire with fire. I'm not typically a violent or aggressive person, but I would kill in a heartbeat to protect my children. Being in touch with that raw emotion, I work on substituting the image of my kids for myself so I can harness that energy and fully protect myself, too.

As a result, my nonviolent values have shifted. Now that I better understand the alarming degree, frequency, and impact of violent female victimization, I've come to believe that we must actively re-spond to violence. We must do this not only to protect ourselves but to neutralize trauma that can lead to lifelong feelings of victim-ization.

Having worked extensively with trauma victims, I can tell you that the work done in traditional therapy is not enough to resolve the feelings that result from violent victimization. Words alone don't and won't fully heal. There must be follow-up action to make the trauma victim feel safe again as soon as possible.

The good news—and you can probably use a little at this point—is that victims of rape and other violent assault have more resources to turn to than ever before. If you have been or become a victim, accept that you can't heal such trauma on your own and get imme-diate counseling from a trauma expert.

Individual needs and circumstances vary dramatically, and there's no one way to better protect yourself. But I can tell you that if I were ever severely assaulted or truly feared assault, I would learn to use mace and a gun. In fact, to test these ideas for this book,

I took lessons at a shooting range. I now know what it feels like to literally take aim and blast the symbolic images of past or potential victimizers.

Shooting is a powerful equalizer that provided a greater sense of release from victimized feelings than I had imagined. Pumping cardboard profiles of your victimizer full of lead can be empowering. Release your rage and return to the shooting range when you're burdened with the flashbacks and nightmares that typically follow traumatic victimizations. If you find you really enjoy shooting, you might even join a competitive club to become more skilled.

I'm not advocating owning or carrying a gun, however, because the chances of it backfiring on you are great. Too many women have been overpowered by men who have turned their gun against them, and too many have seen their children shot accidentally in the home. It's not worth the risk. Shooting another person can also backfire emotionally. No matter how much our victimizer deserves to be hurt, gun violence is so opposite to our cultural conditioning as women that our Traditional Core can become quite disturbed and harass us for years with guilt and doubt if we injure or kill.

If we feel unsafe or have been physically or sexually victimized, we need to learn to use our bodies as weapons. Mace can also be effective, but since it too can be turned against you, be sure to take a class to learn how to use it. Certain canisters and techniques provide better protection and are less likely to boomerang. Your local police department will give you information about classes.

With resources such as mace, trauma counseling, self-defense skills, and a working knowledge of victim psychology, you will be better protected and empowered to prevent or resolve your victimization depression.

8. Rent Heroine Videos.

Women need heroines who take good care of themselves, refuse to play the role of victim, and function powerfully as strong, skilled problem-solvers. While Hollywood typically serves us a steady diet of women in traditional victim roles, there are rare occasions when we're treated to a female film character who can teach us a great deal about coping with and overcoming victimization.

Following are five examples of female role models who can be found in films. Each woman teaches us a different lesson, but they all share a strength of conviction and an inner determination to maintain their dignity and values. As you watch these or other favorite videos, identify what kind of victimization the heroine experienced. What were the sources? What kind of victimization symptoms did she demonstrate? What did she do to resolve the victimization and solve the problems? Which of her strategies could you use?

You can do this exercise alone or with a small group of friends. One client of mine turned this exercise into a six-week film festival that she dubbed "Marilyn's Monday Night at the Movies." She and five friends got together at her apartment every Monday evening for nearly two months to enjoy popcorn, a movie, and some provocative conversation regarding how the heroine rebelled against or overcame victimization.

Whether you do this exercise in a group or alone, be sure to either write down your answers or discuss them in detail so that you get the full value out of this experience. It's not enough to simply watch the movie. The value is in remembering the heroines as role models when you need their strength and support in your own life.

The Silence of the Lambs: Victimization Depression
Clarice (Jodie Foster) teaches us how powerful it is not to become defensive about our emotional vulnerability and how much power we gain by refusing to be victimized again as we were in our childhoods.

Working Girl: Economic Victimization
An ambitious secretary (Melanie Griffith) teaches us how to rise above emotional and economic victimization by learning marketable skills and refusing to quit until she achieves her goals.

Aliens II: Physical Victimization
Ripley (Sigourney Weaver) teaches us to master intense physical and psychological terror and overcome our victim thinking to face even our worst nightmare.

The Accused: Sexual Victimization
A provocative waitress (Jodie Foster) is gang raped and fights back in the courts. She reaches out for support rather than enduring the

pain of sexual victimization alone, learns to express her rage, and perseveres when her initial strategy fails.

Thelma & Louise: **for the ultimate female victimization**

Thelma (Geena Davis) and Louise (Susan Sarandon) learn—and teach us—the importance of friendship and support and how to tap into hidden resources of strength. They also teach us how unresolved rage can cost the ultimate price: death.

After watching some or all of these videos and completing a variety of the Action Therapy exercises, you'll notice some changes in yourself. Your victim voice may grow faint. Your physical movement and your thought processes will become more defined and confident. You'll command more respect as you come to respect yourself more. By resolving Victimization Depression within yourself, you'll invite less victimization from others and live more powerfully and freely than ever before.

·5·

RELATIONSHIP DEPRESSION

It is around losses of love that the clouds of despair tend to converge, hover and darken . . . these are among the commonest causes of female depression.

Maggie Scarff
Intimate Partners

Ayla, a tall, commanding African-American woman in her late 30s, was proud and powerful. A translator of Senegalese at the United Nations, she favored the flowing robes and beads of her parents' native country and loved strolling through the corridors of the U.N. at noontime, savoring the diversity of people and cultures and engaging in intense political and philosophical conversations.

Ayla's commitment to her ideals and her cultural identity were so strong that she inspired those around her. She was seen by many as a charismatic current of positive energy. But even though Ayla could light the lives of others, she quietly struggled with a dark depression that cast imposing shadows on her own life.

Her last lover, Abdul, was dynamic and intense both in and out of bed, but he was also so controlling that she eventually ended the relationship. That was nearly ten years ago, when she was 30. During the last decade, finding a man who appreciated her strength and was willing to work with her in an equal partnership proved more difficult than finding a parking spot in midtown Manhattan. Most of the men she met were either married, gay, or intimidated by her strength and intensity.

Her relationships with women weren't much better. Few of the single women she worked with seemed to share her interests, and most of the married women whose company she enjoyed had lim-

116

ited free time to socialize outside work. The few friendships Ayla managed to maintain were often riddled with conflict and misunderstandings. Whenever problems occurred, Ayla tended to withdraw and retreat to her parents' house. As unpleasant as that environment could often be, Ayla felt comfortable there. Sometimes, it was simply better than being alone.

Ayla felt emotionally bankrupt. Even though she was ambivalent about men, she couldn't help but wonder whether she might have been happier if she'd taken a more traditional path, married, and had children. Now that she was approaching 40, she felt as though her time was running out. She felt that racism and ageism had shrunk her potential pool of suitors more than her own mistrust of men ever could.

Tina and June were more insulated from depression than Ayla. They had relied on each other for the intimacy and emotional security that Ayla lacked. Together, they had escaped the economic struggles, discrimination, and depression that is often experienced by those whose lives flow outside the cultural mainstream. The two women developed a loving, supportive relationship when both were in their mid-20s. For the past nine years, they have lived together in a home they designed and built overlooking a river in Ohio.

Many of their friends considered Tina and June the "ideal couple" because they maintained a comfortable, satisfying division of labor and complemented each other so well in their interests and temperaments. Tina was very much the traditionalist of the two. She rarely missed her former job as a flight attendant and loved staying at home, cooking, taking care of the house and their three dogs, working out at the gym, and organizing their busy social lives.

June, the nontraditionalist, was disorganized and somewhat manic, but she was also extremely effective in her role as a political consultant. Bright and competitive, she loved few things more than waging—and winning—a fierce political battle. For some time, June had earned enough money to support Tina and herself quite comfortably. Since money, status, and winning were critical components of June's self-esteem, her high-powered job had been a perfect fit for her personality. But in the last year or so, a series of political setbacks and losing campaigns had left June riddled with insecurities. She couldn't help but wonder whether she'd lost the magic touch she once had.

June began taking out her frustration on Tina. Before she was home from the campaign trail even twenty-four hours, she and Tina often found themselves locked in confrontation. June began hungering for more of an emotional and financial partner. She wanted the freedom to accept fewer clients, but that wasn't possible unless Tina went back to work. Tina, however, had no desire or intention to look for work outside the home. She was convinced June was just "going through a phase" and resented the fact that June didn't fully appreciate her contribution to their relationship. Tina felt attacked and devalued, and found herself increasingly unable to tolerate June's hostility. Both June and Tina felt misunderstood, unsupported, and inadequate. Their fights and frustration escalated in intensity and frequency because their traditional and nontraditional roles were clashing rather than complementing. As a result, they became even more rigid, polarized, and fixed in their roles. Without compromising to achieve a sense of balance, their depressions deepened and their relationship was doomed to self-destruct.

Dana and Jack know how frustrating relationship pressures can be. Married for four years, they had been together since they met during their last year of college eight years earlier. Jack was one of the few sensitive, "New Age" men Dana had met who wasn't intimidated by her ambition. In fact, Jack was stimulated by Dana's drive, not to mention her scathing wit and offbeat sense of humor. While Jack completed law school at USC, Dana earned her MBA at UCLA.

Jack became a successful family law attorney. Clients appreciated his rare combination of warmth and his ability to negotiate firmly. Dana became a successful bond trader specializing in Japan and other Pacific Rim countries. Both were highly committed to their work and to supporting each other in their careers. Rather than conform to clearly defined roles like Tina and June, they blended roles and shared equally in the financial and household chores. They never fought about housekeeping because they didn't do it. They hired part-time help to do the laundry and cleaning.

But just as Tina and June had, Jack and Dana also experienced problems. Both were so committed to building their careers that they often forgot to build the relationship. After a while, Jack began feeling drained by the demanding, angry clients in his law practice. He had always been proud of his capacity to listen, understand, and inspire trust, but he found himself growing impatient and irritable at work and at home.

What Jack wanted more than anything was a wife who would listen, care, and help him achieve some balance and perspective. But what he usually encountered was a woman who was as absorbed in her own world of demands and deadlines as he was in his. Although Jack was proud of Dana's accomplishments, it irritated him that she always seemed to be studying flow charts or doing marketing analyses on the computer. Part of his frustration stemmed from the likelihood that Dana might outearn him during the coming year. He was even more anxious about their lack of time spent together.

Dana couldn't understand Jack's discomfort. They had agreed to support each other in their work, but increasingly Jack resented what he saw as Dana's selfishness. As a result, their conversations either grew brief or deteriorated into arguments. Sex—or the lack of it—had become a real issue. Jack felt he "deserved" a romantic partner to sleep with after working so hard at the office and being such a "good guy" at home.

Like many nontraditional men, however, Jack was rarely direct about his needs. He tried to be especially sensitive to Dana's needs often at the expense of his own. Dana frequently ignored his indirect sexual advances and encouraged him to go to bed without her. She felt that unless she worked late many nights, she would fall behind. Disappointed and angry, Jack often went to sleep wondering whether he might be happier with a more traditional woman or whether he should simply have an affair with a woman who would appreciate him.

Dana was every bit as frustrated as Jack. She resented his condescending attitude and the unspoken implication that her work couldn't be that challenging and wouldn't take so long if she worked smarter instead of harder. She barely had the energy to take care of herself, yet Jack kept making more and more subtle demands. More than once, Dana wondered whether it wouldn't be easier to simply live her life alone. Even though she loved Jack and knew he loved her, the demands of their professional lives were creating considerable conflicts that neither knew how to resolve.

Ayla, Tina, June, Dana, and Jack are all experiencing Relationship Depressions. **Relationship Depression is the sad, mad, and bad feelings caused by the absence of a meaningful relationship when one is desired, or by the conflict, disappointments, frustrations, and mistrust that are an inevitable part of maintaining meaningful relationships.**

Relationship Depression results from two primary sources:

- low self-esteem that either keeps us from having any relationships at all, or limits us to unhealthy or negative relationships.
- a lack of relationship skills, which typically results in relationships that are unsatisfying and fraught with problems.

Ayla's Relationship Depression grew from needing close relationships and not having them. Part of the problem was cultural: formidable racism, ageism, and sexism. But another part of the problem was personal. Ayla suffered a self-esteem problem not uncommon among professional women. While she possessed high self-esteem at work, she frequently felt incapable and inadequate in developing close, lasting relationships that made her feel good about herself. As a result, she no longer trusted people enough to invest the time or energy necessary to find and build adequate relationships.

Even though June was involved in the kind of relationship Ayla once desperately wanted, she too experienced low self-esteem. She had a relationship yet had no idea how to cultivate it. Because she didn't treat herself well, she didn't know how to treat Tina well. June lacked a number of basic relationship skills. The absence of those skills was a primary source of her growing Relationship Depression.

Neither Dana nor Jack, on the other hand, had much of a problem with self-esteem. Both were typically confident and competent, but they lacked the more advanced skills necessary to maintain their relationship during the inevitable rough spots that every couple encounters.

We can have Relationship Depressions whether we're single or married, in a friendship or romance, or in a platonic or sexual relationship. They can result from past or present relationships, including those we experienced in childhood with our parents, relatives, teachers, and friends. Relationship Depressions only occur if we have an emotional investment in another person and expect our emotional needs to be met by them. These depressions don't occur with strangers, colleagues, or acquaintances because we don't have intimate, loving connections with them.

While both women and men experience Relationship Depression, women are more often vulnerable. We tend to define more of who we are through our relationships, rather than through our achievements as men typically do. We are trained to be more sensitive to the natural ups and downs of relationships and to assume responsibility for them. The pain of others often becomes our own.

Our cultural training has been so thorough that it would feel almost abnormal to many women not to feel this sort of chronic relationship pain. For this reason, Relationship Depressions are the most common of the Healthy Depressions. Victimization Depression is the most destructive, but Relationship Depressions have become so familiar they are a way of life for many women.

The problem is that no matter how good a relationship is, it's constantly evolving. And change typically generates uncertainty, conflict, and periods of Healthy Depression for all of us. There are times when even the best of relationships exact a high price and take more than they give us in return. I've finally accepted, for example, that I'm always going to be vulnerable to relationship loss and disappointment because I experienced so much of it as a child and continue to accept too many relationship responsibilities as an adult. When I do too much for others at the expense of my own needs, I create my own Relationship Depressions.

Over the years I've come to discover that I'm not alone in this vulnerability to Relationship Depression. Many of us grew up in families stricken by loss, addiction, violence, and poor communication. With such backgrounds, we remain vulnerable to relationship loss no matter how much therapy or growth work we do. Our losses have been planted too early and run too deep into the essence of who we are.

It's important to understand that while they never go away, relationship vulnerabilities can become manageable and contained so they don't dominate our lives. These vulnerabilities are another example of when feeling bad is good. They can be converted into a very powerful source of strength, the kind that makes you feel more confident and therefore attracts more intimacy in your life. We cre-

ate this "intimate power" by learning to acknowledge our vulnerability and use it to ask for what we need and want. Converting
vulnerability into intimate power typically works like this for most
women:

Sharing Vulnerability = Intimacy = Connection = More Power

Uncomfortable as it can sometimes be, we create intimacy in two
ways. First, we create it by sharing our vulnerabilities with people
who can understand and won't judge us, and by creating conditions
for them to do the same. Secondly, intimacy is born out of conflict.
If you've ever seriously fought with someone and resolved it in a
mutually acceptable manner, your intimacy bond will forever be
deeper, no matter how frustrated you were or how terribly you
fought.

It is intimacy that creates our feelings of connection, that essential
experience we must have to maintain our physical and mental
health. The exchange of support and validation that connections
provide is empowering for us. The positive side of being relationship custodians is that we have more opportunities than men for the
intimacy and connection experiences that strengthen us. I've seen
so many women find the strength they need to handle a difficult
challenge as a result of the support and energy they've received
from intimacy and quality relationships. Feelings of connection allow us to flex our emotional muscles. We feel whole, energized, and
renewed; we're no longer alone as we face challenges. Consequently, we're more powerful and effective in resolving problems in
the outside world.

It doesn't seem to work quite the same way for most men. Sharing
vulnerability is just not the "male" thing to do. That's why Jack has
so much trouble being direct about his needs and vulnerabilities
with Dana. He'd rather suffer from loneliness and frustration than
tell Dana how much he needs her time, attention, and validation.
Clearly, these cultural formulas are a tragic waste for both sexes.

One of the best ways to break this cycle of loss is to resolve our
own Relationship Depressions. It's only by helping ourselves that we
can fully encourage men to explore their vulnerabilities without
either of us feeling too threatened or needy. Begin by answering the
following questions about your personal and family background to

get an idea of your vulnerability to current Relationship Depression.

RELATIONSHIP DEPRESSION QUIZ

Answer the following questions YES or NO. (If a parent or parents were not your primary caregivers when you were a child, substitute the name of the person or people who were most like parents to you.)

1. My parents were divorced before I was 20. _____
2. One or both of my parents died before I was 20. _____
3. One or both of my parents were very sick with a life-threatening illness or chronically ill for more than a year during my childhood. _____
4. I was physically or sexually abused as a child. _____
5. One or both of my parents were alcoholic or seriously addicted to drugs, gambling, shopping, eating, etc. _____
6. I have been shunned or badly treated at school or work because of my gender, age, race, creed, sexual orientation, or other personal qualities I can't or won't change. _____
7. I've been divorced one or more times. _____
8. My intimate partner had an affair or affairs. _____
9. My friends and family are often unavailable to give me what I need when I'm stressed. _____
10. I'm uncomfortable with intimacy; I seem to choose the "wrong" people or sabotage relationships that may be "right." _____

SCORING

**(0–2) You possess excellent social skills
and had a healthy family background.**

The women who score in this category have indeed been fortunate. If you're among them, you experience very little or no Relationship Depression. You've developed excellent social skills and are quite likely to have had a healthy, normal family background.

But do be sure that if you score in this lower range, it isn't simply because your answers reflect the way you *wish* it was rather than the way it actually was. Seeing our past and present relationships through rose-colored glasses is one sure way to set ourselves up for Relationship Depression. If you find yourself saying or thinking that you had a "perfect childhood," look again. You may have, or you may be kidding yourself because the truth of your life has simply been elusive or too painful to face.

(3–5) You probably experience a moderate degree of Relationship Depression.

You're experiencing the kind of relationship pain and vulnerability familiar to most women. This degree of Relationship Depression seems to be the price we pay as women because our conditioning and assigned position in society is to be the relationship custodians and intimacy maintainers. And that's not all bad. In fact, if we keep them balanced, these nurturing roles offer many rewards. But balance is very difficult to maintain in a culture that is itself so fundamentally out of balance and out of touch with the needs of half its population. Relationship Depression only worsens if we don't know what is happening to us, why, and what to do about it.

(6–7) Beware! You're experiencing a significant degree of healthy Relationship Depression.

If you scored in this range, you've probably had so many losses and disappointments in your past and present relationships that you carry a great deal of unresolved relationship pain. This degree of loss and pain makes you especially vulnerable to Relationship Depression. You're also more likely to be too needy in relationships, which virtually guarantees further relationship problems and ultimately leads to even greater Relationship Depression. Your Relationship Depression is so strong and well developed that it has a good chance of progressing into an unhealthy range if it hasn't already.

One way to evaluate whether this has happened is to complete the Relationship Inventory, which can be found in the action strategies section on page 130 of this chapter. If you find a pattern of chronic failure and dissatisfaction in most or all of your relationships, or have withdrawn from relationships and spend most of your time alone, your Relationship Depression has probably moved into an unhealthy range. If so, professional consultation will help you minimize the negative mental and physical consequences of this depression.

(8–10) Danger! Your Relationship Depression is unhealthy and destructive. Without help, your relationships will continue to be unsuccessful and debilitating.

With your background of relationship pain and loss, you've never had a chance to learn and develop the skills necessary for building healthy, loving relationships. It's important to acknowledge that relationship loss and failure was and probably still is an ongoing pattern in your life. That's an unhealthy and unnecessary condition for any of us to endure and it can have life-threatening consequences. It's nearly impossible to resolve this much relationship loss and pain on your own. Get the help you need from a depression expert. One specializing in interpersonal therapy may be particularly valuable, because this form of therapy focuses on building relationship and social skills. Group therapy may also be very helpful, because it provides a safe place to explore your relationship fears and failures and practice new relationship strategies in a supportive atmosphere.

If the Relationship Depression Quiz has made you feel sad or uncomfortable, you're not alone. You're experiencing feelings many women describe after taking the quiz in the workshops. Because we're women, we are held responsible for relationship pain in our culture; that pain is a chief cause of our greater vulnerability to depression. To protect ourselves from this kind of depression, we need to build and maintain satisfying relationships and know the sources of Relationship Depression so that we can evaluate how much of it is a cultural waste product rather than our individual inadequacy.

Sources of Relationship Depression

1. Females Are Culturally Conditioned from Birth to Be More Vulnerable to Relationship Depression.

The most important, influential source of Relationship Depression is cultural conditioning. From the earliest days of their lives, girls and boys are treated very differently by their mothers and fathers. But haven't times changed? Isn't there a new generation of children being raised by more aware, nontraditional parents? Some eye-opening answers can be found by visiting your local nursery school. At my son's nursery schools in both New York City and southern California, parents who consider themselves contemporary in their childraising techniques encourage their sons to talk about their feelings and their daughters to play soccer.

Yet what we constantly observe are distinct differences in the approaches and attitudes of boys and girls. The little girls are much more relationship and feeling oriented. If one of their playmates has been hurt or is sad, most of the girls will try to do something about it by offering to share a toy, a kind word, or a hug. Many of the boys, on the other hand, will ignore the situation—even if they've caused it—and move easily to the next activity.

This difference becomes even more pronounced in adolescence, when our Traditional Core wields more clout than at any other time of our lives. It's as teenagers that most girls first learn what being female in our society really means: conforming and pleasing others, often at the expense of pleasing themselves. They are culturally encouraged to switch their focus from achievement to relationships. Grades plunge and hemlines rise as the search for validation from others, especially males, becomes a priority.

When female teenagers turn to men, whether their fathers or boyfriends, they often find themselves unable to gain access to the man's softer emotional side. In the male arena of achievement, power, competition, and control, the desire and ability to nurture is rare. So they turn to other women—mothers, sisters, friends, and teachers—and often have difficulty getting what they need because those women can't provide a sense of perspective and validation that they themselves don't have. The result is lower self-esteem and depression for female teens than for their male counterparts.

By adulthood, we're likely to experience Relationship Depression whether or not we have relationships. Recent studies have found that the lack of an intimate relationship with a spouse or boyfriend increases women's vulnerability to depression,[1] just as it did for Ayla. But if we have relationships, the inevitable problems and conflicts can also lead to depression, for two basic reasons. First, as women, we assume a disproportionate responsibility for maintaining relationships, which often drains the energy we need to take care of ourselves. Second, we've been trained to experience relationship problems as personal failures. We tend to measure our value in terms of how successful our relationships are.

Our cultural conditioning has made us especially vulnerable to Relationship Depression, but that does not mean we've been dealt an inherently bad hand. Many of us play it that way, but our training as females also enriches us with qualities and abilities that serve us well throughout our lives. It allows women a quality and quantity of relationships unknown to most men. It makes girls more verbal than boys, better communicators about subjective experience, and more sensitive to others' feelings. All are skills desperately needed in an increasingly impersonal, aggressive world. Women know the wisdom and strength that can be found only in relationships; we just need to channel it more toward ourselves rather than constantly give it away to others.

2. We Deny the Inevitable Pain and Vulnerability of Relationships or We Suffer in Silence.

While successful relationships are critical to our well-being, even the most loving, satisfying ones can sometimes be riddled with conflict and disappointment. Few of us want to be reminded of this basic fact of life. We desperately want to believe that if we just find the right relationship, read the right self-help book, watch the right talk show, or consult the right expert, we'll have the right relationship and therefore escape the pain. So we deny our pain or suffer in silence because we think relationship pain is our fault anyway.

If only it were that easy! Even when we're doing everything right,

128   WHEN FEELING BAD IS GOOD

there are times when relationships feel all wrong. It happens to all
of us. We struggle and fail and quit and heal and try again. Relationships are so complex, dynamic, and ever changing that a particular technique that works at one moment and with one person may
not work even ten minutes later. Relationship needs are challenging and constantly changing, so it's easy to forget the few rules
that remain constant: Try not to hurt the other person. Be trustworthy. Care about the other person as much, but not more, than
you care for yourself. And perhaps most important, accept that conflict is inevitable in order to grow, learn, and achieve greater intimacy.

Conflict is to be expected because any two people who try to
develop intimacy are bound to have differing ideas and needs, no
matter how mature, well intentioned, and socially skilled. We all
experience "flashpoints," those explosive, tense moments of friction
when the needs of two people clash. When both needs can't be met
and compromise or letting go becomes necessary, friction and
sparks are bound to result. The flashpoint creates anger, withdrawal, pain, fear, and depression as part of the experience until
these feelings are worked through by communication and compromise. If the relationship is unhealthy, flashpoints will stir feelings of
victimization, withdrawal, and revenge. We often try to deny that
flashpoints mean anything. Yet, if unresolved, these feelings can
build to an explosive confrontation that often blows the relationship
apart.

While flashpoints create discomfort, denying them can be even
more destructive. If used to grow, flashpoints also lead to a much
greater sense of awareness and intimacy. In confronting and resolving our conflict with another person, we learn much more about
who that person is and whether we can really count on him or her.
These are the experiences that provide the glue to hold relationships together and make us feel closer, more intimate, and more
willing to risk being vulnerable.

3. We Underestimate the Time and Energy Necessary for Exploring, Developing, and Maintaining Relationships.

Different skills are necessary during each stage of a relationship, and many women have never been educated to recognize the need for learning these skills, much less understand when and how to use them. We tend to use the wrong skills for the wrong stage of the relationship, or to hold on to skills that once worked but are no longer appropriate because the relationship has evolved to a new stage. We often move too quickly and reveal a sense of neediness. We believe that we must have a certain relationship with a certain type of person in order to feel complete and adequate. When we operate out of this kind of desperation, our relationships inevitably crumble like a house built on a faultline.

Developing new relationships is often difficult for women because it requires us to take action in a way that is typically foreign to our upbringing. It involves learning to create appropriate social opportunities for ourselves, and requires that we be willing to risk rejection.

It takes a significant amount of time and energy to create and build relationships worth having. Once we've developed one, maintaining it requires hard work, shared goals, patience, empathy, compromise, and a commitment to long-range goals, even if it means short-term sacrifice for the sake of the friendship or partnership. This stage also requires the ability to deal with anger, competition, and conflict resolution. Most women are inclined to avoid conflict, especially with other women, because they're convinced that "fighting" puts the relationship at risk. Even when Relationship Depression is the result of staying silent, it's a choice many women make.

A major problem in contemporary relationships is time, or, more specifically, the lack of it. During certain phases of our lives, personal relationships require a greater commitment of time and energy than our work. For women already faced with role overload, time is our scarcest commodity. Exhaustion, burnout, and Relationship Depressions often feel like inevitable experiences of contemporary life. Yet there are a number of techniques women can use to change this inevitability.

Action Strategies for Resolving
Relationship Depressions

Successful relationships are built on the four stages of learning depicted in the relationship pyramid shown below. The lower stages are larger because they provide the foundation on which all relationships are built. Understanding each step and the progression from one to the next is essential before beginning the action strategies for resolving Relationship Depression.

The Relationship Pyramid

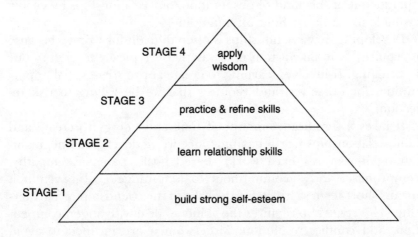

Stage 1, building strong self-esteem and a healthy, loving relationship with ourselves, is the foundation of fundamentally satisfying relationships. Stage 2 involves learning basic relationship skills, including how to communicate more effectively, meet adequate people for friendship and/or romance, keep ourselves from becoming too emotionally vulnerable, strengthen relationships by building trust and partnership around shared interests, and know when to give and take. Stage 3, practicing and refining relationship skills, involves learning how to manage destructive and constructive anger, resolve conflict, build true intimacy, maintain the quality and quantity of relationships we want, and encourage growth in the person you like or love. These skills can be learned only through experience, not through simply reading or talking about relationships. At the apex of the relationship pyramid is Stage 4. Applying wisdom involves consolidation and application of the three previous steps by harvesting our relationship wisdom and directly applying it to every aspect of our lives.

Let's now focus on ways we can convert our relationship pain into sources of strength and energy. The following action strategies have been developed in our workshops and classes, and are the ones that many of my clients and students tell me they've found most valuable. A number of my personal favorites are also included. These exercises can be used by singles, by those in partnerships, and with close relatives and friends.

Some of these strategies will appeal to you more than others. Remember that not every exercise or strategy is intended for every person. Think of the options included here as a menu of choices. Trust your instincts and do only those that sound intriguing to you at the moment. You can always come back to the others later, but try to zero in on at least two of the strategies now. By becoming active and improving your relationship skills, you're already taking a big step toward neutralizing Relationship Depression.

Stage 1: Building Strong Self-esteem

1. Develop Your Independence and Learn to be Alone to Reconnect with Yourself.

In order to build greater self-esteem, we must begin by honestly assessing how much we genuinely like and appreciate ourselves. Do we take good care of ourselves, or do we neglect or even abuse our bodies and minds? Do we appreciate our own company and enjoy being alone?

If we're not careful in tending to our own needs, Relationship Depressions can be compelling examples of when feeling bad is bad and only gets worse. We have no real power or security in any relationship unless we have the strength and ability to leave it. If we're insecure or threatened by the thought of being alone, we will be too needy and unable to attract the kind of people we want to have for friends or romantic partners. In the relationships we do have, we then tend to become especially vulnerable to manipulation, victimization, and abandonment, and are likely to remain in a relationship if it's unhealthy or unsafe simply because we fear being alone.

Being alone for any significant amount of time can feel like punishment or a confirmation of our inadequacy, because one of the ways most of us have learned to judge our worth is by the number of loving relationships we maintain. As a result, we waste the precious "alone time" we do have, using it to wonder *why* we're alone rather than simply appreciating the fact that we *are*.

Instead of sacrificing these important opportunities to grow and reconnect with ourselves, it's essential that we realize that being alone—whether only for a day here and there or for years—can sometimes be our healthiest, most positive choice. Ironically, sometimes being alone is especially important when we're involved in a romantic relationship. Time alone, especially for role-overloaded women, enriches time together.

We know independence doesn't just happen. It must be cultivated and nurtured. But how? Stage 1 is acknowledging how essential it is to build a good relationship with oneself in order to have good relationships with others. Whether you're single or married, set aside some alone time every day, even if it's only ten minutes of solitude every evening before you go to bed or return from work. Use that time to reflect on what's happening in your life and to reconnect with your real feelings and needs. Time alone can take many forms. For some, it may mean a stop at the library instead of going straight home from work. For others, it may mean a long drive and an overnight stay in a place they've never been. However we spend it, successful alone time gives us a richer relationship with ourselves and consequently with others.

Commit to writing or drawing in your Feelings Journal (described on page 305 in Chapter 11) during your ten-minute break. In one year, you'll have invested more than sixty hours in self-reflection and will have a much better idea of the changes you need to make in order to meet your goals.

Graduate from ten-minute breaks to going away by yourself, even if it's only for a day or two. This can be life-affirming and life-changing. It's a great way to break a cycle of unproductive or unrewarding time alone and gain perspective on how your life is progressing.

Your trip doesn't have to be long or expensive. It can be an overnighter at an inexpensive but safe motel. It can mean staying at a friend or relative's house while they're out of town. It can mean going somewhere during the off-season. Ideally, your getaway will last at least several days, but even a day trip is better than no trip at all. Try to get away to a place where you will have space and solitude. It helps to visit beautiful natural settings where you can walk or sit and think undisturbed. John Muir, the famous naturalist who explored Yosemite, said it well when he referred to the process as "going out to go in."

Whatever kind of trip you decide to take, be clear on why you're going. If you're single, don't fall into the trap of wondering whether you'll meet the man of your dreams while you're away. If you're married or have children, don't spend your precious time alone worrying about your husband or kids. The goal of your getaway is to rekindle your relationship with yourself.

Traveling alone was among the most effective techniques I tried during my darkest days as both a single and married person. When I was single, I visited Yosemite twice, hiking to the top of the falls. I carried a canteen, fruit, and a note pad and pen so that I could stop to write or draw whenever I felt like it. Another time I went to my childhood beach house on the Oregon coast to walk on deserted beaches, nap in the sea grass, make clam chowder, read diaries I kept when I was 13, and write in my Feelings Journal about what I was learning and how I wanted to change as a result.

Other times, usually when I was depressed, I drove alone to the desert or mountains to hike, write, and think. Once I was married, I continued to find these occasional alone trips to be just as essential, even just for an overnight getaway at a country inn or city hotel.

These kinds of trips typically provide an infusion of self-esteem, because they are reminders that we can count on ourselves no matter how we feel. They can give us a clearer picture of where we've been, where we are, and where we're going and help us recharge, refocus, and regain energy.

In her book *An Unknown Woman*, Alice Koller eloquently describes the typical struggles so many women face when deciding whether to claim time to be alone and go off by themselves: we're too tired, we don't have enough money, we're too afraid, we don't know where to go, we don't have a goal. Her story is inspiring as she slowly and painfully resolves each of these issues by allowing herself to be alone and feel bad so she can feel good again. After weeks of solitary self-reflection, she began to reconstruct a new identity and a new life that felt far more rewarding than anything she'd ever known.

For those who find themselves uneasy with the notion of being totally alone, there are group trips that build in time alone for personal growth. Vision Quest, for example, originated from Native American and aboriginal cultures as part of the rites of passage from childhood to adulthood. In the contemporary version, people come together for anywhere from several days to several weeks to share workshops and ritual experiences. They use a variety of emotionally expressive techniques, going out into nature—"the heart of Mother Earth"—by themselves and returning to the group to share what they've learned. Outward Bound is another kind of helpful nature experience for women who like physical and psychological challenges. Clients who have done these kinds of adventures have found them empowering and useful in building their self-esteem.

If you're intrigued, you can learn more about these growth experiences by reading New Age magazines or writing, calling, or talking to people in alternative bookstores such as East West Books in New York City or Book Soup in Los Angeles. They'll be able to recommend books, magazines, and newspapers that focus on alternative, nontraditional learning experiences.

If, on the other hand, you have a Relationship Depression from spending too much time alone because you're single or your partner is consistently unavailable, assess what you can do to improve the quality of the time you spend alone. You might begin by turning off the television and telephone and spending time writing in your Feelings Journal. Resolve to use your time alone more intimately and to provide more validation for yourself. Setting aside this kind of time daily can help you better focus on what you need and want during the following day. You can then establish realistic, short-term goals for taking better care of yourself. Write your goals down. The following evening, review how successful you were in accomplishing them. Try this exercise for two weeks and you will feel more in control and focused on your bigger goals in life.

Another important action strategy if you spend too much time alone is to make a commitment to develop better relationship skills by joining support groups or groups focused on helping others. These can be self-help groups, classes, weekend workshops, or groups at your church or synagogue. Or become involved with groups that need your help in promoting a cause you believe in. Volunteer with a group that promotes environmental protection, delivers food to shut-in seniors, or raises money for animal rights.

Participating in these kinds of groups gives you three valuable benefits. First, you'll gain a greater sense of self-esteem from having done something useful. Second, you'll connect with others, which will reduce your vulnerability to Relationship Depression. Third, these group experiences help you cultivate skills that will enable you to achieve more intimate and satisfying relationships, particularly in developing the very important "Family of Choice" described in Chapter 11.

These action strategies offer a way to gain emotional independence by doing something worthwhile for and by yourself or for and with others. You may, however, still find the thought of being alone anxiety-provoking. Many women do. But achieving even the smallest steps in being alone successfully ignites self-esteem, because being alone in productive ways is such a strong self-affirmation for women. With that self-affirmation, we are more able to affirm others and can more easily move into Stage 2 of the relationship pyramid.

Stage 2: Learning Relationship Skills

2. Learn to Communicate More Effectively So That Your Relationships Can Grow.

Trust, both physical and emotional, is the most important element in a successful relationship, whether it's a close friendship or a relationship with a relative or a partner. Unless both people in the relationship feel safe and secure, it's impossible for true intimacy to develop and flourish.

Intimacy is built on the opportunity to be ourselves and share our vulnerabilities, to build trust as we experience the strengths and the weaknesses that each of us possesses. We create this essential safety by staying in touch with our own needs as well as the needs of others, and by knowing how to set boundaries through Power Dialogue and powerful behavior when our needs or integrity are being violated.

Power Dialogue isn't a mysterious, secret language. It's just foreign to most women. As Deborah Tannen described so well in her book *You Just Don't Understand*, men and women communicate in different languages. We use the same words, but how we use those words and what they mean to each of us differs dramatically. What I call Passive Dialogue is the language system taught to women—the native tongue of the Traditional Core. With Passive Dialogue, we learn from our earliest days to go with the flow and by our silence and placating to keep peace. We meet others' needs, often at the expense of our own.

Power Dialogue, on the other hand, is a language in which we set boundaries and communicate our needs and values, and what is and is not acceptable. This capacity to establish boundaries is critical in order for intimacy to develop and the relationship to grow. But setting boundaries is tough for women because our Traditional Core has taught us to have either very flexible boundaries or no boundaries at all. The fact is that many of us have had very little experience using Power Dialogue. We have trouble because in the process of making time for ourselves, we're sometimes forced to ignore or place less value on the needs of others. When this occurs, the Traditional Core tells us our behavior is selfish and unfeminine. If we listen to this voice, however, we set ourselves up for Relationship Depression because we are, in essence, choosing to remain passive, dependent victims of our own inability to identify and communicate our needs.

The first step in developing this relationship skill is acknowledging that you *have* legitimate needs and must set boundaries in order to have those needs respected. This is the most difficult step. When asked to list her needs, Tina, June's traditional partner, asked, "Needs? What're you talking about? I don't really have any needs."

There are many women, like Tina, who have been conditioned to deny or devalue their needs. But in order to grow, we have to make a commitment to understand and acknowledge our needs. To do anything less is to guarantee depression.

The second step is learning to use one of the shortest but most powerful words in the English language: *No.* This one little word can change the course of our life if we learn to say it whenever we're feeling uncomfortable or unsafe in a relationship. We are in unsafe relationships when someone we care about is too competitive, critical, and judgmental with us or demands we do something we don't want to do. It's unsafe and unacceptable if we're threatened with abandonment or violence. It's unsafe to be in a relationship in which another person consistently makes us feel bad about ourselves, whether they mean to or not.

These situations show us where Power Dialogue is needed. Make your "No" statements as brief and to the point as possible, using words, body language, and a tone of voice that leaves no doubt that you mean what you say. Being assertive is much more powerful than being aggressive. By clearly stating how you feel and what you need, you dramatically increase your odds of getting it. In his book *The Performance Edge,* Dr. Robert Cooper suggests the following structure for effective communication, especially when intense feelings are involved:

$$\text{When you } X, \text{ I feel } Y, \text{ because } Z.^2$$

You state what behavior bothers you, how it makes you feel, and why. In a close relationship with a friend, relative, or partner, you might say, "When you raise your voice like that, I feel so upset that I can't remember what you're saying." This is an example of Power Dialogue. You could also say, "When you raise your voice like that, I feel upset and we both lose because I can't think clearly and we can't solve the problem." Other examples of Power Dialogue in a couple relationship might be, "When you threaten to reject me, I feel angry and we both lose because I start thinking about how to reject you first." In a couple relationship or with a relative or friend we might say, "When you put me down, I feel bad. Then you seem to feel bad because I withdraw from you to protect myself."

There are many proven techniques in Power Dialogue. Some that work especially well for women, given our difficulties with assertion, include the following:

The Broken Record. One of my favorite techniques comes from Manuel Smith's book, *When I Say No I Feel Guilty.* To use this approach, you simply say the same thing over and over again, using the same or different words, until you either get a different response or you leave. There are at least a dozen ways, for example, to say, "This isn't working for me. We need to reach a compromise." You may say it nine different ways before you finally hit pay dirt with version number ten when the other person can finally "hear" what you're saying and change his or her behavior. If the other person simply can't or won't hear you, either try another approach or withdraw to protect yourself. Whatever you do, don't back down if what the other person is saying or doing makes you feel unsafe or uncomfortable.

Empathize firmly. Women have been trained from birth to rely on intuition, to put themselves in another person's place and know how they feel and what they need. Use this special ability in Power Dialogue to diffuse intense feelings that typically become unproductive. You can say, "I understand how you feel. It makes total sense to me," and add some detail that shows you really do understand and accept how the other person feels. Or you could respond to the other's comments by validating feelings he or she is having, "If I were in your place, I would feel the same way because . . ."

Whenever you find yourself embroiled in a conflict with another person, ask yourself how—and if—both of your needs can be met without either of you sacrificing essential feelings or desires. Creating compromise and win/win outcomes is the goal. Being "right" and "winning" an argument creates the illusion of victory—you win the point but lose the game, because "winning" distances the other person and often sets the stage for "getting even" later.

Learn to use Time Outs. There are times when effective communication isn't going to happen and conflicts aren't going to be resolved. It may be because both parties are so emotional or angry or needy that both need to be heard but neither wants to listen. When passions rise, objectivity is lost. It might be because one or both of you feel threatened or simply too tired at that moment. Or it could be that you're no longer fighting over the issue at hand. You may be battling an unresolved ghost from the past and reacting as if you are talking to your mother or father rather than your spouse or friend.

Whenever you find yourself in this situation, try taking a Time Out. Most of us associate Time Outs with disciplining children or strategy sessions in sports, but they can serve us well in adult communication, too. Just as they do on the football field, Time Outs enable us to take a break so both parties can reassess their positions and strategies more rationally after cooling down.

Whether we're involved in a conflict with a spouse, friend, or relative, Time Outs are a self-management and relationship technique that really works if both people involved respect the boundaries and make agreements to follow through with them. The best time to discuss Time Outs is when you don't need one, when you're both open, relaxed, and communicating freely. It's important to establish that either person can call a Time Out and agree upon how one is to be called.

In some relationships, for example, it's done by simply saying "Time Out." Other couples use a hand signal or pass a note that says "I need a break." If there's the threat of violence, a place can be designated in the home as a sanctuary where the person who feels threatened can go and not be bothered. You can agree to put a lock on the door if necessary.

Any method is fine as long as you're both clear on what it means. In most circumstances where I've seen Time Outs used successfully, the person calling the Time Out indicates how long he or she needs. Depending on the intensity of the discussion and the issues at hand, it could be five minutes, five hours, or five days. Some Time Outs simply mean that a particular subject is off-limits for a given amount of time. Others mean that no communication between the two parties will occur for X amount of time.

The only way Time Outs can work is if both people have agreed to them with mutual respect for the process of conflict resolution. Once you've made such an agreement, honor it no matter what. Don't allow your temper to rule. Nothing you may want to say during a heated discussion can't wait. During a Time Out, it's often better to remove yourself temporarily from the situation. Take a walk. Go to a movie. Retreat to a safe space and write or draw. Collect yourself and return when you feel more in control.

If you're visiting someone and conflict erupts that you feel unable to resolve during that visit, tell the person that you're too upset to stay. Simply say you need a Time Out and don't give any more explanations or justification. Before you leave, however, be sure to give him or her an idea when you will be in touch again. Make it clear that you're leaving in order to cool down so that you'll be better able to resolve the conflict at a later time.

This last step is a critical relationship skill. It maintains the connection with the person while allowing healthy separations to occur. We have a responsibility to those we care about to make it clear that we are not abandoning or rejecting them or terminating the relationship just because we need time to think or cool down.

One of the most powerful and effective ways to reconnect after a Time Out—or to avoid Time Outs in the first place—is to acknowledge your contribution to the problem, even if you're convinced it was minuscule. Most conflict in close relationships involves about a 50 percent contribution from each party. For example, even if we "didn't start it," we often respond in a way that causes the conflict to continue or to escalate. In contrast, if we just look at our part in the conflict and take responsibility for it instead of spending our time and energy on forcing the other person to accept his or her responsibility and to change, we become free and more powerful no matter what the other person does.

If, after reviewing the situation objectively, you think you behaved badly, be sure to say so. Take the risk of sincerely apologizing. Also accept that if the other person is still angry, he or she may need time and space to absorb your apology or work through his or her own issues before the anger eases. If you can tolerate the discomfort, your admission will create safer conditions so the other person can stop fighting you. Accepting responsibility can be very liberating and helpful in achieving whatever you want: a resolution of the conflict and a return to closeness and the freedom that comes from knowing you have done all you can to resolve the conflict.

3. Use Videos to Examine Relationship Problems and Develop Relationship Skills.

You can learn a great deal about relationships—which ones work, which ones don't, and why—by studying some of the more interesting relationships depicted in films. Among the films I'd recommend for this purpose are:

Fatal Attraction
A fascinating example of how traditional and nontraditional roles are experienced and portrayed in popular culture. In this film, only the nontraditional woman is depicted as unstable, destructive, and dangerous. It's a common undercurrent in film and television, though rarely presented this graphically.

The War of the Roses
This discomforting film shows us how responding to violence and aggression with more violence and aggression can easily lead to tragedy in intimate relationships.

When Harry Met Sally . . .
This contemporary film shows us how nontraditional relationships can work these days. Unlike traditional couples, who communicate mainly through their roles and exchange of resources, nontraditional couples find talking about their feelings and sharing roles essential to building and nurturing their relationship.

Class Action
Maggie, a very successful, very conservative corporate lawyer teaches us that while opposing our parents doesn't free us from them, discovering and accepting who they are does.

The Big Chill
This was the first film to show how a network of close friends in a variety of traditional and nontraditional roles can enable us to create a rich "Family of Choice" that can be as, or more, comforting, supportive, and intimate than the family into which we were born.

4. Do a Relationship Inventory.

Go back to the definition of Relationship Depression at the beginning of this chapter and write it down. It will come in very handy as you do your Relationship Inventory, which will enable you to evaluate the quality of your relationships and determine whether they cause or prevent depression for you.

To begin, write down the names of all family members, close friends, important dating partners, and work partners and anyone else who plays a key role in your current life and with whom you have a close attachment. Include everyone who comes to mind, whether you like them or not. Once you're fairly certain your list is complete, study it and assess whether you're feeling any degree of Relationship Depression as a result of interacting with these people. How does being around each of them make you feel? Over time have you been better or worse off for having them in your life?

What do they give you, and what do they take? What is it that each
of them does to make you feel good or bad?

To take stock of your current relationships, make a Relationship
Inventory List by putting three headings across the top of a page.
Under the heading "Positive," list those people who help most in
preventing depression, who make you feel good about yourself by
appreciating who you are and being there for you when you need
them. Under the middle heading, "Negative," list anyone who is
rarely or never helpful in preventing depressed feelings, who contributes to your feelings of emptiness or meaninglessness by being
unreliable, self-centered, or taking a great deal and not offering
much in return, or simply not being available enough. Under the
last heading, "Toxic," include any of those people who consistently
leave you feeling bad instead of good, who poison your self-esteem
through criticism, exploitation, competitiveness, or attacks. Next to
each name jot down a word or two to remind you why that person
falls into that particular category. The headings on your Relationship Inventory could look like this:

MY RELATIONSHIP INVENTORY

Positive	Negative	Toxic
Create intimacy/ good feelings about me	Create feelings of emptiness/ meaninglessness	Poison my self-esteem

Some of the people on your list may fall into two or even all three
categories. If so, you can list their names in each and draw arrows
connecting them to remind you how fluid these people can be in
stimulating the best and worst in you.

Many of the women in the workshops prefer at this point to
recopy their Relationship Inventory, this time listing the names in
order from most positive to most toxic. What they discover, sometimes to their surprise, is that more men in their lives, including
those they love, fall into the Negative and Toxic categories, while
the women they love often appear in the positive column, a natural
result in our sexist culture.

Until Ayla did her Relationship Inventory, she hadn't fully realized that this was true of most of the men in her life. They were either irrelevant because their traditional training left them incapable of understanding her (her father, for one), or were sometimes toxic (like her former lover, Abdul) because they attempted to restrict her choices and assert their presumed male superiority by trying to make her feel inferior, dependent, and controlled.

The following is the Relationship Inventory that Ayla developed. Some of the labels have been added to identify that person's relationship to her.

AYLA'S RELATIONSHIP INVENTORY

Positive	Negative	Toxic
Sheena (closest friend)		
Maxine (work friend)	Maxine (too competitive with me)	
Charles (childhood friend)	Charles (wimpy and demanding)	
Tanya (friend)	Tanya (too depressed)	
	Kyle (very strict father)	
Abdul (exciting lover)	Abdul (macho/ insensitive)	Abdul (drained my self-esteem)
	Edna (angry mother)	Edna (constantly critical of me)

Ayla's mother, Edna, was in a class by herself. She was the most toxic of all because she felt so threatened by Ayla's independence and "liberated" choices that she handled her discomfort by being consistently hypercritical of nearly everything Ayla did. This pattern had started in childhood and grew worse as Ayla grew more successful. Edna's dislike and mistrust of men had also been highly contagious. As she studied her Relationship Inventory, Ayla realized that when she listed the names in order, she had to list her mother last because theirs was the relationship that benefited her least and was ultimately the most destructive.

For the first time in her life, Ayla could clearly see that there was a great deal she could do to protect herself from Relationship Depression. She began to discuss her feelings with the other participants in the workshop. It became obvious that she wasn't spending enough time with those people who empowered her to feel her best. She was spending far too much time with her parents, hoping they would finally accept her and offer the validation she so desperately needed to build her self-esteem. She knew at that moment it would never happen. They couldn't give her validation they couldn't give themselves.

In the weeks that followed Ayla's awakening, she made a number of changes that greatly improved the quality of her life. She found a support group of other professional women that met regularly to discuss how to build and manage relationships. Ayla made it a priority to attend the meetings no matter how tired she was because she consistently left feeling energized. She also decided to find other people who were interested in sharing living space with her so she would feel less isolated and less dependent on her parents.

Today she shares a large apartment with a single mother of Chinese descent and a black male graduate student in African Studies at the City University of New York. Together they've created an atmosphere in which they all feel the freedom to grow and find out who they really are. Their supportive Family of Choice has become strong enough to insulate each of them from Relationship Depression at home and often in the outside world. They have formed a unique and healthy extended family. Ayla discovered that while she needed intimate connections, they didn't have to be in the form of a romantic relationship with a man in order for her to feel full, happy, and connected to others.

Stage 3: Practicing and Refining Relationship Skills

5. Make a Relationship Damage Doll to Resolve Relationship Wounds.

After you've completed your Relationship Inventory, you'll have a much clearer picture of who has contributed most to your Relationship Depression. You're also likely to have more upset feelings about them and what they've done. To deal with those bad feelings, make a Relationship Damage Doll. Since this is one of the exercises typically done in our workshops, it can seem particularly silly out of this context and you may wish to skip this strategy. But if you're in the mood to be a risk-taker, give it a try. The dolls are fun to make and can be very helpful in recognizing and letting go of relationship pain.

Begin yours by making a list of all the people who have drained you, used you, hurt you, or abandoned you during the past five years. You may find you've encountered very few rejectors or abandoners, but have connected with people who have consistently wanted too much from you. It's best to deal with the recent past if you're doing this process alone so you'll have more success confronting and resolving your adult relationship issues. If you're intent on dealing with a Relationship Depression from childhood, I would encourage you to seek support from a professional. Childhood damage is much harder to resolve on your own and the exploration process can easily put you at risk for Unhealthy Depression if you don't have an experienced guide to pace your journey and support you along the way.

After you've made your list of the recent rejectors, abandoners, or hangers-on, lie down on a large white sheet or long piece of butcher paper and have someone outline your body with a pencil or a marker. If no one is available to help you, draw a basic human form. Cut your figure out of the sheet. You have the beginnings of your own Damage Doll. Now make the relationship damage you've experienced as an adult as tangible as possible by adorning your doll with symbols you make to represent the following categories:

The Heartbreakers. Cut out red hearts. Break them or rip them or make jagged lines through them.

The Controllers. Make paper chains to symbolize their need to control and restrict you.

The Emptyers. Cut holes in your doll to show how the emptyers have robbed you and left you feeling empty inside. Or, make a flap instead to symbolize that you may look OK on the outside but inside there's only emptiness.

The Destroyers. Make knives and clubs to symbolize the physical or emotional damage done by these violent, aggressive people. Destroyers try to hurt because they think they're entitled, or because aggression is their habit, or they don't know any alternatives.

The Hangers-On. These are people who've needed to merge with us and lead their lives through us rather than being independent and responsible for themselves. They want to make us responsible for their well-being and won't let go, even when we're not interested in spending time with them. Attach extension cords and plugs to your Damage Doll to represent how these people plug into you, operate off your current, and drain you of your energy and ability to operate independently.

In addition to the symbols suggested here, create your own. Make objects that represent the varieties of relationship damage you've experienced as an adult. Write the damager's name on each symbol and attach them all with tape or pins wherever they seem to fit best on your Damage Doll. List the names of all the damagers again, this time where you have more control, such as under your foot or fist. Many of the women who've done this exercise in the workshops list the damagers' names under the doll's foot because that's where they would like to put their damagers before they kick them out of their lives.

When you've made sure that all the people who have hurt you are included, stick the doll up on the wall, sit back, and study what you see. Ask yourself the following questions and write down your feelings and reactions as they come to you, without judging or editing them:

What kind of damage patterns do I see?

What kinds of damage do I seem to invite?

Who caused multiple damage?

What do I feel as I look at what has happened to me over the past few years?

What have my painful relationship experiences had in common?

How does this pain of the recent past keep me from moving on with my life and making new and better relationship choices?

Keep your doll on the wall for a while as a reminder to think about and analyze the patterns in your relationship pain. This exploration process may take a few hours, a few days, or even a few weeks. The more time you spend with it, the more benefits you're likely to derive. You can even try to relate to your doll, hold and comfort her as you grieve over the damage she has endured, or pat her as you walk by as a sign of reassurance and healing. Focus on what you've learned from the damage; write it down so you don't forget. Once you feel you've gotten as much as you can from this exercise, let go of the damage by letting go of the doll. You may want to take a photograph of it first so that you'll always have a visual reminder of what it has taught you.

Some of my clients have held funerals for their Damage Dolls. Others have built a fire at the beach and burned theirs up. I know women who have ripped their dolls into thousands of tiny pieces and flushed them down the toilet or sprinkled them in the ocean like cremation ashes. Some have gone through old photo albums and thrown out pictures of the relationship damagers along with the scraps of the doll. How you destroy your doll isn't as important as appreciating the symbolism of the process of letting go of as much relationship damage as you can. Acknowledge that the time has come to let go of the damage and pain. What better time than now to trade in your Relationship Depression for Intimate Power?

6. Create an Intimate Power Getaway for Someone You Love.

Practicing and refining relationship skills involves learning what Intimate Power is and practicing the steps to develop it. Intimate Power is knowing how to convert our vulnerability and the vulnerabilities of others into the power of being able to meet our needs as well as theirs. Unlike the traditional model of power, which is built on control and need—"If you do what I want, I'll give you what you want"—Intimate Power stems from our ability to influence and lead others by example and by the quality of our ideas rather than by force or coercion. It springs from our capacity to communicate feelings honestly and effectively, from allowing ourselves to be vulnerable with those we trust, from validating others for who they are as well as for what they do, and from creating win/win situations in which our needs and the needs of others are met. Intimate Power is a particularly effective power tool for women.

Control isn't the goal of Intimate Power because control isn't intimate. What's more, it usually backfires because it sets up resentment and power struggles. Instead, the goal is to create a climate of safety and acceptance enabling both people in the relationship to be more powerful and effective in getting what they want.

Creating Intimate Power takes more awareness than time. At work it can be done in just a few moments: complimenting a co-worker on a job well done or an attractive dress or tie, remembering a birthday or anniversary with a card or brief call, helping out even when it's not your job, bringing a little gift or food for someone who's sick or depressed, and using humor whenever possible. Shared laughter connects people faster than virtually any other experience, so practice seeing and saying things in a humorous light to build more Intimate Power.

One of the best ways for couples to develop Stage 3 skills is for one of them to surprise the other with an Intimate Power getaway. It can be a one-nighter at an inexpensive motel down the street or a three-day weekend at a five-star resort a thousand miles from home. What matters most is that the person planning the getaway caters to the whims, desires, and fantasies of his or her partner, even if it means putting his or her own on the back burner for a weekend. As difficult as that may sound, it works. Creating an Intimate Power getaway for someone you love is one of the most important and effective action strategies for developing Intimate Power.

Although this strategy is most often used by couples, a number of women have found Intimate Power getaways to be very effective in reestablishing or deepening their connection to "significant others" —close friends or relatives, especially mothers and sisters. By sharing time in which the primary goal is to connect with the other person and understand him or her better, we're able to build more intimacy and create conditions that will enable us to work out conflicts at a later time.

Dana and Jack never would have believed that a single weekend could turn their marriage around, but that's exactly what happened. Dana had first heard about the Intimate Power getaway from a friend at the brokerage firm who had planned one for her husband. The timing for the weekend was ideal. She was beginning to understand that Jack's anger, which stemmed from his feeling chronically ignored and unimportant, was making her life tense and unhappy. Her choice was either to improve the relationship or leave. Dana decided to plan an Intimate Power getaway for Jack's upcoming birthday.

Planning the weekend took more time and energy than Dana had anticipated. In addition to the time, it also cost money she couldn't really afford. But after reflecting on the sorry state of her relationship with Jack, she decided she couldn't afford not to.

Early in the week, Dana told Jack she had a surprise planned and asked him to be free at four o'clock on Friday afternoon. She explained that someone would call him at work with instructions about where to go and what to do. Jack was amused, intrigued, and even a little anxious. He thought Dana had been so self-centered lately she might not even realize if she was hurting him with her "surprise."

Promptly at four, Dana called Jack's office. She put a handkerchief over the mouthpiece of the phone and proceeded to use a deep, commanding "Mission Impossible" voice to tell Jack what his "mission" was. The only problem was that despite several rehearsals, she began laughing so hard she couldn't speak. She hadn't lost control or laughed that hard in months. It suddenly occurred to her that maybe she'd already gotten her money's worth.

As Dana's infectious laugh grew, Jack was reassured and immediately much more willing to do what he was told. He arrived in the lobby of the hotel as requested at precisely four forty-five. He didn't know what he was looking for, but when he saw it he was stunned. There, at the opposite end of the hotel lobby, stood Dana in high heels and a trenchcoat.

Dana felt incredibly self-conscious. She hadn't worn a pair of heels that high in six months and had never been playful or bold enough to go out in public wearing only high heels, a coat, and a smile. But she also had a strange new feeling of energy. Without a word, she motioned for him to follow her. They rode the crowded elevator in silence. Once inside, Dana took Jack by the hand and led him to the bathroom, where the tub was filled with bubbles and surrounded by evergreen-scented candles. Next to the tub sat a bottle of champagne in an ice bucket. Soft, mellow music played in the background. Dana slipped out of her raincoat and proceeded to slowly, silently undress Jack. She kissed him, popped open the champagne, and passed him a tray of caviar, crackers, and the Peanut Chews candy bars he had loved as a kid. As they toasted, she finally spoke: "Welcome. I love you." As Dana said those words, she thought to herself, "At least I hope I do."

They stayed in bed most of the following day. They ordered from room service, read magazines, talked, and made love with a passion neither had felt in some time. Sunday morning, they enjoyed a relaxed brunch and took a long walk in the park. Rather than raise the serious, practical subjects Dana preferred, she honored her commitment to herself and allowed the conversation to be easy and relaxed, sprinkled with some of the silly jokes Jack liked to make.

By Sunday afternoon, Dana appreciated what it meant to possess Intimate Power. So did Jack. They were both amazed at how getting out of their routine and focusing on connecting with each other enabled them to abandon their typical roles and simply enjoy the time together. Weeks later, they were both happier as a result of their special weekend. Jack, encouraged by Dana's gesture and willingness to heal and nurture the relationship, began to help with the cooking, shopping, and supervising of their house cleaner. As Jack became more supportive, Dana found herself more willing to shift her priorities when Jack needed her and became more sexually and emotionally available. And thanks to the lessons they've learned, their marriage is stronger.

Some women couldn't do what Dana did that weekend without feeling devalued, used, or too passive. If that's how you feel, it's important to honor and respect your feelings. Never feel you have to justify them. Remember that in creating a fantasy for your partner, never do anything that could jeopardize your or his physical or emotional health. To do so will only defeat your purpose.

With whatever behavior is comfortable for you, there are three ingredients essential to achieving the Intimate Power time—focus, fantasy, and fun. Focus time and energy on creating intimate situations with your partner where the two of you can be alone with no distractions. Make your time light and playful. The Intimate Power getaway is not the time to resolve relationship problems. A new environment is very helpful in creating a fun, intimate atmosphere, but you can also plan a special evening at home if time or money is an issue. Dana and Jack decided these evenings were such an efficient way to nourish the relationship that one of them would surprise the other with a fantasy evening every few months. By using their vulnerability to become closer and stronger, Dana and Jack had learned how to cultivate Intimate Power.

Stage 4: Applying Relationship Wisdom

7. Create Your Own Relationship Wisdom List.

Many of us overlook a wonderful opportunity to learn from the experiences, stories, mistakes, and life lessons of others. When is the last time you tapped the wisdom of a friend, neighbor, coworker, older relative, or casual acquaintance? Start by explaining to the other person that you think she has a perspective and wisdom that you could benefit from. Tell her exactly what you want to do—learn from her experiences. You can start with: "Can you advise me on something?" The following are questions to consider:

> What one thing do you know about relationships today that you wish you'd known a year ago or when you were my age?
>
> What is the biggest relationship mistake you've made, and what did you learn from it?
>
> What advice would you give to someone entering her first relationship? What advice or tips do you wish someone had given you before you first started dating?

If she tends to get analytical or starts to intellectualize rather than talk from the heart, steer the conversation back to her experiences so that you can directly benefit from her wisdom and gut-level insights. Encourage her to share the first thing that comes to mind. It's up to you to keep the momentum of the conversation going. As the other person becomes more comfortable talking about things she's learned along the way, don't be surprised if you find yourself in the midst of one of the more stimulating, enlightening conversations you've had.

As you speak with others, men as well as women, use their thoughts to stimulate your own. Write down your own Relationship Wisdom List from all that you have learned over the years about what works and doesn't work in relationships. Write down inspiring sayings from books or magazines, or briefly describe experiences you have or hear about that teach relationship lessons.

These lists provide an essential source of comfort to help you get through the inevitable rough spots of any close relationship. Focus on the three most important relationships in your life. For each, make a list of the rewards and benefits you enjoy from being involved with that person. When the inevitable conflicts occur, think about or return to your list for inspiration, hope, and a reminder as to why you're willing to invest energy in a relationship that is sometimes difficult.

Then work on applying your wisdom in the world by working for a cause you believe in. When you are doing this, you have reached Stage 4 of the relationship pyramid. Examples of Stage 4 women are Gloria Steinem; Mother Teresa; physician and author Elisabeth Kübler-Ross, who first described the stages of dying and brought the hospice movement to the United States; Barbara Marx Hubbard, internationally known writer, activist, and founder of Global Family; and Peggy Charren, founder of Action for Children's Television, the force behind passage of the Children's Television Act of 1990 and numerous other reforms for children's television.

All these women are in their mid to late 50s or older and are dynamos of energy and enthusiasm. They and their counterparts find Stage 4 so empowering and satisfying that many of those who are single report they don't need or want a long-term committed relationship because it is too restricting and distracting for achieving results and actualizing their vision. Their intimate connection is to a larger extended family of people who share their drive and ideals to make the world a better place. This feeling of connection and purpose provides more than what they need to protect themselves from Relationship Depression and build Intimate Power for themselves and others.

These exercises offer emotional support so we can trade our Relationship Depression for Intimate Power. As we shed our skin of culturally conditioned powerlessness and assume responsibility for our emotional well-being, we'll experience the freedom and strength that makes Intimate Power so priceless. Whenever relationships seem elusive or become stormy, we can maintain our vision of what we want for ourselves. Don't hesitate to try or redo some of these exercises whenever you need support or ideas. Keep working until you achieve the positive results and the positive relationships you want. With time and effort, they will be yours.

·6·

AGE RAGE DEPRESSION

The past is finished and the present is where I can make all the changes. . . . I don't spend any time holding grudges or worrying about the past. . . . The more time I spend in anger or pity or any of those things, without having an outlet to change something, it is erosive to my body.
  Virginia Satir, the "Columbus of Family Therapy"

Janet and her best friend, Gwen, had bought their tickets for the hit musical *Les Misérables* nearly four months in advance. They were both looking forward to their evening at the theater, but where they were going wasn't nearly as important to either of them as the fact they were going together. The women had been friends since they were neighbors thirty years ago, and while they now lived ninety miles apart, both were within an hour's drive of New York City. For nearly eight years they'd designated the first Wednesday of every month as their "women's night out."

Janet and Gwen always had fun together, but this time, over a glass of wine after the show they talked more openly and honestly than they ever had before. Their communication was sparked by a show-stopping song, "I Dreamed a Dream," sung by a defeated, disillusioned character named Fantine. Fantine's song describes how easy it is to waste dreams when we're young because we have so many to choose from and we often assume that an abundance of choices will always be ours. But a broken, bitter Fantine discovers that life can sometimes betray our dreams and turn what we thought would be heaven into living hell.

"I can't remember the last time I was touched as deeply as I was when I heard that song," Janet recalls, wiping tears from her eyes.

"I felt like the person who wrote it had peeked into my soul. I hadn't wept like that since Frank died. I realized while talking with Gwen that in many ways that song captured the way I've been feeling about my life for the past couple of years. I remember a time when I thought that the future was nearly unlimited. Whatever didn't happen today would happen tomorrow. It never occurred to me that tomorrow wouldn't come. I thought by the time I was in my fifties, my mother would be gone, the kids would be out on their own, and Frank and I would finally have the time and money to live our dreams."

In the past two years, however, life has indeed killed many of Janet's dreams. At 58, an age Janet anticipated would be her "prime time," she has little time to enjoy the pleasures she had deferred to the future. Frank, her husband and partner in a successful catering business, had a stroke one October afternoon while doing yardwork. Six days later he was dead. The youngest of their five children, 25-year-old Gary, lives at home and continues to try Janet's patience. And Janet's 81-year-old mother, Dorothy, who she is now convinced will live to be well over 100, is a chronic drain on Janet's limited emotional and financial resources. Dorothy is a master manipulator who knows Janet's hot buttons and doesn't hesitate to push them.

"To tell you the truth, when I looked to the future, I never saw my mother as a part of it," admits Janet. "I know it sounds awful, but I never thought my mother would live long enough to need me this much. She's been in ill health for the better part of twenty years, she's hard to get along with, and she loves to whine and nag. Nothing is ever right. She drives me crazy! I've never felt so much stress."

"Spending as much time as I do with my mother reminds me how devastating the aging process can be," Janet explains. "It's discouraging, restrictive, and very frustrating. Sometimes when I'm feeling exhausted or depressed or stiff from my own aches and pains, I just keep it to myself. I feel guilty if I complain because I know Mother is feeling a lot worse. And I know she won't sympathize with me, anyway."

If my own grandmother, Muriel, were to meet Janet, I know exactly what she'd say. "Young lady," she'd undoubtedly begin, "count your blessings. Widowhood is a new chapter, but it's certainly no end to the book! And quit talking about old—*I'm* old! Old for you is thirty years away. When you're 90, you might have something real to complain about."

My grandmother isn't a complainer, but if she were she'd have plenty of reasons. In her younger years she was very active and independent. She worked in Chicago as a bank teller, cared for a chronically ill husband, and raised two daughters. She was also an entrepreneur. During the Depression she began selling her chicken pot pies to local restaurants, civic groups, and neighbors. Her business thrived until World War II, when tire rationing literally brought her growing enterprise to a screeching halt.

As times changed, so did her body. Her arthritis is so crippling now that she sometimes has trouble maintaining her balance. The last time my family and I visited her, we took her out to her favorite restaurant for dinner. As she was getting out of the car, she lost her balance and fell. Fortunately, she landed in a flower bed instead of on the concrete. Embarrassed and angry that her body had once again betrayed her, she let go with a string of colorful curses. We were all momentarily frozen in shock. Within seconds, though, my grandmother must have realized how ridiculous she looked sprawled out in the pansies. She began to chuckle. "I'm in no mood for a nap," she laughed. "Pull me up so we can eat!"

As we later sat eating dinner, my grandmother apologized for losing her temper in front of the children. "I get so frustrated sometimes," she confessed. "In my heart I still feel like a young girl. I still want to make chicken pot pies and go swimming in Lake Michigan. But my body won't let me. Sometimes I feel so trapped. Humor helps, but it's just not enough."

Janet and Muriel are both experiencing their personal variations of Age Rage Depression. **Age Rage Depression is the healthy range of bad feelings women experience as the result of growing older in a society that has conditioned us to believe that female aging represents little else but loss.** At the core of these cultural teachings is a belief that as we grow older we become less attractive, less able to concentrate, less able to see, and less physically capable, and we have less money, less happiness, and fewer friends and family.

Even though age brings with it the wisdom of decades of life's lessons, the process of growing older is dreaded by the vast majority of women in our culture. And with good reason. Women are doubly burdened by aging. Not only do we experience the inevitable physical and social losses, as do men, but we're also saddled with a culturally imposed burden. While aging men often enjoy greater respect and are perceived as dignified and wise, women are fundamentally devalued as they age.

All of us live with the evidence of the pain and loss of aging. A great deal of what is written in books and magazines and shown on film and television screens focuses on the negatives of growing older. What has virtually disappeared are the positive experiences of aging. To balance the scale, much of this chapter focuses on "age gains," ways we can enrich and improve the quality of our aging experience.

Am I suggesting that aging is wonderful—that wrinkles, physical limitations, and the losses we inevitably experience as we grow older are fun? Not a chance. I hate the signs of aging as much as anyone I know. As do most women my age, I see wrinkles around my eyes that weren't there ten years ago. I really wish they weren't there now. Some of my friends, who were vital and dynamic ten years ago, have slowed down. A few of them have died young, victims of the AIDS epidemic. There are so many things I wish were different.

While we can't change these losses, we can change how we perceive them. Most of us have learned to equate aging with a loss of options and independence. And if we think that way, we typically behave that way and create a self-fulfilling prophecy.[1]

Learning to cope better with the inevitability of aging is a unique developmental challenge that will give us new strength at a time when we genuinely need it. We're living in exciting but frightening times. As psychologist Daniel Levinson, who has extensively studied what he calls the "seasons" of men's and women's lives, has written, "There is no accrued cultural wisdom to help us with our ever-expanding range of choices as we become pioneers in a new phase of human history."[2]

We are poised to enter a new era in which femininity can equal genuine power and aging can finally be equated with wisdom and respect. As the Baby Boom generation ages, those of us who are part of it could fundamentally redefine what aging means for women and men by the sheer magnitude of our numbers and by applying what we've learned about how to effect social change. Aging can mean focusing on internal gain instead of the current focus:

external loss. Rather than become invisible as we age, we can become more visible and valued by harnessing our life experience into practical knowledge for social and individual change.

To effect such change and to make each of our highly individual, personal journeys more fulfilling, we need to appreciate the overall span of our life development from birth to death and know what to expect during each developmental passage. Our life journeys are fluid, winding rivers of constant change. If you've ever gone white-water rafting, you may appreciate this analogy, because you've experienced firsthand the unpredictable power and flow of a river. You know how quickly the river can turn from a placid stream into a raging, life-threatening current, and how important it is to have at least a general idea of what is coming up around the next bend.

In his excellent book *Adulthood and Aging*, Douglas C. Kimmel calls aging the "River of Life"[3] and very briefly describes the value of such a term. We have expanded the concept and applied it in the workshops as a visual analogy that can help each of us see where our lives have been and where they're going. Each of our Rivers of Life follows a different course. Some are intense but short, others are gentle and long. There are always at least two strong currents constantly flowing, one moving toward darkness and despair, the other flowing toward life and growth. Every turn in our river presents unique challenges. As we resolve each challenge successfully, we earn navigational rewards and enter the calm waters of consolidation before moving into the next stage of growth.

During periods in which we appreciate the flow of our lives, we drift downstream for awhile, enjoying the ride and the view. But rest assured there are rapids ahead that must be negotiated and resolved in order to continue growing and living well. Each of these growth passages contains its own treacherous currents of bad feelings. Each has a Healthy Depression that is a natural part of the passage. These Depressive Passages must be resolved or we end up beached in a swamp of Unhealthy Depression at each stage of our development.

As we age, our rivers seem to pick up speed and time passes much more quickly. At the end of the journey, we all face a Waterfall of Transition: death and whatever it represents to each of us. Death may be a much-dreaded brutal crash onto the rocks below. For some, it's too risky to plunge into the unknown, so they frantically and futilely swim upstream in a last desperate attempt to avoid being swept over the edge. The curious and hopeful can dream of being reunited with previously departed loved ones. For others, the Waterfall of Transition is a welcome relief, a liberating dive into an unknown sparkling pool of mysterious light and energy. Some believe they are leaping into the outstretched hands of God.

Whatever the end of the journey means to us individually, we must each navigate our own River of Life by coming to terms with the realities of aging that make us most vulnerable. Women of any age are aware that aging in our society robs us of choices, options, alternatives, and power, none of which we possessed in abundance in the first place. This robbery of female choices is a masterful form of cultural punishment, because we're being judged and devalued for something we cannot prevent or change: growing old.

Rather than entertain the possibility that aging represents a different kind of beauty and newly minted wisdom, women are encouraged to blindly accept the notion that female aging has to mean decay, lost sexuality, and uselessness. Feeling bad about these sexist cultural assumptions is a healthy response to the negative reality women experience as we age. The secret is converting this pain into gain as much and as often as possible and moving beyond those negative feelings.

To do this, you need to know where you've been and where you're likely to be going on your own River of Life. Drawing the flow of our life from start to finish is useful to gain a clearer perspective of the actual and potential rapids, swamps, and navigational rewards we may face along the way.

In this chapter, there is no quiz to assess how much Age Rage you may be experiencing. That's because it's a safe bet that whatever your age, you have a significant amount of anger and depression when you think about or directly experience aging in our culture. A diagram of your River of Life will give you a better diagnosis of your aging issues and vulnerabilities than a quiz.

To help you visualize this process, let's look at the River of Life Janet drew in one of the workshops. When she first began drawing it, she stopped and said she couldn't do it. Few people are eager to do this work at first because it forces them to confront their past, present, and future. With a little encouragement, Janet eventually made a few tentative marks and then became increasingly absorbed

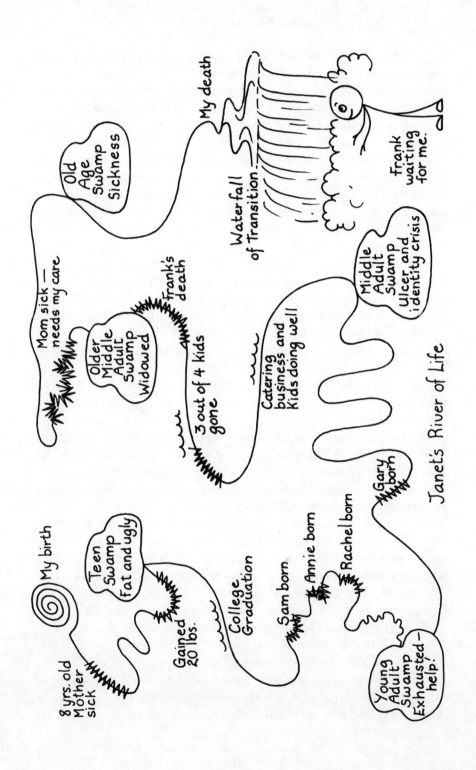

Janet's River of Life

in the task until she was one of the last in the room to finish her drawing. Janet began with the basic diagram from this chapter and added her own individual experience.

As Janet studied her drawing, she was amazed to see some patterns she hadn't recognized before. Since adolescence, she has frequently ended up in the swamp because she often felt helpless in the face of life's challenges and withdrew into the identity of the victim, just as her mother often does. Now she found herself stuck again in the swamp of middle adulthood by playing the victim role with both her mother and son. This was particularly disturbing because the Waterfall of Transition had never seemed so close. After studying her River of Life, Janet was determined that she wouldn't die a victim, too. She would make changes at home to allow herself more time for activities she enjoys and insist that both her mother and son take more responsibility for themselves.

The River of Life drawing helped her to see not only how quickly her life was passing, but how many people she was carrying in her boat and how much they slowed her down. She encouraged her son to get his own apartment and insisted that her mother begin developing outside interests. Dorothy now attends the local community center for seniors and takes the senior community van to most of her doctor's appointments. To celebrate, Janet traded in her large sedan for a little silver sports car. It is a two-seater, and too low for her mother to get in and out of comfortably. Whenever Janet takes her mother to the doctor, she uses her caterer's van. Janet loves the new sense of independence that her little car symbolizes. Even though she still has family responsibilities, she now has a separate, free life of her own.

Now draw your own River of Life by either using the diagram in this book or making up your own. To begin, trace or photocopy the diagram included here or, using it as a guide, make your own version by dividing a long piece of rectangular paper (at least legal size, preferably a longer piece of butcher paper or poster board) into five sections: childhood, adolescence, young adult, middle adult, and older adult. Then read about the Depressive Passages for each developmental stage that everyone must navigate before successfully completing each of these stages and continuing to grow.

A Depressive Passage is a term I've developed to explain the predictable, common phase of bad feelings we must experience as we

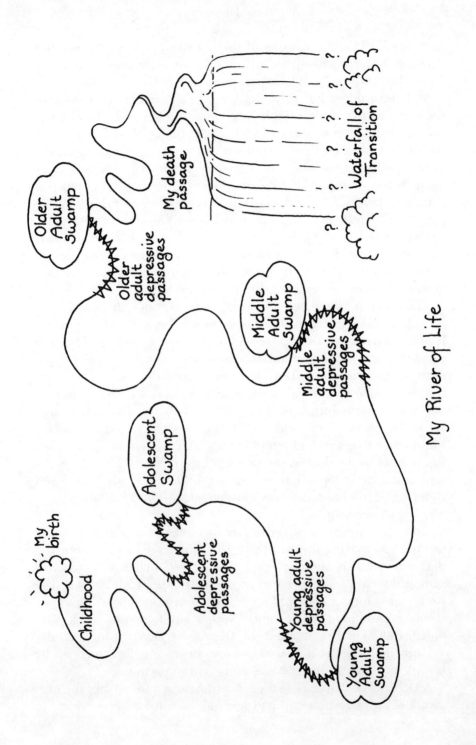

My River of Life

pass through the stages of adulthood before moving on to the next level of development. These are not the normal developmental passages we all encounter. Rather, Depressive Passages are the typical phases of bad feelings most women must resolve in order to reach the next age and stage of maturity.

The problem, however, is that many women find certain Depressive Passages difficult to resolve and find themselves mired in a swamp of Unhealthy Depression, where they stagnate and even die if they don't find their way back on the course to healthy development. Mental health professionals call these "developmental arrests," meaning that part of our development is frozen, and we can't proceed to grow in those areas until they're thawed and resolved. By understanding what to expect—and appreciating the rewards for successfully navigating each passage—you'll be more aware and better equipped to deal with the challenges of each developmental stage.

Knowing and appreciating your Navigational Rewards is critical to understanding why the journey through the Depressive Passages is so worthwhile. If you're afraid of water, imagine you're in a safe lifeboat and have a life preserver to face the journey. Which sections of your river are likely to be unsafe? Where could you drown by not being adequately informed or prepared for the problems of aging? Where are the rest stops along the way and where are there resources for you to continue your journey? With realistic expectations, we'll handle unavoidable turbulent water with much greater navigational skill. Consider the following Depressive Passages and Navigational Rewards for each stage of development as you draw your River of Life.

Adolescence

Depressive Passage: The adolescent passage is one that often involves our first serious loss of self-esteem. As teenagers, women begin to understand that in our culture, being female means being less and having less freedom, privilege, ability to earn money, and less protection from physical and sexual abuse.

Navigational Rewards: If we successfully navigate this passage, we gain a sense of competence and mastery that no one can ever take away. We avoid feeling like second-class citizens. We appreciate the strength and beauty of our bodies, regardless of what shape they're in and begin to free ourselves from the cultural punishers and their arbitrary standards of perfection.

Young Adulthood

Depressive Passage: In our 20s and 30s, we typically experience bad feelings generated by economic discrimination and the exhaustion and conflict raised by trying to juggle our careers, relationships, and family development, or remaining comfortably single. No matter what we choose and no matter in what order we try to have it, most women are left feeling they didn't get it quite right.

Navigational Rewards: There is an integration of different parts of who we are, so that by the time we reach our 40s we're in a position to operate at peak performance. We become more capable of work, love, and play than ever before. We're beginning to understand what we really need and who we are, no matter what our family, friends, and culture tell us we "should" want and "should" do. Owning ourselves and our feelings generates an incredible freedom and energy to give back to ourselves, to our relationships, and to the world in the last two phases: middle and older adulthood.

Middle Adulthood

Depressive Passage: During this passage we endure the first visible, physical signs of aging. We see age marks and wrinkles on our face and hands. Our vision may be less crisp than before. We're confronted with the reality that no matter how hard we try, we're not physically capable of doing everything we used to for as long as we used to. We worry about becoming helpless, useless, old, and poor. Friends and family die.

Navigational Rewards: We experience greater mental health and ability to cope with stress, more rewarding relationships, more time to pursue our own interests and experiment with new activities, more work fulfillment, more opportunity for creativity, more time to experience nature, and a general feeling of strength and confidence many women have never known until this stage in their lives.

Older Adulthood

Depressive Passage: This is a time when we begin to experience multiple losses as a result of physical deterioration, illness, and death. We suffer an assault on our self-esteem as a result of living in a culture that demands we become increasingly invisible as we age. Many of us experience a reduction in our standard of living. Some slide into poverty. Our bodies feel like prisons and we feel like we are a burden to those around us.

Navigational Rewards: The Navigational Rewards of this passage are among the richest life has to offer. We can cultivate the deep well of wisdom that comes only from age, and have the time, opportunity, and satisfaction to be creative, help others and teach them valuable life lessons, and give back to our environment. We know so much more about how the world works, we know what's important and what isn't worth our energy. Spirituality takes on a new, richer meaning and can be a source of great consolation for some of us. If we've navigated this Depressive Passage carefully, we gain a deep sense of peace and contentment.

Keeping in mind these Depressive Passages and Navigational Rewards, chart your own River of Life on the diagram, filling in your individual experiences as Janet did. As you add these experiences from your past, think about your entire life cycle. Use memories to draw up to your current age. Continue to draw where you may go in the future as you age by anticipating what is coming up and assessing your potential for positive experiences as well as your vulnerabilities to poverty, illness, isolation, boredom, dependency, or despair. Think about your wishes and desires. What aging gains and losses did your mother and grandmother experience? They provide excellent clues about what may also happen to you. Write down your vulnerabilities and fears on your drawing. Then, with your River of Life in front of you, examine the potential sources of your Age Rage Depression and change or modify your drawing as new ideas or associations occur to you.

Sources of Age Rage Depression

1. The Cultural Punishers

There are three primary sources of cultural punishment for women as we age: the health care system, the cosmetics industry, and the media. Each of these cultural punishers makes a significant and powerful contribution to developing and promoting Age Rage Depression in women, because their presence is so pervasive that it's impossible to escape them.

When influenced by these punishing cultural forces, the inescapable natural process of aging becomes a loss that defines us as less adequate with every passing year. We are often treated like children by a male-dominated medical community that over-prescribes drugs and underserves the specific health needs of women. We are sold magic remedies the cosmetics industry claims will help us avoid wrinkles and retain our "youthful radiance." We are bombarded with images of beautiful models who are presented as ideal women—thin and young. If you were to accept the media version of society, you'd have no choice but to accept the notion that women over 50 are or should be an endangered species.

Let's look more closely at how each of these experiences serves as a form of cultural punishment that encourages and maintains Age Rage Depression for most women.

The Health Care System

Age Rage Depression is caused in part by the systematic discrimination against women by the American health care system. When it comes to quality medical care, our voices are weak. Consequently, aging women aren't a medical priority. In her book *Women Over Forty*,[4] Dr. Jean Grambs calls aging women the "invisible women." She points out that finding information and research on older women has been difficult because everything has been standardized according to men. Women have been studied considerably less as a separate population with unique health needs. Before 1970, women's health was barely studied at all. Reflecting this cultural punishment, the National Institutes of Health spends just 13 percent of its $7.7 billion budget on women's health needs,[5] although women pay a significant part of the bill for NIH research with their tax dollars. The prevailing notion seems to be that if it's good enough for men, it is more than good enough for women.

What we're learning, of course, is that nothing could be further from the truth. Women do have very different health needs that may require different kinds and dosages of medicine. For example, women experience less heart disease than men before age 50. Men develop heart disease ten to twenty years earlier than women of the same age. But after 50, the heart attacks we do have are more likely to be fatal. Why? One explanation is that physicians don't monitor older women for heart disease as closely as they do older men. They are slower to spot problems and recommend surgery for women. They don't appreciate the increased risk for heart disease that results from the loss of estrogen after menopause.

Yet in spite of these medical differences between men and women, when your doctor gives you a diagnosis or prescribes medicine, he or she is basing these recommendations primarily on knowledge about men's diseases and medication needs. It is becoming increasingly clear that we need to be our own health researchers and managers. It takes time and effort, but it's the only way to keep health care from making us feel worse instead of better as we age.

The Cosmetics Industry

In Chapter 8 on Body Image Depression, we'll explore in detail how the powerful cosmetics industry has gracefully and artfully assumed the mantle of supreme cultural punisher of women. When it comes to aging and women, this particular cultural punisher plays an especially important role because it creates and promotes the notion that the natural process of aging is something that can and should be repaired, fixed, corrected, masked, delayed, and avoided, all through the use of their beauty products, of course. Some of these products are useful, but they are too often marketed as the ultimate solution to a situation that has no remedy.

We are so willing to buy into the impossible dream they're selling that we abandon reason and purchase products we don't need and often can't afford. Women over 50 spend more on health- and personal-care products than any other age group.[6] They're a ripe market and the industry exploits them. Advertising slogans such as

"Beauty doesn't have to end at 50!" have continued to encourage retirement-age women to try to look younger by constantly dipping into the cosmetic industry's bottomless fountain of youth.

There is no real evidence, however, that the products manufactured and marketed by the cosmetics industry to reduce wrinkles or eliminate cellulite make any substantial difference, even though billions of dollars are spent on advertising to convince us otherwise. As *Newsweek* reported in 1990,[7] the promises of "reversal," "renewal," or "repair" of aging skin were virtually "all fraudulent," so much so that the Food and Drug Administration required twenty-three cosmetics companies to stop immediately their false advertising about these products.

The effect of these marketing techniques is to send a message that it's unthinkable for us to accept the signs of aging, that we must do something about them or we have failed our mission as women. The subtle and sometimes not-so-subtle message is that in order to be attractive, we must erase or cover up all signs of who we've become over time because aging is unacceptable. We constantly see and hear this message; it seeps into our being. Faced with this endless barrage, it's no wonder that so many of us feel so bad as we age.

The Media

The media is the eyes and ears of our culture. And with rare exception, it sees and hears only the young. Advertising uses models fifteen years younger than the targeted audience.[8] Clothing advertising pretends there are no women in America over 30, yet middle-aged women buy more clothes than any other segment of the population. Even magazines geared to older readers rely heavily on younger models. When Frances Lear risked launching *Lear's,* the first magazine targeted specifically to older women, she was taken to task for using younger models. But she knew that because youth is what sells, youth is what had to be used to attract advertisers and keep her new magazine afloat.

In television and film, older actresses are usually relegated to what are appropriately known as supporting roles—their purpose is to support the younger, often male characters whose adventures are central to the plot. There are rare exceptions. Geraldine Page and Jessica Tandy both won Academy Awards for Best Actress during the last decade for their respective performances in *The Trip to Bountiful* and *Driving Miss Daisy*. The vast majority of the stars of movies and television, however, are under 40. On television, fewer than 3 percent of the characters are over 65, even though people over 65 make up more than 12 percent of the American population and spend more time watching TV than any other age group.

It is the same behind the scenes. Writers for film and TV are considered "pushing it" by ages 30 to 35. "We're talking extreme ageism here. If you haven't made it by 40, your career is over," says entertainment attorney David Colden in a *Los Angeles Times* interview. The media, more than most other forms of popular culture, supports the assumption that men mature and grow wiser, while women simply age and fade.

2. Aging Violates the Traditional Core.

Our Age Rage Depression is fueled by the powerful external forces of cultural punishment, but the issue runs much deeper. The Traditional Core is built on the assumption that the only desirable woman is a young woman. Aging then becomes a fundamental violation of the Traditional Core because the Traditional Core was never allowed to grow up. As long as we're youthful and nurturing, caregivers to all, everything is fine.

But youth is a stage we all outgrow. Women are living longer than ever before. The fastest growing segment of the U.S. population, in fact, is women over 80.[9] For the Traditional Core, such changes aren't "real." The Traditional Core operates in deep denial by either pretending nothing is happening to our aging bodies or buying into the notion that the results of the aging process can be "cured" with just the right facial cream, surgical technique, special exercise, or food.

When these solutions don't work, the Traditional Core makes us feel even more helpless and inadequate. It never once helps us question the fundamentally inaccurate and unhealthy assumptions on which female ageism is based. It never encourages us to learn to value the resources and advantages of aging. Instead, the Traditional Core and our cultural punishers make aging the most consistent experience in a woman's life that invites dependency and development of a victim identity. As we are more naturally impaired by physical aging, it has become acceptable for us to become much more dependent than is necessary on medical authorities, adult children, friends, and family. We increasingly see ourselves as victims, in part because we are, and in part because there's comfort in assuming an identity that is familiar.

What if we didn't allow ourselves to be victimized by aging? Imagine the force of our collective rage if older women everywhere absolutely refused to feel devalued by their age, and instead directed their fury outward to our culture in the form of nonnegotiable demands for equality in social, medical, financial, and political systems. Our sexist culture would have little choice but to change fundamentally. The energy and influence of the Gray Panthers and the lobbying power of Association for the Advancement of Retired Persons illustrate how effective collective action can be. Changing how we think about aging and demanding that others treat us with the respect and the dignity we have earned is one of the best ways to neutralize Age Rage.

3. Economic Discrimination Against Women.

Another source of Age Rage Depression is the economic status of aging women and their potential for inadequate income. Women over 65 represent the largest group living below the poverty line.[10] Women's vulnerability to poverty reflects pervasive and persistent sexism: years of nonpayment for household work, intermittent employment resulting in limited or nonexistent retirement income, limited access to higher-paying jobs, and the reality that 80 percent of full-time working women still earn "less than $20,000 a year, nearly half the male rate."[11]

Although women are making significant inroads in combating this inequality in certain areas, some studies suggest the financial future is increasingly bleak for many young women. According to a study by Peter Uhlenberg, professor of sociology at the University of North Carolina,[12] by the time most women now in their early 30s are elderly, they're more apt to be divorced than widowed, and they're even more likely to be in economic peril than today's elderly. The grim reality is that Age Rage Depression is more likely for the current generation of young women than ever before.

• • •

Rather than feel angry or depressed over what we have lost or will lose, we need to accept our feelings as appropriate reactions, understand why we have them, and use those feelings to motivate ourselves to harvest the riches of aging. We have to be willing to invest in our own futures as older women. Among our best tools to do this are the action techniques, which can be used to identify the currents of rage flowing from our Traditional Core and channel that anger into productive action and creative solutions.

The following strategies will help you if you're afraid of aging, stuck in a particular phase of the aging process, or want to let go of your depression about aging. They'll show you how to convert these bad feelings into an appreciation for the remarkable journey your own River of Life offers once you learn to enjoy the ride. To remind yourself of the perils and potential of your own journey, keep your River of Life drawing visible as you work with the following action strategies.

Action Strategies to Resolve Age Rage Depression

1. Learn and Apply the Secrets of Quality Aging.

There are specific strategies for "quality aging" that are critical to learn now—no matter what our age—in order to improve our quality of life in later years (and successfully navigate our River of Life). These are life skills that are very helpful to learn and apply during the earlier phases of our lives, but they're especially important later when we must cope with the challenges of aging. Among the proven strategies of "quality aging" are:

- Carefully planning ahead, especially financially, so you remain in maximum control of your life.
- Developing and maintaining a strong social support network of family, friends, and colleagues.
- Eating a low-fat, high-fiber diet and keeping aware of the latest nutritional information.

- Developing a personal exercise program combining aerobics and weight work, and/or a brisk walk and making it as regular a part of your day as eating or sleeping.
- Organizing your daily schedule so you don't enter an unfocused or unplanned day; make definite one-year and five-year goals that you actively work toward no matter what your age.
- No smoking, no matter what.

In one study of quality aging, the researchers found that for women, "aging was a career . . . a serious commitment to surviving, complete with standards of excellence and clear long-term goals whose attainment yielded community recognition and inner satisfaction."[13] Erik Erikson, one of the most esteemed and influential voices in modern psychology and human development, believes quality aging is "a determination to keep old age licked. If you're going to keep on living you better keep on growing. Once in a while I get a little pain, but it doesn't stop me from doing things."[14]

That determination is a common thread that Jane Brody, health editor for the *New York Times,* observes among her healthy, active older friends. Not one of them leaves vigor to chance. All pursue "mental prowess" and work hard at the strategies of "successful aging." From them, Jane learned to appreciate the gains of age so that on her fiftieth birthday, she proudly wore a button that read: "50: The Legend Lives On."[15] Now *that's* quality aging!

2. Make Your Own "Age Gains List."

To better recognize and appreciate these benefits of aging, make a list of all the rewards you can enjoy as a result of quality aging. Quality aging is living in a mentally and physically healthy way to minimize the losses of aging and maximize age gains. Age Gains are the realistic rewards we can expect from getting older if we follow the guidelines described in this chapter and other books on mental and physical health for the later years. I've started the list for you by summarizing some of the key points from the existing research on aging. To remind yourself of the easy-to-forget reality that aging has many rewards, copy the following list.

AGE GAINS LIST

1. Aging enables women to become more integrated, balanced, and active.
2. Wisdom comes only with age—and effort.
3. Intelligence actually increases as we age if we stay active and committed to learning.
4. Chronological age doesn't define how "old" you are; attitude and activity level do.
5. Most older women have less dissatisfaction and psychological stress than at any other time in life.
6. We trade PMS (premenstrual syndrome) for PMZ (postmenopausal zest).
7. There will be more and better work opportunities for older women workers in the future.
8. Most of us lose our fear of death after middle age.

Now read the following summary of what experts have to say about each of these Age Gains so that you can evaluate them for yourself and internalize those that make the most sense to you as part of your future.

Realistic Gains of Quality Aging

**Aging enables women to become more
integrated, balanced, and active.**
Women become more active, assertive, and work-oriented as they age, while many men become more gentle, more submissive, less interested in power, and more interested in learning about intimacy and relationships. Aging enables women to become more whole and balanced. A recent Lou Harris/*Lear's* magazine study of women 60 to 65 who had a household income of at least $40,000 found that a number of positive qualities increase with age: a "sense of success, of eloquence, of courage, of serenity, of grace, and of attractiveness."[16] Aging seems to provide us with an opportunity to reclaim missing or undeveloped parts of ourselves.

Janet, the theater lover we met at the beginning of the chapter, is a wonderful example. After applying several of the strategies outlined in this chapter, she mustered the courage and creativity to pursue a lifelong dream of taking acting lessons. To do so she had to overcome her mother's ridicule—"It's a little late to become a starlet, isn't it, dear?"—and her adult son's complaints—"When are you going to stay home and cook a meal?"

She has been delighted to discover not only that her acting has brought energy and sparkle into a life that had become drab and draining, but that she's good at it, too. She had never felt as attractive and accomplished in her life as when she landed the leading role in a community theater production of *On Golden Pond*. Since then, she has been involved in some phase of every production staged by her local theater company.

Wisdom comes with age—and effort.

Erik Erikson and his wife, Joan Erikson, have developed a highly productive writing partnership that has continued into their nineties. The Ericksons suggest that old age is the struggle between one's sense of integrity and a feeling of despair about one's life during the phase of normal physical disintegration.[17] Wisdom, the Eriksons suggest, is the result of that struggle. It's the classic example of when feeling bad is good because experiencing bad feelings is essential for gaining wisdom. Curiosity and risk taking are also essential wisdom builders. So is making mistakes. Some of the wisest people are those who take risks, make the biggest mistakes, and then invest the time and effort to apply what they've learned.

Since most of us would rather hide our mistakes, you probably won't be surprised by the Ericksons' belief that "Lots of old people don't get wise, but you don't get wise unless you age." Wisdom is one of the most important gains of old age. We need what the Ericksons call "vital involvement," the energy and action essential to change, learn, and grow before we earn wisdom and age successfully.

Intelligence increases as we age *if* we stay active and committed to learning.

Research supports the Ericksons' theory. New learning exceeds the rate at which we forget. The research on lifespan development of human abilities shows that people who have compelling interests and activities and remain socially connected actually increase their IQ scores as they age. It's only when we withdraw from the world because of depression or sickness that "what goes out exceeds what comes in, and crystallized intelligence declines," according to Dr. Janet Belsky's summary of the research in *Here Tomorrow: Making the Most of Life After 50*.[18]

We have a choice regarding the quality of our aging. Observes Karen DeCrow, former president of the National Organization for Women: "At 50, one realizes that many people will go to any extreme to avoid significant intellectual work. They lapse into the occult, search out dangerous and uncomfortable sports, and turn to the soap opera of personal battles."[19] If we fall into the trap DeCrow describes and lose our motivation to learn, our brains indeed deteriorate and our IQ scores actually drop. An active commitment to learning and growth, however, nourishes our brains throughout later life. So next time you have a problem, remember that actively embracing and solving it is an opportunity to feed your brain with the stimulation necessary to grow more brain cells.

Chronological age doesn't define how "old" you are: attitude and activity level do.

There are enormous physical differences in people of the same age between 65 and 90. This is because the difference between "typical" and "quality" patterns of aging is significant. Quality aging means understanding the aging process and learning to take very good care of yourself so that you're not restricted as society assumes older people have to be. Healthy 71-year-olds can be nearly as vigorous and capable of exercise as 21-year-olds, even if they are a little slower. Pete Hamill, a veteran New York newspaper columnist, described this process very well in *Lear's* when he wrote of his admiration for aging women after a visit to Rancho La Puerta health spa:

> But the serious people were extraordinary. They pushed their bodies in the exercise class, working through pain, often for small gain. . . . Most of them were in their 40s and 50s, successful in their lives, and it was obvious why this is so: they had will, determination, intelligence and the best kind of toughness. Time and time again, these older women outperformed the younger ones, who tended to give up too eas-

ily. They did this without being grim; they laughed at themselves, at the absurdity of paying so much money to be denied food and forced to torture their aging bodies.[20]

These women understood what Karen DeCrow said about 50 and beyond: "At 50 one knows what was vague at 30. You will not have enough time to do everything, so you must do what is important."[21]

Most older women have less dissatisfaction and psychological stress than at any other time in life.
The stereotype of older women is that they're too sick, too poor, or too alone to enjoy life, but women who fit this description are clearly a minority. Indeed, in a Lou Harris nationwide poll conducted several years ago, one-third of women over 65 interviewed said it was the best time of their lives.[22] Other studies have also reported high levels of satisfaction if the women questioned weren't poor or quite sick. In a *Los Angeles Times* poll,[23] those over 65 were far happier with their lives than younger people. In fact, nearly two-thirds said they were very happy with "the way things are going" with their personal lives.

When we're older, we're better able to handle setbacks and have a greater ability to cope with illness. In one study, for example, people between 20 and 49 were more likely to cope with setbacks either by becoming a victim, flying into a rage, or escaping into fantasy.[24] After age 50, most women are well aware that anger, fantasy, and adopting a victim mentality waste time and energy. Strength from life experience and our growing wisdom allow women after 50 to wrestle more effectively with the Ten Commandments of the Traditional Core. We're increasingly able to break free of our traditional cultural conscience so that victim mentality and behavior are no longer our habitual and expected response to stress and conflict.

Social purpose, mastery, and generativity (our ability to stay productive and continue contributing something of value to the world and to others) become more important as we enter and pass through middle and older age.[25] The Study of Adult Development at Harvard University and Dartmouth College has found that we are four times more likely to use "mature defenses" in mid-life than in earlier phases. These "mature defenses" include altruism, humor, suppression (pushing out of consciousness unnecessary bad feelings and memories), anticipation (looking forward to positive experiences), and sublimation (channeling negative feelings into constructive action and then taking active responsibility for our emotional and physical well-being instead of expecting others to do it for us). Mature psychological defenses are some of the best Age Gains: they are essential for reducing stress and increasing life satisfaction. Mature defenses come only with age, growth, and effort.

We trade PMS (premenstrual syndrome) for PMZ (postmenopausal zest).

Events and experiences that our culture often perceives as aging losses are, for many of us, aging gains. For years, it was thought that most women plunged into a dark depression after their children left home to pursue their own lives. We were told this phenomenon was so common that it was even given a diagnostic name: "empty nest syndrome."

Recent research shows us that just the opposite is true. Most women are happier with themselves and their marriages after their last child leaves home. An eight-year University of Nebraska study found that no matter how "good" the kids were while growing up, the marriage gets better once they're gone. Women generally feel relief because they did most of the work, and now they have more time for themselves and feel they've "earned" it.[26]

Menopause is another middle-aged milestone that is supposed to plunge us into depression and despair. Even mental health professionals supported this stereotype for many years. One of the most famous female analysts, Helene Deutsch, called menopause "woman's last traumatic experience as a sexual being," "a mortification that is difficult to overcome," and insisted that "mastering the physiological reaction to organic decline is one of the most difficult tasks of a woman's life."[27] As part of the same cultural bias against women, a diagnostic category was developed in psychiatry in the early 1900s called "involutional melancholia," which was the depression middle-aged women were supposed to develop in response to menopause, empty nest syndrome, and aging.

The psychiatrists had to eliminate this diagnostic label about fifteen years ago because after reviewing the existing research studies, they simply couldn't find support for the syndrome. The reality is that most women don't experience depression as a result of meno-

pause and other milestones of middle age. The New England Research Institute, after tracking 2,300 women for five years, reported
that most "expressed relief at the loss of concern over pregnancy,
contraception, and menstruation."[28] Eighty-five percent of the
menopausal women surveyed report they were never depressed
about menopause. Another study compared a group of premeno-
pausal and postmenopausal women and found no difference in
their levels of anxiety, anger, stress, depression, and job satisfaction.
While the losses of middle age do trigger depression in some
women, it is important to remember that they are the exception
rather than the norm.

Most menopausal women trade depression and PMS for what
anthropologist Margaret Mead called PMZ (postmenopausal zest),
the tremendous release of energy that becomes available to women
after menopause.[29] PMZ gives us new sources of energy for further
achievement in both relationships and career because we're less
constricted by the cultural and physical restraints (i.e., the fear of
becoming pregnant or the limitations of raising young children)
that reduced our choices so significantly in the earlier years.

Margaret Mead certainly capitalized on her PMZ, doing some of
her finest work after 50, as did many of the women 40 to 65 featured in the Lou Harris/*Lear's* magazine poll mentioned earlier. In
this nationwide survey of seven hundred women, most reported an
increase in energy with age. Fifty-nine percent of women ages 60 to
65 said they were energetic, compared to 53 percent of those ages
50 to 59. Three-quarters of the women surveyed worked for pay,
including 42 percent of those women between the ages of 60 to 65.
Only 3 percent wanted to work less while 51 percent of the women
wanted to start their own business. Volunteer work created the same
feelings of energy and satisfaction.[30] Aging gave all these women a
new freedom, energy, and clarity to pursue what they really wanted
to do, whether it was in traditional or nontraditional arenas.

**There will be more and better work
opportunities for older women workers.**
Companies will increasingly value and need the older woman's sea-
soned work experience. In *Megatrends 2000,* John Naisbitt says,
"Women may have missed out on the industrial age, but they have
already established themselves in the industries of the future."[31]

Women will enjoy better working conditions and will be tapped as leaders more often than ever before because they have finally reached "a critical mass in virtually all the white-collar professions, especially business."[32] We already make up 30 percent to 50 percent of the employees in such vital branches of business as accounting, computers, and banking. Although clustered within the lower-status jobs in most of these fields, the fact that we have become a "critical mass" positions us to unleash enormous power and opportunity for women when we mobilize our numbers.

Considering that a labor shortage is anticipated due to the "baby bust" and a shortage of white male workers, older women workers will be increasingly in demand. Immigrants and young people will satisfy some of the demand for lower level jobs, but as the "graying of America" continues, the skilled work force of the nineties and beyond has to become older. In the next eight years, in fact, the number of workers 45 and older will increase three times faster than the rest of the labor force. The number of women workers will grow twice as fast as men. By the end of this century, women will hold nearly half of all the jobs in America.[33]

One of the reasons for this growth is that older women offer more maturity, perseverance, a greater sense of responsibility, and an ability to get along in groups from their experience raising a family or an impressive independence honed from being single and surviving so long in a male dominated, couples-oriented society. Older women's skills are also a better fit in the emerging Information Era than they were in the Industrial Era, where size and strength worked to men's advantage. Social and communication skills will count far more than muscle tone in the work world of the twenty-first century.

Most of us lose our fear of death as we age.
In the *Handbook of Aging and the Social Sciences,* Richard Kalish reported that only one out of four adults over 65 feared death. This is compared with 55 percent of people between 18 to 24.[34] Another study has shown that the older people are, the less they fear death and dying. Death itself is seen more often as a "long sleep" than a terrifying event. Most older women face death "without storminess and disruption . . . as if they were dealing with a developmental task that they were coping with adequately."[35] For many, the accep-

tance of death provides an irreplaceable wisdom about life and is a
source of ultimate freedom.

As the current research on aging clearly illustrates, there are
many realistic rewards to be enjoyed. Now that you're familiar with
some of them, make your own personal Age Gains list. With a little
effort and creativity, you can probably come up with at least five to
ten realistic Age Gains to look forward to. Your personal list might
include such opportunities as time to travel and pursue new hobbies, to move to a place you've always wanted to live, to seriously
pursue creative activities or go back to school, to donate your time
to a worthwhile organization or cause, to develop your spirituality,
or to pursue the pleasures adult children and grandchildren can
offer.

Tape a copy of the list from the book and your own list on your
bathroom mirror for a while until you become comfortable and
familiar with it and believe what it says. These lists remind us of the
power and wisdom the past year fulfilled and how much the next
year can deliver.

3. Anticipate Realistic Losses and
Adopt Practical Coping Strategies.

The perils of aging center around loss. As we enter middle adulthood, it is critical for us to understand which losses are realistic at
what age, and to acknowledge that we can cope with the great majority of these losses. Otherwise, we're bound to become overwhelmed. Study the following list of realistic losses and realistic
coping strategies, which show the predictable losses of aging and
some proven, successful coping mechanisms. This will help keep the
losses from growing out of proportion and will help you to have a
sense of control about how to develop coping skills by recognizing
what can and cannot be changed. You may also find it useful to read
Fact Book on Aging by Elizabeth Vierck (ABC-CLIO, Santa Barbara,
1990), a book I found very valuable for summarizing the realities of
getting older.

FEMALE AGING: REALISTIC LOSSES / REALISTIC COPING

Loss: Our mental functions are slower with age.

1. Electrical activity in the brain slows. EEG is one cycle slower.[36]
2. Slower functioning of central nervous system.
3. It takes longer to recover from stress and regain equilibrium.
4. It takes longer to retrieve information from our memory banks.

Coping: An older mind functions as well, just not quite as quickly.

1–4. The older mind still works fine but simply slower. It just takes a little longer to process and remember things. Much of the assumed atrophy of the brain's functioning can be traced to a lessening of novel stimuli as we age. We don't lose our knowledge or our ability to learn. Our capacity for learning increases as we age faster than our memory fades.[37]

Loss: Our bodies work less effectively.

1. Vision and hearing decrease. By age 50, 75 percent of us will wear glasses. By 65, 95 percent of us will wear glasses and 29 percent will have hearing impairments.[38] Also by 65, 60 percent of us will have major impairments in our sense of smell, and our taste buds will atrophy and become less efficient.[39]
2. We lose heart and lung capacity; we feel winded easily and tire with exertion.
3. We are more sensitive to heat and cold and more vulnerable to damage from exposure to extremes in temperature.
4. We have more trouble sleeping than we used to and wake up more easily and earlier than we wish.
5. Skin loses elasticity and becomes wrinkled, baggy, and often very dry; develops brown spots.
6. Hair loses pigment and grays; also, for many of us, there's a loss of teeth from gum disease. Thirty-four percent of those 65 to 74 have false teeth and after 75, almost half of us have. We

are twice as likely to develop cavities after 55 as when we were children.[40]

7. We become flabbier and fatter. Women typically gain 25 percent to 35 percent in weight during their middle years. Men gain 5 percent to 16 percent.[41]

Coping: The limitations can be adjusted and often repaired.

1. Glasses, hearing aids, and eye surgery for glaucoma are common and readily available. Cataract surgeries are 90 to 95 percent successful.[42] Significantly increasing the amount of light or carrying a small flashlight to read in dim places can be very practical and helpful. Accept that your capacity to smell and taste may be less, so compensate by eating healthy foods you really enjoy.

2. With regular exercise, we can compensate for these losses and be nearly as fit and energized as in our younger years.[43]

3. Pay extra attention to climate; wear appropriate clothing when going outside; avoid extremes by staying inside midday or visiting temperate climates. Or use climate as a challenge to overcome and a consequent source of self-esteem. At 84, Katharine Hepburn still swims year-round in the chilly waters of the Long Island Sound.[44]

4. Relaxation exercises and meditation contribute significantly to better sleep. Even with the typical problems of aging, 80 percent of those over 65 sleep more than six hours a night.[45]

5. Stay out of the sun; use sunscreen; learn to appreciate wrinkles as badges of courage and life experience.

6. Learn to value your new hair color or change it; for teeth, floss, use a Water Pik, and see a dentist often.

7. Weight gain is not inevitable. Commitment to diet and exercise neutralizes the tendency to gain. Weight gain has less to do with age and more to do with being sedentary as we age. Unfortunately, most older women don't act on this knowledge. Only about one-fourth of senior women regularly exercise or play sports.[46]

Loss: We're more vulnerable to illness.

1. We are more vulnerable to illness but not significantly until we are much older. Four out of five of us have one chronic condition such as arthritis, hypertension, heart disease, or hearing impairments.[47]

2. Women are more vulnerable to osteoporosis (a decrease in bone mass, making bones more fragile and porous). By 65, 25 percent of us will have fractures, mostly caused by osteoporosis.[48]

3. Women are more vulnerable to serious heart disease. Nearly 60 percent of us have it by the time we reach our 80s. We are two to three times more likely than men to suffer a second heart attack within five years.[49]

4. Women are more vulnerable to rheumatoid arthritis, our most common chronic condition. By 65, 80 percent of all people suffer from osteoarthritis, where the lining of the joints breaks down and we feel pain and stiffness.[50]

Coping: Better nutrition and exercise help tremendously.

1. Average life expectancy is now 78 for women. It's not until 85 that the incidence of disabling disease goes up significantly and we have a 60 percent chance of a chronic disabling disease.[51] Before then, we typically live free of serious illness, *if* we take care of ourselves. The usual chronic conditions can all be treated and are not disabling.

2. Osteoporosis can often be prevented through dietary and behavioral changes if detected early. Drink at least three glasses of milk a day, take calcium tablets, or eat calcium-rich food. Eight hundred mg. of calcium per day is recommended, especially as we reach menopause and our estrogen levels dip. Vitamin D, low-dosage estrogen, and exercise with weights also retard bone loss.[52] Smoking and drinking each double your risk for developing osteoporosis.[53]

3. Physician partnerships (described in Chapter 9), health knowledge, regular exercise, and good nutrition will significantly reduce our risk and symptoms.

4. Keep up on arthritis research and breakthroughs. It was re-

cently found, for example, that two Extra-Strength Tylenol taken four times a day was as effective as the typically prescribed arthritis drugs, which can cause ulcers and loss of kidney function.

**Loss: We experience increased fears
as we're more vulnerable from aging.**

1. Increased fear of crime. Older women fear being victims of crime far more than older men.
2. Fear of abuse. About 2 million seniors, many more women than men, were victims of elder abuse in 1988. "The most common forms . . . in order of severity are: neglect, physical abuse, financial/material exploitation, emotional abuse/neglect, and sexual abuse."[54]
3. Fear and reality of losing loved ones.
4. Fear of retirement.
5. Fear of being "abandoned" in a nursing home. Women are considerably more at risk; three out of four residents of nursing homes are women. This is partly because the primary caregivers for senior women are adult children while the primary caregivers for senior men are their wives.[55]
6. Fear of being poor.
7. Increased feeling of being less valuable.

**Coping: Acknowledge that fears are normal;
then move into problem solving.**

1. The reality: People 65 and older are less likely to be victimized by crime than any other age group.[56] If you are victimized by violent crime, however, you'll have more problems recovering so plan to be more careful and cautious.
2. Elder abuse can be prevented by building a strong support system outside your family, since family members account for over 50 percent of the abuse.[57]
3. You have a two-thirds chance of being widowed by 75, but the readjustment may not be as difficult as you imagine. Widows are in no different psychological health ten years after being widowed than those still married. Many widows choose not to

remarry even if given the chance.[58] Children, friends, and relatives will probably be available; almost 80 percent of us have at least one living sibling.[59] In one study, three-quarters of women from 50 to their late 80s had children who lived within a half-hour drive.[60] We expect we'll be lonely when we're older, but research suggests that with effort, the opposite is true.

4. The average retirement does not cause unhappiness or ill health; the typical feeling is relief, anticipation, and enthusiasm along with manageable fear and loss.[61]

5. The majority of older women do not live in nursing homes. Among the general population, you have a 40 percent chance between 75 and 80 and a 46 percent chance between 85 and 90 of living in a nursing home if you're a woman.[62] However, it is critical to stay fit and take good care of your health to minimize the risk of institutionalization.

6. Poverty may be one of the most realistic fears for older women. Fifteen percent of older women live below the poverty line compared with 8.5 percent of men.[63] Women endure a large decrease in income when they enter old age, so early financial and career planning is an essential survival skill, especially for ethnic minorities, who face greater economic discrimination.

7. With effort, education, and a strong collective voice, we can change the definition of aging in our culture, reject the emphasis on youth, and truly appreciate the gains of aging.

4. Take Greater Control of Your Life by Confronting Your Death.

A critical step in effectively dealing with your River of Life is accepting that it eventually leads to a Waterfall of Transition: death. By developing our understanding of death, we become less afraid of it when we're younger and gain more control over the quality of our life and death when we are older. Learning about death also provides a buffer against Unhealthy Depression, because our discoveries help us see that we have nothing to fear. Rollo May, an eminent psychological theorist, said it well: "The confronting of death gives us the . . . positive reality to life itself. It makes the individual existence real, absolute, and concrete."[64]

How do you see death? Once you've given some thought to these issues and have actually drawn your Waterfall of Transition, attach it to the end of your River of Life sheet, hang it on a wall, and study what it means. Make a commitment to developing a positive image of death for yourself, especially if you're uncomfortable with what you see. There are a number of action strategies you can do to develop a positive image of death.

Study what death means in major religions. Talk with ministers, priests, and/or rabbis about death. Their perspectives and experience will be enlightening, whether or not you happen to identify with or share their beliefs. Read one or several of the religious books that discuss death: the Bible, the Koran, the Torah, the Book of Miracles, or books about Eastern religions to find the ingredients to develop your own concept and theory about death.

Rent videos that feature death as a major theme, such as *Ghost, Flatliners, Longtime Companion, Defending Your Life, Whose Life Is It Anyway?,* and the classic *Harold and Maude.* These and other films explore death in positive, life-affirming ways. Watch and discuss them with family and trusted friends. Borrow from them the elements that ring true to you to help develop your own positive image of death.

Another approach to examining death is to read Elisabeth Kübler-Ross's classic work, *On Death and Dying* (Macmillan, 1969), or her later book, *Questions and Answers on Death and Dying* (Macmillan, 1974). She was the first to clearly identify and describe the predictable feelings experienced by those facing serious illness or death: denial and isolation, anger, bargaining, depression, and acceptance. They don't have to come in a particular order and not everyone has every one of these feelings. But knowing the typical reactions to illness and death provide comfort that we're not alone in our feelings and knowledge about what to expect.

Another comfort in exploring death is to learn about hospices, which are becoming increasingly common in the United States. They provide settings in which terminally ill patients are cared for with support and dignity. Hospice personnel work on helping the patient learn to regulate medications so that he or she has greater control and is pain free, and they provide a positive environment where a patient never has to be alone or to hide his or her illness or symptoms.

Preparing for the details of your death mentally and materially, no matter what your age, will help you and those you love exercise as much control as possible in facing what is ultimately an uncontrollable event. Make out a legal will to insure that your material possessions are given to those you wish. Give clear written instructions about the type of funeral and burial you want. Prepare a living will so that no one will have to guess whether you would want to have your life sustained through extraordinary means. These kinds of mental and legal preparations will give you an invaluable sense of strength, peace, and acceptance about your own mortality.

5. Cultivate Intimate Relationships as a Buffer for the Predictable Losses, Especially Widowhood.

Emotional intimacy is vital for successful aging. The more connected we are, the healthier we stay. That's why one of the most important strategies for resolving Age Rage Depression is investing yourself in developing and maintaining close personal relationships.

One thing is virtually certain for most women: even if you're married, you're likely to be alone as you advance in age. There are three times as many widows as widowers[65] and women typically outlive their husbands by fifteen years.[66]

Widowhood is a distinct era of life, and you need to be prepared for the likelihood that although you may be married today, you probably won't be tomorrow. Widowhood has several stages, and nearly any woman who has survived the loss of a husband will tell you the first three years are the most painful and difficult. Many clients have told me that the initial pain of losing a husband is so severe they seriously feared they wouldn't survive it. As Dr. Janet Belsky describes in her book, *Here Tomorrow: Making the Most of Life After 50:*

> Losing a loved one is similar to a severe physical wound. The pain is unbearable at the beginning, then gradually subsides. As the wound heals, there are many days when the agony is nearly forgotten and others when it reappears full force. Although people differ in how long the healing takes, sooner or later recovery generally is complete. A scar remains, but the person is able to resume a full life.[67]

It doesn't work this way for everyone. One-third of widows suffer "unlimited grieving" and one in five never fully recovers from the loss, although the intense grief does subside. Some even lose the will to live and die of "Broken-Heart Syndrome." But it doesn't have to be this way. There are a number of steps you can take to make sure you aren't stuck living in an emotional death camp after losing a spouse.

Right after the loss, it's critical that you stay active in the funeral or memorial arrangements and remain available to talk with friends and relatives who can help you begin the transition to this new stage in your life. Funerals are a rare opportunity to have space and support for your grieving and for Healthy Depression. According to research conducted by psychologist Neil Krause at the University of Texas, supportive friends and family are "more important in preventing depression after the loss of a spouse than during any other crisis in our lives."[68]

The worst stage for men is generally right after their wife's death, but the time of greatest vulnerability for women survivors is typically two to three years later.[69] If you're older when the loss occurs, however, you're in the best shape to handle it and least likely to become ill. Again the research shows that older women are more emotionally resilient and better able to cope with loss.[70] The healthy adjustment typically requires moving through a Depressive Passage of fear and loneliness, but most women learn how to cope with the changes of old age and discover this stage isn't nearly as bad or lonely as they anticipated. In fact, 72 percent of people over 65 feel "satisfied with life" according to a Lou Harris poll and 60 percent do not experience any major fears as they face the future.[71]

Even if you're divorced or have never married, you still face the same process as you lose close friends and relatives. And you still face the same developmental challenge as widows—to build and maintain enough quality relationships that you never feel totally alone. It is critical to have at least one trusted confidant to act as a buffer against the losses of life.[72] Healthy living habits are not as important for longevity as social factors. "There is no disease that kills people at the rate loneliness does," according to Drs. Robert Ornstein and Charles Swencionis, two well-respected health psychologists.[73]

Women without close personal relationships are much more likely to experience aging the way many men do. Men die younger, are more depressed in old age, and are more at risk for suicide.[74] They become more depressed when they retire and lose work as a source of self-esteem. Most older men in our culture never learned the relationship skills necessary to develop true intimacy and find themselves emotionally isolated as they age. Most older men report having only one real confidant: their wives. If she dies before they do, they're especially vulnerable to sickness and death.[75] Insurance companies will tell you that their highest-risk clients are older men who have recently lost their wives. Women, on the other hand, usually can count four or five confidants to turn to for emotional support when facing a loss.

How do you nourish intimacy? You begin early in life by understanding how important relationships are for your emotional and physical health. You make a commitment to develop intimate relationships with a number of appropriate men and women you like and trust, and practice the strategies recommended in Chapter 5, on Relationship Depression and in Chapter 11, on how to create a Family of Choice.

6. Reclaim Your Sexuality.

Even though our cultural standards regarding aging and sexuality have evolved somewhat over the past twenty years, there's still a strong societal undercurrent that suggests that people over 50 aren't expected to be or supposed to be sexually active and fulfilled. It's generally assumed that interest in sex—not to mention the enjoyment of it—diminishes with age. We live in a culture that still assumes our main value is to attract men and have babies. When the culture considers us less attractive because we have aged and can no longer bear children, it's assumed that we're no longer sexual since there's no longer a "need" for us to be.

It's essential that we understand female sexual response in the later years and not allow our sexual energy to be turned off by the cultural spigot. Sexuality is a wonderful source of energy, creativity, and fulfillment that women can tap. Whatever losses in sexuality we experience are far more likely to be psychological than physical in nature. If we accept the cultural party line of the Traditional Core that says women are "dried up" and no longer sexually attractive after a given age, we're allowing ourselves to be robbed of a very rich bounty.

Masters and Johnson and a number of other credible sex researchers have found that women's sexual response changes little with age. Older women are just as physically capable of achieving orgasm as younger women.[76] Arousal and performance do not decrease by much and in fact may even become better after age 50, when women tap into their increased self-confidence and greater sexual experience and no longer fear becoming pregnant.

While there are physical changes that result from reduced estrogen after menopause, there are solutions to offset most such changes. Drier vaginal walls, for example, can be remedied by using a lubricating jelly, which offers the added benefit of heightening sexual sensation. Your doctor isn't likely to share such suggestions, however, because many doctors feel awkward discussing sex, especially with older women. But this and other information is available from books, women's health groups, older female confidants, and specialists trained in the psychology and physiology of older women.

Make a commitment that you won't allow your sexuality to evaporate simply because you're divorced, single, widowed, beyond menopause, or married to an inattentive husband. Keep your sexual vitality by having a sexual relationship that you create and nurture. How? The possibilities are endless. Here are a few ideas:

- Masturbate. Buy a back massager at a department store or from a mail order catalog and use it as a vibrator. In some cities, adult sex toys, once referred to as "marital aids," are sold in upscale boutiques and through home parties.
- Develop and savor sexual fantasies about men or women you work with or see around town. Don't judge the fantasies. Simply experience and enjoy them.
- Explore nonpornographic, sexually oriented novels, magazines, and videos. You can find the books in the fiction sections of most mainstream bookstores under "Anonymous" or in the Human Sexuality sections of most contemporary or New Age bookstores.
- Flirt with men or women of all ages. Join a social or dance club to keep you sexually connected to the world.

You may be surprised where your newfound sexual independence leads. There is an increasing phenomenon of middle-aged women becoming single through divorce or death of a husband and turning to another woman for the first time for intimacy and sex.

While little research has yet been conducted on this trend, we're seeing it in cities and small towns across the country. As one of my clients who made this choice explained, "The available women in my age range are so much higher quality than the few available men that women are, at this point in my life, a more desirable alternative for a sexual or life partner."

Another alternative that a growing number of older women explore is sex with younger men. In our 40s, sex becomes more physical and less tied to the feeling that we must love someone to have sex. In summarizing new research in this area, an article in *Harper's Bazaar* stated that "sexually, a woman in her 40s has more in common with a man in his 20s than she does with men her own age."[77] In a study from researchers at the University of Kansas and Florida State University, results showed that 61 percent of women surveyed between the ages 22 and 35 reported they primarily have sex to express love. On the other hand, 62 percent of the women surveyed between the ages of 36 and 57 stated their reasons for having sex were more physical than emotional. Sixty-nine percent of the men in the younger age group reported their reasons for having sex were more physical than emotional, while 50 percent of the older men said love and intimacy were their primary sexual motivators.[78]

One of the reasons for this reversal in experience and motivation between men and women is that both men and women have testosterone, a chief source of sexual energy, when they're young.[79] As men age, however, their testosterone decreases. In women, testosterone levels remain constant, so while aging women produce fewer female hormones like estrogen, the fact that our testosterone level stays the same gives many older women a sense of heightened sexual drive while male sexuality diminishes.

There are also psychological factors at work that can make women sexually stronger in later years. After 35, many women shed previous sexual fears and inhibitions. They just don't seem relevant or serve their purpose anymore. Women who had problems having orgasms in their 20s and early 30s often find that after 35 they freely enjoy more frequent and fulfilling orgasms than ever before.

Don't waste this source of pleasure and power. Be inventive and exploratory. Find safe, healthy outlets for your sexuality and refuse to allow cultural punishment to rob you of the most basic and satisfying of human experiences. If you're in a committed relationship or long-term marriage, use your increased sexual potential to excite a husband or lover who may need more stimulation due to his reduced testosterone levels. Be playful and willing to take the lead, if you don't already. You may find your partner more receptive and willing than you imagined. By reaching out to him now, you will encourage him to reach back to you in a more intimate manner in other areas of your life.

7. Learn from Role Models of Quality Aging.

Harvest the wisdom that women before us have gained as they learned how to age well. Make a list of five or six women you feel have aged successfully. Some of the women typically mentioned in the workshops and classes are:

> Martha Graham, who continued to dance until age 75 and created new dances until her death in 1990 at 96.

> May Sarton, who at age 83 wrote her first book, which became a best-seller.

> Georgia O'Keeffe, who painted until she was in her 90s and spent her final years on her bleak, beautiful desert with a much younger male companion.

> Eleanor Roosevelt, who continued to influence social policy and encourage new program development into her 70s.

> Imogen Cunningham, who captured the essence of the female spirit in her photographs well into old age.

> Grandma Moses, who illustrated 'Twas the Night Before Christmas when she was 100.

> Tina Turner, who resurrected her career as a rock star in her 40s and still has, in her early 50s, what one music publicist describes as "the best legs in America."

Read autobiographies of women who have aged well and list the strategies they used for quality aging. Discuss their strategies with friends to see what makes sense and what doesn't. Then make a list of the best strategies you can actually apply in your own life and post them as reminders that you do have power and there are unique rewards for aging.

8. Tap the Wisdom of Your Family and Friends by Doing "Quality Aging" Interviews.

Instead of relying solely on books, make a point of focusing on those you know personally. Bring the harvest of wisdom closer to home by turning to your own family and friends. Talk with the older women. Sit down with your older living relatives—grandmothers, mother, aunts—and do an age interview to learn from their experiences. If, because of distance or death, none of the older women in your family are available, reach out to older friends or neighbors.

By talking with older women face to face and listening to their experiences and observations, you're certain to benefit from their wisdom and gain new insights into what getting older can mean. Once you start talking with them, the conversation usually flows quite naturally. Older people who are encouraged to talk about themselves usually welcome the opportunity to share. Be sure to ask them about their impressions of you. What advice would they give you about problems or concerns you have? What would they suggest you do? This approach makes it clear that you honor and value their perspective, and gives them power and involvement so that they don't feel simply like interview subjects. As they become more comfortable and open, ask questions such as:

- What is it like to be your age? What do you like and dislike about being your age? How is it different from what you anticipated?
- What was the best age of your life? Why? What was the worst age? Why? What made the best so much better than the worst?
- What was the attitude toward women in the various stages of your life? How is it better or worse today? Have we made progress or have we lost ground?

- What do you know now that you wish you'd known when you were a young woman?
- What can I do to age successfully? What do you do?
- What mistakes have you made? What have you done that made aging more painful or difficult? What would you do differently if you had it to do over?
- How do you feel about death? What do you think happens when we die? When do you think you will die? How? Is there anything I or anyone else can do to help you face that experience?

Some of my clients have videotaped their interviews. Video is a wonderful way to relive the conversations and treat yourself to their wisdom whenever you choose. If videotaping isn't practical, or if it makes the person you're interviewing uncomfortable, try using a small audiocassette recorder. When neither are appropriate, take notes. If the women you want to interview are hesitant to participate, assure them how important and helpful the information will be to you, how much you value them as a role model and how much you appreciate the opportunity to learn from their experience.

If the women you talk with are willing to have you share their stories with others, compile their thoughts and insights into a female family history and give copies as birthday presents to all the young women and men in your family. You might also go through the interviews and select the quotes and comments that most moved or enlightened you. By writing them down and keeping them visible on your desk or on your refrigerator, you'll continue to stay inspired and equipped as you face your own aging process.

9. Watch Videos on Quality Aging.

Don't restrict yourself to books and family interviews to learn about quality aging. A number of films feature the stories of real and fictional women who have aged with dignity and passion.

Harold and Maude
A wise and daffy character in her 80s (played to the hilt by Ruth Gordon) teaches a suicidal 18-year-old boy how to laugh, love, and live.

The Autobiography of Miss Jane Pittman
A slave of 110 (Cicely Tyson) remembers her life and her struggle for liberty that began with the Civil War and ended during the civil rights movement.

On Golden Pond
A film about family and relationships, it poignantly depicts the frustration and fear of a woman (Katharine Hepburn) caring for her aging husband as he faces his final days.

Fried Green Tomatoes
Jessica Tandy plays an 83-year-old rest home resident who helps heal a younger woman's broken spirit by sharing her own remarkable life story.

Driving Miss Daisy
An aging Jewish woman (Jessica Tandy) comes to terms with her own pride and prejudice as her rich twenty-five-year relationship with her black chauffeur unfolds.

Each of these characters has lessons to teach us about how to grow older gracefully and with purpose. All stayed active and vital until their deaths. All stayed connected to people they cared about. All became teachers to others and remained generative. All stayed creative and in control of as many aspects of their lives as possible. Some had physical limitations or illnesses, but didn't focus on them except to get appropriate medical care. To these women, every day was important because they had a sense of purpose.

Writing this chapter has been a remarkable education for me. I am considerably less anxious and afraid of aging and death than I ever have been. I can't say that I welcome either, but I'll feel more ready as each plays a more significant role in my life. I finally completed a will, reviewed my life insurance, and updated all of my physical exams. I began a systematic exercise program to help minimize future physical problems and maximize my quality of life. I hope this chapter has infused you with the same kind of hope and support to convert what you've learned about aging into action. Take responsibility for making quality aging another career, regardless of how old or young you are. If we women act and speak together, we have the power to fundamentally change the experience of female aging in this country from an unhealthy one to a healthy and rewarding one.

· 7 ·

DEPLETION DEPRESSION

Sometimes I get too compulsive about my work and don't take care of me as well as I'd like. When I don't set enough limits . . . I can feel low. It isn't actually depression, but I can quickly get in touch with those old feelings of powerlessness and loneliness.

Claudia Black, a founder of
Adult Children of Alcoholics

It was a bright, sunny Wednesday morning. But to Alice, it still seemed too dark and dreary to climb out of bed. The helplessness and anxiety she'd experienced in her dreams left her feeling tense and lethargic. As she lay there, attempting to rally the energy to begin another day, she thought of a favorite old Billie Holiday song, "Good Morning Heartache." In the song, Holiday describes a heartache so persistent that she finally gives up fighting and invites it to sit down and join her.

On days like these, Alice, 38, wanted nothing more than to pull the covers over her face and snuggle into a friendly pillow. The last thing she wanted to do was to deal with all the people and responsibilities awaiting her. She didn't want to be a wife or mommy. She didn't want to be the caretaker of the dogs, the CEO of a hectic household, or a friend to anyone. And she certainly didn't want to be a pediatrician. She could hardly tolerate her own kids on days like these.

As tired as she felt, Alice knew from experience that staying in bed would make her feel even worse. So out of bed she crawled, dreading the day she was about to face. After a busy morning at home policing an active 4-year-old and consoling an irritable, teething toddler, she rushed off to the clinic, where she was greeted by a seemingly endless parade of more whining, crying kids.

Alice adores children, but because she felt so frazzled and overextended, each child began to look more like a little monster than a sick little patient. Throughout the afternoon, she felt increasingly drained and miserable. Between nearly every appointment, she would duck into her office to catch her breath and munch on a handful of M&M's.

Alice knew that all the candy really provided was unwanted calories, but it was also a source of immediate gratification and energy, one of the few ways she could get instead of give and have at least one thing *she* wanted and when *she* wanted it. By the time Alice had finished seeing her last patient, she'd finished the entire one-pound bag she'd opened just six hours earlier.

Alice had no choice but to keep pushing. When she returned home, her "second shift" began. After feeding the kids, giving them their baths, and reading a rousing rendition of Dr. Seuss's *Green Eggs and Ham*, she greeted her husband, Paul, who was just returning from a long day of his own. She put a frozen lasagna in the microwave and went about making a salad. She was so stressed and frustrated that she actually had to make an effort to keep from raising her voice as she told Paul about her busy day.

Alice didn't work every night, but that night she felt driven to check off at least two tasks from her ever-growing "To Do" list. So she was at the kitchen table by 9:30 P.M., sorting phone messages, tending to a pile of paperwork, and drafting a speech. She finally collapsed into bed a few minutes before one A.M. Although she was exhausted from having done so much, and frustrated by the reality that she'd have to do it all over again in less than five hours, she also got a rush and even a sense of pride out of being able to somehow "do it all." What she didn't realize was that "doing it all" was doing her in.

Alice had been developing a Depletion Depression for the past several years. Her perfectionism, her deep commitment to her children, and her draining work schedule combined to create intense multiple demands on her time. Role overload was second nature to her; she didn't realize she was often feeling bad because she was getting so much done. She usually dismissed whatever bad feelings surfaced as the result of not getting enough sleep and promised herself that soon she'd take a day off to "catch up."

It never occurred to Alice that she was dangerously depleting her internal reserves by pushing herself at such an unrelenting pace without taking time out to take care of herself. And the candy and cookies she was using to fuel herself were endangering the good health she had always enjoyed, by making her too heavy and channeling her appetite away from healthy, nutritious food.

Alice is not alone. In fact, millions of contemporary American women know how she feels. Depletion Depressions have reached near epidemic proportions as we move through the nineties. Most of us are time-starved: we have too much to do and not enough time to do it. Never before have women had so many choices and so many demands to meet all at the same time.

Our Traditional Core encourages us to be traditional wives and mothers, safe and secure in an Ozzie and Harriet world where men are the breadwinners and women are the bread bakers. Yet these days less than 14 percent of American women fit the traditional family model. Many women feel unable to abandon traditional roles, however, so they maintain these roles and add all the necessary new ones to keep the Traditional Core quiet and appeased. We've been taught to believe we're inadequate or unfulfilled unless we "have it all," which now has come to mean continuing to nurture the Traditional Core despite the intense demands of an increasingly untraditional world.

Many of us find ourselves in the roles of executives, entrepreneurs, volunteers, lovers, friends, mentors, mothers, and organizers, often all at the same time, in our relentless quest to appease our Traditional Core. The result? We have become a nation of exhausted women. Virtually every woman I encounter experiences at least some degree of Depletion Depression. When asked how they're doing, most women—if they're honest with you—will tell you they're tired or even exhausted.

Depletion Depression is defined as the bad feelings we experience from being chronically tired, overwhelmed, stressed, and drained by the role demands and role conflicts confronting contemporary women. The typical symptoms of Depletion Depression are sleep deprivation, chronic fatigue, overeating, smoking, perfectionism, forgetfulness, irritability, taking pills or alcohol to sleep or calm down, physical problems caused by stress, always feeling behind, making too many mistakes as a result of doing too much too fast, and frequent bouts of impatience from having to wait in line or in traffic or being slowed down by a person who isn't moving rapidly enough and is "in the way."

Women are susceptible to Depletion Depression no matter how traditional or nontraditional their lifestyle. Mothers who work outside the home are prone as a result of juggling the multiple demands of working hard and feeling responsible in two places at once. Mothers who stay home often become just as depleted from the continual demands of children, housework, and the lack of adult support and validation of their traditional role. Single women find themselves exhausted because they're striving to excel professionally and socially in a culture that places a high premium on couples' relationships and often views single women as irrelevant or potential poachers of married men.

Married women without children are pressured by family and culture to have children to escape being defined as inadequate. Some feel driven to do too many other activities to compensate for not having kids. Divorced women and lesbians are still viewed by some as failures or damaged goods. The cultural assumption is that if the women were the effective relationship custodians they were supposed to be, the breakup wouldn't have happened or they would have made the obvious "superior" relationship choice: men. When we don't conform to these traditional cultural biases, it is draining to maintain our self-esteem and sense of adequacy. One of the results is chronic Depletion Depression.

Depletion Depression is clearly the price many women pay for survival in the nineties. Feelings of strain, frustration, exhaustion, and withdrawal are normal responses in this age of the anxiety attack. These conditions produce Healthy Depressions in many of us like the one Alice had. Her feelings were an appropriate reaction to the constant, multiple demands she faced. Despite the demands and negative feelings she experienced, she was still able to function adequately, if not at optimum levels, which is why Alice had a Healthy rather than Unhealthy Depression.

A week or so after Alice's most recent depleting day, she developed a red rash on her neck that her dermatologist diagnosed as stress related. She was ashamed that her stress was so visible. But her inflamed skin mobilized her to examine the source of her stress and look at how unrealistic her schedule and expectations were. She finally realized that if she continued living the way she was, her bad feelings would intensify, she would escalate into an Unhealthy Depression, and would ultimately burn out or break down.

Just like Alice, it may be time for you to make some changes. You can begin by evaluating how much you're at risk for Depletion Depression by taking the following quiz to identify Depletion Depression before it expresses itself as a physical symptom, illness, or an Unhealthy Depression. Even if it doesn't escalate into a major problem, feeling depleted frequently is a second-rate way to live. What's more, it's unnecessary. The action strategies in the last part of this chapter will show you how to alleviate your Depletion Depression or at least keep it within manageable bounds when it's unavoidable.

DEPLETION DEPRESSION QUIZ

How much of a role does Depletion Depression play in your life? Answer the following questions YES or NO.

1. Do you consistently average less than seven hours of sleep a night?   _____

2. Are you a principal caregiver to an aging relative, or a mother to one or more teenagers or young children under 6?   _____

3. Do you often feel that no matter how much you do, you never get enough done?   _____

4. Are you frequently quite irritable or impatient when you have to stand in line, get stuck in traffic, or have to fix the "small" things that typically go wrong in an average day?   _____

5. Do you dread holidays, birthdays, anniversaries, and other events because they mean more work and organizing?   _____

6. Do you play more than two roles daily or often find yourself doing several things at once (talking on the phone while fixing dinner and watching the kids)?   _____

7. Do you find yourself losing or forgetting important things like keys, money, appointments, or directions because you're always racing the clock?   _____

8. Do you often overeat or eat "junk food" to give yourself

energy, comfort, or pleasure; and/or do you light up a
cigarette when you're stressed or tired?   _____

9. Are you in a significantly unhappy relationship at work
and/or at home?   _____

10. Are you the only "minority" in at least one group important to you (i.e., are you an ethnic minority, a lesbian, the only woman in a group of men, the only nontraditional woman in a group of traditional women, or
vice versa)?   _____

Total number of questions answered YES: _____

SCORING

**(0–2) Your life is in balance and you deserve
congratulations!**

The degree of Depletion Depression you experience is negligible to
nonexistent. You've done a terrific job balancing your needs and
the needs of others to escape the tyranny of the negative Traditional
Core. Savor and appreciate what you've done because it's a rare
accomplishment. Think about what strategies you're using to stay
balanced. You may want to write them down so you can easily reinforce your strategy during particularly stressful times.

(3–5) Caution: You're vulnerable!

Although your life may feel somewhat balanced, the demands on
your time—and your degree of Depletion Depression—are problematic. Make careful choices and think twice before committing
yourself to anything new until your life simmers down and you feel
less overextended. Focus on priorities. Challenge yourself to see
how many tasks you can delegate to others and how many you can
simply dissolve by letting go of the expectation that they must be
completed.

**(6–7) You have a significant Depletion Depression
that could easily become unhealthy.**

You're seriously pushing your physical and emotional limits. You're
doing more and enjoying it less. Your chances of becoming ill or
developing a variety of physical symptoms are high. You're proba-

bly much less effective in relationships than you care to admit because you can't spare the time and energy to maintain them properly. If you don't make some immediate changes and reduce your daily stress and role overload, you run a clear risk of burning out and ending up with an Unhealthy Depression.

(8–10) Danger: You're running on empty!

The demands on your time and energy are extreme, and are placing you in danger of a physical and/or emotional breakdown. You're exhausted and totally overextended. It's likely that you have moved or are moving into an Unhealthy Depression. Seriously examine why you're trying to do so much and be all things to all people. Short- or long-term counseling, depending on your degree of vulnerability, will help you examine the answer to this all-important question and will challenge you to sort out your priorities, clarify your values, establish your boundaries, and learn how and when to say no.

What can you do if you're struggling with Depletion Depression? The first step is taking some time to understand why you're feeling the way you do. Look beyond the obvious reasons such as lack of sleep to explore why you're so willing and likely to use yourself up. Then work with action strategies that will help you reduce your degree of depletion, achieve better balance, and build up your immunity to Unhealthy Depression.

Sources of Depletion Depression

1. Women Are Experiencing Greater Role Overload Than Ever Before.

A woman's work is never done. It's an old adage, but it's never been truer than it is today. As wives, we typically come home from work to face another shift at home. Women perform 75 percent of the housekeeping chores and often operate as the CEO of the household by managing the couple's social calendar and finances and performing or supervising most of the multiple tasks necessary to eat, sleep, and live in a comfortable home. Role overload makes it increasingly difficult to stay organized. The more chaotic our lives feel, the more depleted we become.

Even in relationships in which the women and men believe in "equal roles," one study showed that the women averaged thirty-two hours of child care and housework per week, while their "liberated" male partner averaged less than eleven hours doing similar chores.[1] Another study by a University of Wisconsin researcher found that although traditional men put in the same number of hours at work as their female counterparts, they worked considerably less at home because they "hated chores." Nontraditional women put in fewer hours tending to child care and housework, but still averaged a fifty-eight-hour work week between their job and household responsibilities. In her book *The Second Shift*,[2] sociologist Arly Hochchild points out that men are "having their cake and eating it, too," enjoying the benefits of their wives' salaries but rarely contributing to maintenance of the household they both need for emotional and physical survival.

Being or becoming single provides no refuge from this depleting role overload. Single women face significant work pressures and time demands because it takes a great deal of planning and effort to maintain an active social life while also struggling up the corporate ladder or keeping up with the pace of the assembly line or typing pool. The constant grind often leaves single women feeling so depleted that they can barely manage the basics of their lives, much less reach out to others to date or build new relationships.

The holiday season is an especially high-risk period for Depletion Depression, since it's the favorite season of the Traditional Core. We have more performance demands, more interpersonal commitments, and greater expectations between Thanksgiving and New Year's than at any other time of the year. Many of us become so exhausted afterward that it takes weeks or months to recover our energy. "Winter blahs" are often unrecognized Depletion Depressions.

It's no wonder that women—whether single, married, or divorced, with or without children—often feel they're on stage, expected to perform every role. But unlike theater, our lives rarely have an intermission. What's more, we hardly ever get recognition for a brilliant performance. Rather than occasionally stopping long enough to give ourselves an ovation, we end up immediately throwing ourselves into the next role because the culture's current demands for female performance are insatiable. Not only are we the star of our own show, we're expected to be the supporting actress, director, stage manager, usher, and janitor for the lives of everyone around us.

2. Women Are Experiencing a New Kind of Economic and Emotional Fatigue.

To be a woman in the nineties is to feel fatigued and depleted to an unprecedented depth and degree as the result of our economic and emotional struggles. It's a common bond that unites virtually every woman I know and meet regardless of her age, race, occupation, or economic standing. If you're female, chances are you're chronically fatigued in a way that women from previous generations were not. Our unstable economy, global competition, escalating prices on everything from food to college educations, low-paying jobs, a lack of job security for our husbands and ourselves, and unprecedented divorce rates have forced the majority of women to assume or share the role of primary economic provider and to become very tired in the process.

For the first time in history, most women must earn money to survive or to maintain an adequate standard of living for their family. And for many of us, the effort doesn't seem to pay off. According to a recent survey quoted in a *Newsweek* article called "Living on the Edge," only 62 percent of American households currently report that their standard of living is satisfactory, the lowest level since 1963.[3] We have come to the grim realization that our children may not necessarily live better than we do, or as well, despite our efforts to change current economic and political realities.

The need to earn money compounds feelings of depression for many women, because the role of breadwinner becomes yet another demand on an already long list of obligations and expectations. For many women, the necessity to work outside the home directly conflicts with their desire to stay home and raise their young children. According to recent Bureau of Labor statistics, for the first time more than half of all American women with children 1 year old or younger are in the labor force. This is a drastic increase from the late seventies, when less than 30 percent of mothers returned to work before their child's first birthday. Among women currently giving birth to their first child, nearly 30 percent are single mothers. This is more than double the rate of single mothers found in the 1960s. The great majority of these mothers are the sole economic and emotional providers for their children,[4] making them prime targets for Depletion Depression.

The depleting fatigue results not only from this excessive role overload, but from the realities of the workplace. As we saw in the chapter on Victimization Depression, women consistently face firmly entrenched economic discrimination that is every bit as depleting and psychologically draining as it is financially oppressive and unfair. If you think things have changed for the better due to women's liberation and other factors, you're overlooking a major source of your Depletion Depression. Consider the following statistics: the number of women working two jobs has increased 500 percent since 1970, yet during that same time their average hourly wage has slipped nearly 5 percent. According to the *New York Times,* the average working woman is paid only 60 percent to 70 percent as much as the average working man.[5]

Another factor contributing to our fatigue is, quite predictably, too little sleep. In her book *Losing Sleep,* Lydia Dotto suggests that "we are battling a global epidemic of sleepiness."[6] A recent report in *Time* echoed Dotto's sentiments, citing mounting evidence that "sleep deprivation has become one of the most pervasive problems facing the U.S."[7]

The vast majority of American women average only five to six hours of sleep a night, rather than the seven to eight hours that sleep experts tell us we need to function most effectively. Over time, the effect of sleep deprivation is a depletion that's not easily repaired. "Catching up" by sleeping for ten or twelve hours on the weekend only partially offsets the chronic loss. When we consistently get two or three hours a night less sleep than our bodies need, we're setting ourselves up for Depletion Depression, because we have less energy, think less clearly, and become much more vulnerable to illness, accidents, irritability, and conflict.

3. Being Responsible for Children in a Culture That Provides Few Supports.

Parents, regardless of how old their children happen to be, are more vulnerable to stress than ever. The National Commission on Children reported in the fall of 1991 that 88 percent of the adults surveyed feel it's more difficult to be a parent now than at any previous time in history. Eighty-seven percent of parents report financial difficulties and 81 percent admit they don't begin to spend enough time with their kids.[8]

There are two major reasons for the level of stress so many parents feel. One is that we live in a society that continues to favor status, money, and career success over relationships, children, and parenting. The other is the depressing reality that our child care options continue to be so limited and expensive. "In study after study, America's working mothers have identified adequate child care as the factor most important to their peace of mind, yet the number of companies that offer child care remains tiny," states psychologist Dr. Faye Crosby, author of *Juggling: The Unexpected Advantages of Balancing Career and Home for Women and Their Families.*[9]

During recent Senate hearings, it was reported that more than 75 percent of the mothers surveyed feel they do not have access to adequate child care. Many have simply given up. As a result, there are more than 10 million "latchkey kids" who are completely unsupervised after school.[10] The research suggests that parents who leave their older children home alone tend to have a tougher time and more problems with their kids. A *Journal of Pediatrics* study released in late 1990 showed that adolescent "latchkey kids" seemed to suffer much higher levels of stress and more frequent clashes with their parents than children who had more parental supervision.[11] Another study showed that older kids who were often left alone were more prone to depression, drinking, and sexual activity.[12] Mothers who must work are typically blamed for abandoning their children and creating or allowing an atmosphere that promotes "problems." The result: a major case of Depletion Depression with a dash of Victimization Depression added for good measure.

Women who are at home taking care of their children when they'd rather be working outside the home are also at high risk for Depletion Depression. Mothers who work outside the home and have mixed emotions about their decision have less depression but more stress. It's no wonder that approximately 12 percent of mothers with small children have major Unhealthy Depressions, and more than 52 percent experience milder general depressions.[13] My clinical and life experience suggests that up to 90 percent of women with preschoolers have varying levels of Depletion Depression, regardless of whether they stay home with their children full time or work outside the home and have quality child care.

4. Although We're the Majority, Females Are Still Treated as a Minority.

Even though U.S. Census figures show that females make up more than half of the American population, women are still perceived and treated as a minority. And as we know, perception feels like reality when enough people see it the same way. Whether we're different from the perceived majority due to the color of our skin, our ability to move without handicap, our sexual orientation, or our socioeconomic standing, most women have experienced feeling like or being a minority. And since discrimination and feelings of inadequacy are so natural to many of us, women often have trouble acknowledging how difficult and depleting it is to be treated this way. Yet research clearly shows that being in a minority position makes us more vulnerable to feelings of depletion and stress.[14]

If you're female and a member of an ethnic minority group, you're at even greater risk for depression because racial discrimination is so inherently depleting. For example, Hispanic and Asian women who come to this country are especially vulnerable to stress and depression due to the depleting experiences of migration and subsequent culture shock. They find that their former training to be passive and obliging doesn't fit well in a culture where women must be assertive for emotional and economic survival.[15] Another study found that depression was 42 percent more commonly diagnosed among black women than among white women at a large outpatient clinic.[16] These figures suggest that we're in double jeopardy for Depletion Depression if we are female and also happen to be part of an ethnic minority.

5. Women's Vulnerability to Low Self-Esteem and Codependency.

Chronic low self-esteem is not unusual among women. Even the most high-powered and confident among us suffer painful bouts of poor self-image. Moments of low self-esteem are a natural by-product of the Traditional Core and the way our culture feels about women. This is particularly true if we function in traditional roles. The Traditional Core drives us to do more and be more in order to prove our value and earn the love of others, since we typically have fewer sources of self-esteem outside our relationships and home.

Our devaluation of ourselves is rooted in centuries of sexism and being dominated and controlled by men. Many of us learned low self-esteem by imitating our mothers, who were born in an era where women didn't dare raise their concerns or their conscious-ness. We continue to allow our esteem to be drained by what has recently been labeled "codependent behavior," which is simply the current pop psychology label for the ancient codes of behavior pre-scribed by the Traditional Core.

The Traditional Core encourages us to spend our time, money, and energy rescuing and taking care of other people, especially those who engage in negative, self-destructive behavior—taking drugs, drinking too much, eating too much or too little, uncontrol-lable gambling, never meeting deadlines, or simply living life irre-sponsibly—because we think they are the ones who need us most. Even if we're not active participants in their behavior, we often be-come a passive part of the process by serving as codependents or enablers. This can drain and deplete as much as the addiction itself.

Low self-esteem and our tendency toward codependency are sig-nificant sources of Depletion Depression because they fuel our need to do more and be more to justify our worth, to guarantee that we will be cared about and loved. Many of us secretly fear that if we rely strictly on our inherent value as human beings, we'll be abandoned or rejected because there is nothing there. We do for others in the vain hope they will reciprocate and fill in the pieces we lack in ourselves.

When we understand the sources of our Depletion Depression, it's easier to accept why reducing this particular depression is such a formidable challenge: it means swimming upstream against very strong cultural currents. But a slow, steady stroke provides enormous payoffs. As you do some of the following action strategies and begin to free some time for yourself, you may feel some anxiety at first. That's to be expected. After moving full steam ahead for months or even years, many women feel guilty, lazy, or selfish if they relax with a satisfying book, take a nap, spend part of an afternoon watching a movie, go for a long walk, or linger over coffee with a good friend.

This anxiety and discomfort with giving to yourself is another example of when feeling bad is good. You're challenging the Traditional Core and that seldom feels good initially. But you'll soon begin to appreciate that doing less can give you more—more of the depth and focus that ultimately leads to a stronger sense of purpose, a stronger sense of self, and more control over your life.

Action Strategies for Depletion Depression

1. Get and Stay Organized.

How much time do you spend looking for misplaced keys, papers, bills, or clothes? Do you often feel that your life is disorganized and chaotic, and that the disorder slows you down and gets in the way of your ability to effectively manage responsibilities? How messy is your closet, desk, or office? How much hassle and frustration do you experience when your lack of attention to detail results in mechanical breakdowns, late notices, missed opportunities, or hurting loved ones?

If these are common experiences for you, your disorganization is feeding your Depletion Depression. The women who most need to organize their lives are usually the ones who insist they don't have the time, but getting and staying organized are the first steps to regaining greater control of your life. When you live a life bursting with role overload, it's essential that you're immediately able to put your hands on the things you need. When you're already feeling bad, not being able to find your car keys or checkbook can make you feel more helpless and even more depleted. It's an added burden you simply can't afford.

Tackle the disorganized areas of your life one at a time. For some women, it's the office. For others, it's a "closet from hell," a briefcase, or the kitchen. Whatever area of your life is causing the greatest frustration and depletion is the one that deserves your attention first. Devote several consecutive evenings or an entire weekend to cleaning out your desk, organizing your closet, filing your papers, or answering correspondence.

Organize your living space by creating or simplifying systems. Keep a notepad and pen near the phone. Develop the habit of putting your keys in the same place every time you walk through the door. As you go through the mail every day, put bills to be paid in one file so that you don't have to launch a hunt every time you go to pay them. If you don't already have one, perhaps now is the time to buy a time management system like Day Runner or Filofax to organize your calendar, address book, checkbook, and other important notes in one place.

These are just a few of many strategies you can use to simplify your life and use your time more efficiently. If you're really committed to reducing your Depletion Depression by streamlining your life, read books on the subject, such as *How to Get Control of Your Time and Your Life* by Alan Lakein (NAL-Dutton, 1989) or *Getting Organized* by Stephanie Winston (Warner, 1991) and practice their suggestions.

Another important step in getting organized and assuming more control is taking a few minutes to make a list of all the things you feel you "should" do. Once your list is complete, prioritize the items in order of importance. Cross off the two items at the bottom and simply decide that they're not important enough to do at the moment. Many of us spend too much time tending to the low-priority items because they're easier to do. We become experts at making "have to's" out of choices. When we begin to see how many of the demands on our time are really choices rather than necessities, it becomes easier to clarify what's important to us and what really must be done.

2. Validate Your Contributions by Rewarding Yourself with Money or Time.

Women who function primarily in traditional roles often seek validation from their husband, children, friends, and relatives because other sources of self-esteem—such as status, money, and other benefits of working outside the home—are unavailable to them. Unfortunately, other people are rarely able to give us the support or acknowledgment we want and deserve. They often don't know how, since they too are products of a culture that simultaneously reveres and devalues the traditional role.

When we're feeling overextended and unappreciated, Depletion Depression flourishes. One of the best ways to safeguard against it and also validate yourself is to "pay" yourself in time, money, or treats for the work you do. Calculate the number of hours you spend providing services for your home and family, find out what the going rate is for such services, and figure out what you are earning. Then pay yourself extra money and/or take extra time just for you to compensate yourself for your services.

Kate, the traditional wife and mother we met in Chapter 1, did exactly that one Saturday night at one A.M. She stood alone at the sink, loading the dishwasher and washing glasses and pans after a large dinner party that had taken a day to prepare and an hour to eat. Everyone else had gone home or gone to bed, and she felt angry, exhausted, and abandoned. How could she channel her Depletion Depression into an action strategy, she wondered? She decided to calculate how much it would have cost to have the dinner party catered.

After she added the numbers, she made plans for the money she had "earned." This process produced energy to cheer her up and help Kate see that her "have to" of finishing the dishes that night could easily wait until morning. To complete her plan, the next afternoon she bought a new dress with the money. When her husband, Bill, objected to the amount of her purchase, she explained how she had earned it. After several similar experiences, she made her point. Both Kate and Bill began valuing her time and effort much more. For the first time in a long while, Kate no longer felt like an indentured servant. When they next had company over, Bill was much more willing to help out.

If you can't afford to pay yourself in dollars, pay yourself in time and do something you really want to do. It will be much easier to make the time for yourself when you are more aware and appreciate how much you've truly earned it. No matter how you pay yourself, make sure you create specific rewards for the work you do. You'll feel considerably less depleted and depressed because you will have taken action to validate your own worth and work whether anyone else does or not. Seeing you validate yourself will make it easier for those around you to follow your example.

3. Learn the Art of Sleep Exchanges.

Although a good night's sleep is one of the most obvious solutions for overcoming Depletion Depression, it's usually the first trade-off women make. Our Traditional Core tells us the sacrifice is worth the price because it gives us time to do more for others. The implied message is that if the loss is our loss, it's fine because no one else is suffering. We also cheat sleep because staying up later affords a luxury many of us rarely enjoy: an uninterrupted half-hour or hour to do exactly what we want, without responding to the demands of others.

We drain ourselves by assuming that sleep is somehow a disposable commodity. In fact, it's absolutely essential for keeping depression at bay. To reduce sleep deprivation, learn the art of Sleep Exchanges. Sleep Exchanges are a bartering system with yourself in which you consciously trade something less valuable, such as other obligations or activities, for the rest you need.

To develop Sleep Exchanges, evaluate how you spend the few hours before you go to sleep. Begin by making a list of everything you do from five P.M. until you finally turn the lights out to go to bed. Keep a thorough list every evening for a week. You'll soon discover how and where you squander or waste your time. This will enable you to begin reclaiming some of it.

Commit to eliminating one or two activities from your list every night. Alice decided to give up returning nonessential phone calls at night. She found that she could handle them more efficiently during the day, anyway. Other women commit to watching one less television show or delegating more household chores. By eliminating nonessential activities, you should be able to go to bed at least thirty minutes earlier. Apply the same strategy to your morning routine, if possible, and you may find you're able to sleep ten or fifteen minutes later. Those who become skilled at the art of Sleep Exchanges report more productive lives and less depletion than they have previously known. Protecting seven or eight hours for sleep quite naturally becomes one of their highest daily priorities after they experience the benefits of Sleep Exchanges.

4. Learn and Practice Visualization Techniques.

Visualization techniques are worth learning, remembering, and practicing as a way to wind down mentally, refocus your energy, and ward off depletion. There are times when transporting yourself visually to a place of tranquillity can renew your energy and soothe and calm you like nothing else. Visualizations can even be a critical survival tool, as demonstrated by the released American hostages, who survived years of isolation in Beirut by mentally transporting themselves to more comforting places and conversing with the people they put there. They realized the only thing their captors couldn't control was their minds. Exercising mind control kept them from becoming too depleted to survive.

You can easily learn to use visualization when communication or other direct action is impossible or when you simply need to relax to recharge after a depleting experience or day. Begin by visualizing a scene from the beach, mountains, desert, forest, or any other peaceful, relaxed setting you especially love. Make the visualization as real as possible to all your senses. Not only do you want to see the place, but you want to smell it, hear it, touch it, and feel it.

I last used this visualization technique while stuck on the subway under the East River in New York City. The train lurched to a stop and the lights went out briefly. Knowing we were trapped beneath the river triggered waves of claustrophobia and helplessness. Since there was nothing I could do but wait, I retreated emotionally by visualizing one of my favorite places, a beautiful sandy beach where clear water crashes onto large black rocks and sends sea spray flying into the sun.

The visualization was so compelling that I could smell the salt air and feel the sand between my toes. By staying on the beach in my mind and using deep breathing techniques, I was able to derail my anxiety until the train began moving again. By exercising what little control I could, I was able to keep the delay from draining me of precious energy I needed once I returned to my business above ground.

This visualization technique can be used to conserve energy in many frustrating situations, especially those in which we're victims of circumstance. If you're stuck in a line, in traffic, in a plane circling an airport, or on hold on the phone, you'll find that such visualizations can really help transform frustration into relaxation and preserve your energy for more satisfying activities.

5. Sweep or Burn Your Troubles Away.

In our workshops, we used to only visualize the following two exercises. But we've discovered, once again, that action exercises are more powerful than intellectual exercises in reducing anxiety and depletion. So I would encourage you to actually *do* one or both of these exercises whenever you need to reduce your level of stress and depletion. They take very little time—usually less than five minutes—and have elements that appeal to both traditional and nontraditional women.

Cut out squares of paper. On each square write down a worry, disappointment, or an event that is still bothering you. Keep it simple. A few words or a sentence is plenty: "Financial pressure never stops," "Relationship ended," "I blew that test" is all you need. Make as many squares as it takes to clean out your head and your heart of as many problems and concerns as possible.

Take all your worry squares and throw them up in the air. As they fall, notice how it feels to be showered with so many worries and negative feelings. If it doesn't feel good, resolve then and there that you don't have to live with so many. Commit that you'll no longer invest energy brooding over decisions or events from the past. Instead of fearing or worrying about the present or future, move into action to begin solving these problems.

Start immediately by taking a broom and sweep all your worry squares, all those concerns and cares, into a single pile. Instead of sweeping your problems under the rug, as many of us have been taught to do, scoop them up when you feel ready and throw them away. When you do, pay attention to how you feel. Are you relieved, or do you feel some loss at letting go? Lean the broom up in a corner and leave it there for a while. Let it be a symbol that you have tools and resources to deal actively with your problems.

If a broom isn't handy—or if you're not handy with a broom—another way to do this exercise is to torch your troubles. Rather than use worry squares, write down all your worries on a single sheet of paper. Take your worry list and some matches with you to the bathroom. Stand over the toilet and light your list. Watch it slowly burn. Turn off the lights if you can do so safely. Let the darkness be symbolic of your depression, and let the warmth and glow of the flame be symbolic of the energy you're committing to making changes in the way you live.

When you're ready to really let go, feel the symbolic power of flushing your worries down the toilet. Make a promise to yourself before leaving the bathroom that you're going to actively confront a problem on your list by taking one manageable step toward problem solving.

Besides being fun, economical in terms of both time and supplies, and useful in helping you experience your problems in a creative new way, you can do this exercise anywhere and anytime you're feeling stressed and overwhelmed. You need to exercise caution with any fire, but there's something about burning your troubles away that is relieving and rejuvenating. The action therapy of burning or sweeping anxiety away will energize and empower you.

6. Take "Time Outs" to Renew Depleted Energy.

For kids, a Time Out can be the ultimate punishment. In Chapter 5, on Relationship Depression, a Time Out was a way to diffuse aggression so that constructive communication could replace hostility and aggression. But when it comes to Depletion Depression, a Time Out is a loving and necessary personal gift that only you can give yourself. This strategy is different from the solitary trips we discussed in the Relationship Depression chapter, because these Time Outs are much briefer, can be used daily, and require considerably less time and planning.

The first step in taking personal Time Outs is to schedule mini-breaks during the day. This is difficult because many of us have been programmed by our Traditional Core to believe that such behavior is "selfish." In fact, Time Outs enable you to recharge and refocus, which in turn enables you to better help others as well as yourself.

Aim for at least one twenty-minute break or two ten-minute mini-breaks during the day. During that time, check in with yourself and ask several questions to help you focus on getting what you need: Am I doing what I really want to be doing? Will my behavior make me feel better or worse? What do I need to do next to realize my goals for today?

In her book *The Female Advantage: Women's Ways of Leadership,* Sally Helgesen notes that many of the most successful women in America schedule mini-breaks throughout their workdays.[17] Frances Hesselbein, chief executive of the Girl Scouts of America, takes time during her lunch hours to sit and read a good book. She also sets aside several minutes before important meetings to review what she wants to accomplish or expects to learn and to check her appearance. Other successful executives schedule fifteen-minute breaks between meetings in order to refocus. This "deliberate pacing" tactic is very helpful and leaves the women who use it feeling more effective, productive, and satisfied.

7. Learn to Accept Your Limits.

Learning to accept your limits is critical to prevent or resolve Depletion Depression. The most effective women have learned to accept the limits of their energy and ability to produce. They also learn to give up their perfectionism. As a good friend of mine summed it up: "I have a lot to do in my life. If I don't let go of this perfectionism I won't live long enough to do it."

Alice found this to be her major challenge because she hates to restrict herself or say no, especially when it means letting go of great opportunities or not doing things perfectly. Accepting limits and establishing boundaries is a reminder of her vulnerability. The bottom line is that limits make her feel limited, old, inadequate, and unlovable. She usually feels that no matter how frazzled she is, she "should" be able to do more. Most of us won't allow ourselves the same slack we give others. Like Alice, we expect to have done it right or perfectly in the first place. With that expectation, we guarantee Depletion Depression will be our constant companion.

Once you gain a clearer understanding of the need for limits, you may even begin to appreciate their value just as Alice did. After arranging her schedule, she went on a day trip to the mountains to hike. She returned with new energy, better able to take control over the quality of her life. She began to plan and structure her time by taking mini-breaks at work. She quit scheduling patients back-to-back, convinced Paul to share more responsibility for the child care, let the answering machine take most of her calls, and did the Sleep Exchange exercise.

Alice found her new boundaries provided a sense of balance and peace in her life that she found much more rewarding than her frantic scrambling. She still had an occasional bad day but she had freed herself from the Depletion Depression that had drained her of her creativity and joy for living.

8. Learn to Apply the Exchange → Loss → Gain Formula.

The same principle used to exchange activity for more sleep can be applied in other parts of our life as well. Although we all understand the premise of trade-offs, most women find that making them effectively can be very difficult. For one thing, it often means delegating certain tasks to others, which is in direct conflict with traditional female training. A technique that has worked successfully for many clients is applying the Exchange → Loss → Gain formula. The strategy is to write down what's really important to us, what we're willing to exchange to get it, and the losses and gains we're likely to experience as a result of the exchange. Here are several examples of exchanges from clients who have used this solution successfully:

EXCHANGE → LOSS → GAIN FORMULAS

EXCHANGE:	Hire a weekly, biweekly, or monthly cleaning service.
LOSS:	Money. I may need to limit my spending in other areas such as dinners out and entertainment.
GAIN:	Time, energy, peace of mind. I'll no longer have to spend my Saturdays cleaning and I won't have to worry about a dirty home the rest of the week.

EXCHANGE: Limit the kids' after-school activities and have them pitch in with assigned household chores and meal preparation.

LOSS: I may feel guilty about not doing it all myself and restricting my children's free time. They may be angry or defiant with me. I will be anxious. It will take more time to make them do it than if I do it myself.

GAIN: More time and energy. I'll be less depleted, more relaxed and more available for talks and to help with homework. My children will also be learning responsibility and new skills. Family bonds will be strengthened.

EXCHANGE: Delegate a work project or share the responsibility with others.

LOSS: I may lose control—and possibly some of the credit.

GAIN: Time to concentrate on priority projects and responsibilities. I'll also learn a lot about the person or people who handled the project, which provides valuable knowledge of their abilities and work ethics. I can then build better work teams. I'll feel less drained and more connected to those I work with.

Writing down the Exchange → Loss → Gain formula is an effective way to clearly see the benefits of your trade-offs so that you're more apt to remain committed to them. If you don't write down and appreciate the exchanges, letting go can feel like too great a loss. You'll feel the loss and stop making the trade before you've had time to experience the reward. To save energy obsessing about what to do and being stuck in indecision, use a Exchange → Loss → Gain chart whenever you need to make a big decision or know something has to give but are too overwhelmed to decide what it is.

9. Use Five-Minute Intimacy Breaks as One of the Ultimate Replenishers.

Talking in depth or even just briefly with a close friend or family member about what's going on in your life is an extremely helpful step in resolving Depletion Depression. It's also a luxury of time we often feel we can't afford. But talking provides an outlet for our pain and anger. It helps us manage stress and clarify our priorities. When you are unable to take the time to talk at length, you can achieve the same results with short telephone conversations—what I call Five-Minute Intimacy Breaks.

Alice learned through experience that such an intimacy break created positive energy when she was feeling angry or frustrated. She would call one of her good friends, telling her first that it was a five-minute conversation to seek support and blow off a little steam. After checking to make sure the friend had the time and energy to manage it, Alice told her exactly what was going on and why she was so upset. She could rant, rave, cry, complain, and analyze. By expressing her feelings closer to when she felt them, she was able to diffuse her feelings of depression and depletion. What's more, the short phone sessions often led to some wonderfully productive follow-up conversations and practical problem-solving as well as an opportunity for the talk partner to have a turn at venting her or his feelings. Sometimes just leaving a message on the answering machine helped until Alice could talk later with her friend. Alice learned that rather than forgo intimacy because she realistically "didn't have time," it was an essential element in protecting her from Depletion Depression.

The purpose of each of these exercises is to encourage you to value and take better care of yourself. When you do, you'll find you're much less likely to allow yourself to become depleted, no matter how overwhelming the demands happen to be. And when you do feel depleted, you'll be much more likely to take action rather than to accept depression as your fate. By taking this kind of responsibility for your own well-being, you can claim and retain the joy of living you've earned and deserve.

·8·

BODY IMAGE DEPRESSION

Beauty is a currency system like the gold standard . . . it is an expression of power relations in which women must unnaturally compete for resources that men have appropriated for themselves.

Naomi Wolf
The Beauty Myth

Within minutes after Ali walked into my office, it was clear she was vulnerable and in pain. She avoided eye contact and was agitated and edgy, which was unusual for her. Ali, 36, is typically quite animated and intense. She has a wicked wit and penetrating insights that her friends find entertaining and stimulating, but often she's perceived as too aggressive.

After divorcing a husband who "just didn't give me enough," Ali tried to build a new life for herself. She cast a wide net for friends but was often disappointed with those she pulled in. Dependent and needy, Ali had to have people around her to feel adequate and complete. More than anything, she hated being alone, which is why until recently she had always thought her job was a perfect match for her personality.

She has worked for nearly four years as an executive assistant to a motivational speaker. While excellent at helping motivate others, Ali had great difficulty motivating herself to control her binging. Whenever she felt alone, isolated, or disappointed in a relationship, she bought a junk food feast of Häagen Dazs ice cream, cookies, and Coca-Cola and devoured it all. Her high-calorie, high-fat binges gave Ali the quick fix she craved. By "treating herself" and medicating her feelings with food, she felt a temporary sense of relief

221

from her emptiness and loneliness. The food was her companion and friend when no one else was around. But inevitably the next morning Ali woke up feeling guilty and disgusted. She often decided to fast for the entire day to offset her previous night's binge, and would jump into her sweats and running shoes and go for a punishing six-mile run.

As it turns out, this binge/exercise syndrome had become a habit for Ali, especially when she found herself alone. Ali had begun to panic because her food binges were occurring more frequently and lasting longer. She had put on nine pounds in two months. It was also becoming ever more difficult for her to muster the energy to exercise, and her fasting left her feeling hungry and deprived. For Ali, food choices were like men—sometimes she loved them, other times she saw them as her darkest enemy. Food protected and persecuted her, often in the same day.

Kathy, on the other hand, prides herself on eating well. In fact, she considers looking healthy and fit to be as much a part of her job as wearing a uniform. As a nutritionist for a large Atlanta hospital, she's seen firsthand the devastating effects of severe dieting, eating disorders, and poor nutrition. At 29, Kathy is enormously pragmatic and unburdened by the usual female concerns about eating. She cannot fully understand how or why some women do such harm to their bodies and their self-esteem by using food so destructively.

But while Kathy is comfortable with food, she's not comfortable with her body. Even though she has a trim, athletic body that many of her friends consider nearly "perfect," Kathy has always been extremely self-conscious. She grew up feeling that her breasts were too small and her nose was too big. Although she dates regularly and has a number of male friends, she's convinced that her "physical flaws" are the primary reason she has yet to meet the husband she feels is missing from her life. When her grandmother died and left her $10,000, Kathy decided to "invest" the lion's share of her inheritance in "fixing a few things that God didn't get quite right." She made plans to spend her next vacation recuperating from cosmetic surgery.

The very notion of spending a week or more recuperating would have made Joyce, an attractive 21-year-old college junior, shudder. A self-proclaimed "party girl," Joyce attended a California college ranked by *Playboy* as one of the top ten party schools in the country. The party atmosphere was what attracted Joyce to the school. If they offered a major in socializing, Joyce would have graduated Phi Beta Kappa.

Joyce is bright but lazy and unmotivated to study. Her priorities were to be a popular presence on campus and to attract "Mr. Right." To accomplish her goal, she spent more time at cheerleading practice than she did in class. She also spent a great deal of time and money buying clothes. Nothing was more important to Joyce than her appearance. She had often heard her father, a wealthy advertising executive, comment that "packaging sells the product." She was convinced that how she packaged and presented herself was more important than who she was as a human being, at least to the men whose attention she craved.

In college Joyce began having trouble maintaining her weight because she was careless and impulsive about what she ate. With each pound she gained, Joyce felt worse about herself, as if each pound was proof there was something fundamentally weak and wrong with her. When her cheerleading coach commented that Joyce was looking "a little chunky" and suggested she start taking better care of herself, Joyce was devastated. She became withdrawn and irritable to a point that her sorority sisters were concerned. Several of them encouraged Joyce to try the solution that had worked for them: vomiting.

Joyce found the idea more than distasteful, but one night after heavy drinking at a fraternity house party, she felt "too bloated and fat" and returned to the sorority house to sheepishly try her new solution. Even though she felt ashamed at even the thought of sticking her finger down her throat, she felt a sense of relief and control after actually doing it. Before long, she was joking with her best friend about her new "diet plan" that allowed them to eat whatever they wanted. Joyce didn't realize until several years later that her "easy way out" would not only plunge her into an Unhealthy Depression, it would lead to a full-blown eating disorder that could eventually threaten her life.

Ali, Kathy, and Joyce are very different women leading very different lives. But a common thread weaves their stories together. All three of them are experiencing a Body Image Depression. **Body Image Depression is defined as the negative feelings of shame, contempt, and disappointment in our bodies that most women experience as we attempt to meet impossible cultural standards of physical perfection, beauty, sex appeal, youth, and fashion.**

We are conditioned from infancy to believe that the major source of our worth is how attractive we are to others, especially men. A disproportionate premium is placed on being beautiful, pretty, attractive, cute, and sexy. While we may like the personable and outgoing "Miss Congeniality," it's no coincidence that the woman deemed most *beautiful* is named "Miss Universe" and goes home wearing the crown. The pressure to be physically perfect and remain forever young are two of the most consistent sources of depression among women.

When we're told, "How beautiful you look!" what we hear is "How good you are!" Even today, as we advance through the nineties, for a vast majority of women beauty remains the primary currency of our value and worth. It is viewed as our most prized resource in attracting a man and our most powerful weapon in competing with other women. Women have learned that by being thin, dressing fashionably, and wearing the right amount of the right makeup, we can get more of what we want.

Those women who are either born beautiful or learn how to play the game often attract power and abundance. In fact, research shows that people consistently rate women more intelligent than they really are if they're more physically attractive.[1] Those who are deemed unattractive by the culture can easily pass through life feeling and/or being undervalued and shortchanged. The depressing reality is that the cultural pressures for female perfection are so strong and pervasive that even if we resist or reject them, they still continue to haunt most of us.

And we can be our own worst enemies. When it comes to our appearance and the appearance of others, we are often more instantly judgmental than in any other area of our lives. How many times have you assessed another woman—a new coworker or a new mother at the playground, for example—and prejudged who she was or how capable she would be based on her physical appearance and the first impressions they stirred within you? How often have you felt inadequate because you thought you didn't look as good as those around you and that they were silently judging you? With these attitudes and judgments, we've all helped maintain and perpetuate the unrealistic standards that so hurt us by buying into the cultural expectation for women: to somehow, some way become and remain physically perfect.

To develop a clearer sense of how big a role Body Image Depression plays in your life, take the following quiz. The results will be most helpful if you answer the questions as honestly as you can. If they stir up discomfort by reminding you about your own Body Image Depression, take comfort in the fact that you're having a healthy response to the negative realities of the cultural punishers of women's bodies. Your bad feelings will provide the energy and motivation to change. Keep in mind that realization is the first step toward resolution.

BODY IMAGE DEPRESSION QUIZ

Answer the following questions YES or NO.

1. Do you think about the shape, condition, and/or size of your body on a daily basis? _____

2. Stand in front of a mirror and study your body for several minutes. Do you wish your body looked significantly different than it does today? _____

3. Do you feel fat no matter how much weight you lose or how much positive feedback you receive about your appearance from others? _____

4. Do you often feel intimidated by women you judge as thinner, better dressed, or more attractive? _____

5. Have you ever vomited or used laxatives to discharge food, or become so thin that your health has been affected (i.e., irregular or interrupted periods, fainting, or difficulty sustaining energy) because you were so unhappy with your body? _____

6. Do you often change clothes a number of times before deciding what to wear or feel frustrated that you "have nothing to wear," even though your closet is full of clothes you have chosen? _____

7. Do you either dread the idea of shopping and trying on clothes or feel deprived unless you're well dressed? _____

8. Have you ever seriously considered having a facelift, breast augmentation, or any other elective cosmetic surgery because it would make you feel better about yourself? _____

9. Are you self-conscious if you go out without wearing makeup, the "right" clothes, and doing your hair? _____
10. Do you ever attempt to hide your body from your intimate partner or hide from yourself by avoiding looking in the mirror? _____

Total number of questions answered YES: _____

SCORING

**(0–2)　You appreciate your body
and have a healthy body image.**

You enjoy a very healthy, positive self-image. You're at peace with your body and appreciate its female power. You've successfully resisted the endless barrage of negative cultural images about the female body and have maintained high self-esteem. Body Image Depression is not a problem for you. Congratulations on not being hooked on "perfection."

(3–5)　Caution: You're vulnerable.

You probably experience Body Image Depression more often than not. Pay careful attention to the suggested action strategies featured later in this chapter. They'll help you better understand why you're especially susceptible, and they offer specific ideas on what you can do to reduce your vulnerability.

**(6–7)　Beware: You probably have
a Body Image Depression.**

You have a negative body image. You're rarely happy with your physical appearance and do whatever you can to compensate for what you perceive as your flaws and shortcomings. Years of negative cultural conditioning have taken their toll. It's time to confront your Body Image Depression head-on before it gets worse and deteriorates into an Unhealthy Depression.

**(8–10)　You're in trouble; your Body Image Depression
is unhealthy.**

You seem to have a significant unhealthy Body Image Depression. You've been damaged by the cultural and media images of how a woman should look and the hostile, negative messages about your appearance you probably received or receive from family and friends. It's quite likely you're unaware of how much self-hatred these experiences have created within you. Professional help is essential if you are going to resolve your negative, self-destructive feelings about your body. If you don't get the help, it's likely you'll become more destructive of your body. Whatever self-esteem you've salvaged will slowly evaporate.

If you answered YES to five or more of these questions, you have cause for concern. But there's also cause for hope. You may be experiencing a Body Image Depression, but there's a great deal you can do to confront and resolve it. You're definitely not alone in your struggle for a more positive self-image. Of all the women I've met and talked with over the years, at least 95 percent experience some degree of Body Image Depression on a regular basis, and virtually every woman can identify with the pain and humiliation of believing at some point in her life that her body and appearance are inadequate, although in reality both are just fine.

But it doesn't have to be that way. We can break the cultural bonds that restrict us and rob us of our energy, power, and self-esteem. We can learn to appreciate our physical selves whether or not we conform to the cultural ideal. We can absolutely refuse to allow ourselves to be defined as inadequate because our bodies aren't perfect. The exercises in the last half of this chapter can help do this. But first, it's important to gain a better understanding of where all this body hatred comes from.

Sources of Body Image Depression

There are three major sources of Body Image Depression: our negative Traditional Core, which conditions us to embrace physical appearance as a measure of our worth; our families, which may have contributed years of negative feedback that was forgotten but nevertheless left scars; and our culture, in which five major cultural punishers—the diet industry, the cosmetic industry, the fashion industry, the cosmetic surgery industry, and the media—combine to exert undeniable influence over how we look, feel, and think.

1. Our Negative Traditional Core.

From birth, the negative Traditional Core codes us as adequate or inadequate depending on how "good" or "bad" we look. Traditionally, beauty and quality of appearance are the first and most enduring qualities people notice in women. According to the Traditional Core, external appearance should be the very root of our self-esteem and the source of how well we can expect to be taken care of in the world of men.

While men find their primary source of self-esteem stems from what they do and how well they perform, women's self-esteem is directly connected to how attractive we are to others. As Elissa Melamed observes in the book *Meditations for Women Who Do Too Much:* "Men look at themselves in mirrors. Women look *for* themselves."[2] Career accomplishments, educational achievements, and other successes pale in comparison to the significant validation our Traditional Core receives when someone thinks we look good and approves of our appearance.

The Traditional Core isn't all negative. It also has positive influences on our development. It drives us to exercise and be careful with our diet. It encourages us to look as good as we can. But the dark side of the Traditional Core is so filled with self-doubt and fear about our bodies and what to do with them that Body Image Depression is the natural, inevitable result.

2. Our Destructive Family Ghosts.

Another significant source of Body Image Depression is the influence our family had—and may still have—over the way we feel about our body and our appearance. Remarks made to us by our mother, father, sisters, brothers, aunts, uncles, cousins, and grandparents while we were growing up can and do have a lasting effect. Their teasing or cutting statements about how we look live deep inside us. Do any of the following stir memories from your past?

"Why don't you do something with your hair?"

"You can't be my sister—you're so ugly you must be adopted!"

"Fatty, fatty, two by four, can't get through the bathroom door . . ."

"Why don't you eat something, dear? If you get any thinner, you're going to make yourself sick."

"You're not going out in public wearing that, are you?"

"Go in that bathroom and scrub some of that makeup off. You look like a hooker!"

"You're a pretty little girl, dear, but you look like a boy. It's time you learn how to wear a dress."

Whenever these messages—or an adult variation of them—are repeated, the echoes stir up the family ghosts and the insecurity they evoked all over again. What they *said* becomes how you *are* and how you *feel* about yourself now. Like so many women, you may find it difficult to tell the difference between someone else's aggression or criticism and your own physical and emotional reality.[3]

3. The Five Cultural Punishers.

The combined messages of five powerful forces have convinced women over the years that they're inadequate unless they package and present themselves in certain culturally sanctioned ways. It's a form of cultural punishment that ignites insecurity among women and then fans the flame. Clearly, the economic exploitation of women's insecurities has big payoffs for certain industries. Take a minute to review the phenomenal profits these industries enjoy, in part because of the money they earn from women who are encouraged to feel bad about our bodies and appearance.

PROFITABILITY FOR THE MAJOR
CULTURAL PUNISHERS OF WOMEN

Diet Industry[4]	$33 billion
Cosmetic and Toiletries Industry[5]	$18.5 billion
Fashion Apparel Industry[6]	$181 billion
Cosmetic Surgery Industry[7]	$300 billion
Media	Billions—so powerful and pervasive, it's difficult to establish accurate figures.

As you can see, creating and feeding body image insecurity is big business. That's not to say, of course, that all the products and services reflected in these numbers are unhealthy or culturally punishing to women. A number of these services and products have their place and purpose and can be useful to women. A facial can be relaxing and good for your skin. We all need clothes that feel good to us, and it can be a treat to buy a bottle of perfume, a new shade of lipstick, or a gym membership.

The problem isn't buying a particular product; it's that so much of the spending women do on their appearance is not rooted in healthy needs. Instead, it's the result of women trying to conform to unrealistic ideals, trying to look a certain way so they'll be accepted and valued more highly in a fundamentally unhealthy culture.

Let's take a closer look at each of the cultural punishers.

The Diet Industry

What's wrong with losing weight? After all, the benefits of shedding excess pounds are many. Maintaining a proper weight and doing regular exercise is great for our health, increases self-esteem, personal power, and control over our lives.

But these are not the primary reasons most women diet. Women diet because we have been culturally conditioned to believe our bodies are not acceptable the way they are. Says actress Tyne Daly: "I realized that in our culture if you don't have a penis, the only true contribution you can make is to lose twenty pounds. Any of your other accomplishments pale in comparison. Ask Oprah Winfrey. It doesn't matter how smart or how rich or how kind she is to the less fortunate. The most important thing is that she lost weight (and gained it back)."[8]

No matter how much we weigh, we're told we could be thinner, leaner, and tighter. And we buy it. A 1990 study in *Time* indicated that 58 percent of the young women polled thought they were overweight, though only 17 percent actually were.[9] A 1992 study from the Centers for Disease Control found that in a representative sample of nearly 12,000 high school students, more than one-third of the girls thought they were overweight, compared with only 15 percent of the boys. Forty-three percent of the girls—even some of those who thought they were the "right weight"—were dieting, leading to nutritional deficiencies that put them at significant risk for future health problems.[10]

You might assume that as women move out of the turbulence of adolescence into adulthood, our self-images stabilize. That's not the case. A recent *Family Circle* survey showed that although only 27 percent of adult women surveyed were overweight, 78 percent thought they were. Eighty-eight percent of these women felt their bodies were so inadequate that they were reluctant to wear a bathing suit. The survey also indicated that two times as many women as men consider themselves overweight, and more than 75 percent of women questioned admit to hating one or more parts of their bodies.[11]

So what do we do about our body hatred? Instead of rejecting the cultural assumptions that created it, we accept it and diet to change it. While most men diet for health reasons, most women diet to look better. An *American Health* survey[12] showed that while only 40 percent of the men surveyed choose a healthy diet to look better, 60 percent of the women said that appearance was their major motivation. Only 36 percent of the women said they were motivated by health concerns, yet living longer was the reason that 53 percent of the men counted their calories.

The problem with this approach is that diets don't work. Studies have consistently shown 75 percent to 90 percent of women dieters regain the weight they lost within two years.[13] On liquid diets, such as the one on which Oprah Winfrey lost eighty-seven pounds, 98 percent of women do exactly what Oprah did. They put it all back on—and then some. I was one of them too. I once lost forty pounds on Optifast but quickly regained all the weight I'd lost—and more— once I began eating regular food again. The program didn't begin to address or resolve the reasons I was overeating in the first place. Starving created a tidal wave of deprivation that came crashing down on me once I had the opportunity to feed myself again and make up for all that lost time and all those lost goodies.

The Federal Trade Commission recently demanded that makers of the liquid diets, including Optifast, stop making unsupported claims of long-term success when, in fact, "for many dieters the weight loss is temporary."[14] It is even more depressing to realize that with all the diet plans and programs on the market, women are more likely to be overweight today than thirty years ago. As a panel of experts at the National Institute for Mental Health concluded, "We're getting fatter because we're dieting."[15] The diet industry has indeed become quite skilled at its unique brand of cultural punishment and manipulation: helping women continue to feel like failures no matter how much or how well we control our eating.

The Cosmetics Industry

Lipstick. Blush. Eyeliner. Mascara. Eye shadow. Nail polish. The industry that markets and manufactures these products calls them cosmetics. But most women call them makeup, which raises an important question: When we apply these products to our bodies, what are we "making up" *for*? The fact that we don't have the flawless, unlined complexion at 40 that we may have had at 16? That our features aren't as perfectly proportioned as the women we see on the covers of *Vogue* or *Glamour* or *Mademoiselle*? That we're not naturally red-lipped and rosy-cheeked?

The double standard in our culture is as fascinating as it is disturbing. The men's grooming market has become big business in recent years, but imagine how conspicuous a man would be if he were to go out in public wearing eye shadow, eyeliner, blush, and lipstick. Yet women who wear no makeup can be more conspicuous than those who do. It is expected of us. A female service representative for Continental Airlines was suspended in 1991 after protesting a company policy that required female employees to wear makeup, on the assumption they would look more attractive to the flying public. Only after the dispute generated widespread adverse publicity for the airline was the policy discontinued and the employee reinstated.

Like the diet industry, the cosmetics industry is a highly successful cultural punisher of women. It perpetuates the myth that we are attractive and culturally acceptable only if we paint our faces. And a vast majority of women buy the message. By shifting the tone, color, and "look" of beauty from season to season, the cosmetics industry literally keeps us coming back for more to "make up" for our culturally defined deficiencies.

The Fashion Industry

The fashion industry is another multibillion dollar cultural punisher, built on the assumption that a woman isn't adequate unless she's fashionably dressed. Images of tall, thin women are used to model styles the average woman can't wear because she doesn't have the body of an adolescent boy with breasts. Ninety-five percent of fashions are designed for women well over 5'4" and well under a size 12, yet fewer than one in four American women fit these specifications.[16] The average American woman is 32 years old, 143 pounds, and wears a size 10 or 12 dress. Thirty to 40 million women deviate even further from the fashion standard and wear a size 16 or larger.[17]

Most of us don't question the insanity of these cultural "norms" and expectations. Instead, we do exactly what we're supposed to do —we invest time, energy, and money in playing the fashion game, a game in which the rules are ever changing. Rather than spend the money on experiences that provide us with real power—education, trips to visit people who love us, dance or sports lessons, or personal-growth workshops—too many of us strive to stay in style. And style, of course, is ever changing. One season fashion dictates short skirts, the next season they're out of style, only to be replaced by mid-calf designs that will themselves be obsolete within months.

The Cosmetic Surgery Industry

The cosmetic surgery industry has exploded into a $300 million-a-year business. That's because women are culturally encouraged to dislike what they see when they look in the mirror. In the past three years, nearly 2 million women have relied on the surgeon's scalpel to cut away their discontent. The nineties are fast becoming the surgical era for women as the Baby Boomers age; 85 percent of cosmetic surgery patients are female.[18] Cosmetic surgery is becoming more affordable and, therefore, a volume business catering to the insecure, dissatisfied, and those who believe that looking better will somehow translate into a happier, more satisfying life. Says comedian and talk show host Joan Rivers, an enthusiastic proponent of cosmetic surgery: "Looks count. Forget 'inner beauty'. If a man wants inner beauty, he'll take X-rays."[19]

Responding to these cultural pressures, women turn to doctors to redeal the hand that nature, time, and genetics have dealt them. The industry is partially built on the assumption that a woman is deformed as she ages. A man is considered deformed only if he loses a limb.

Kathy, the dietician who was convinced that her small breasts had helped keep her single, did use her inheritance to have her breasts augmented. The surgery and recovery went fine. She returned to work two weeks later, bursting with pride and chemical sacs. Everything was great for a while. Gradually, however, Kathy began to realize that she still hadn't attracted the man of her dreams. Her breasts began to hurt and felt as though they were turning to stone. Eventually, they became so hard that her doctor had to perform a second surgery to crush the calcified chemicals and replace them with new sacs.

According to Naomi Wolf in *The Beauty Myth*, in just three years as many as 1 million American women have been cut open and had sacs of chemicals implanted to create the illusion of rounder, fuller, bigger breasts. Although 70 percent of these procedures have some kind of complications and certain silicone implants have been pulled off the market because of the high risks, many women still accept the notion that the bigger the breast, the more adequate the woman.[20]

And the standards keep getting higher (or lower, depending on your perspective). Surgeons describe the B cup that was typically requested just a decade ago as inadequate these days.[21] Now the request is for a C and increasingly a D. One can't help but wonder whether these are breast sizes or the grades for the women's levels of self-esteem.

Large breasts apparently aren't the only tools some women feel they need to survive or thrive in the nineties. More than 100,000 women have already had the fat sucked out of their thighs, buttocks, and chins through liposuction, an expensive procedure that was nonexistent even ten years ago.[22]

These women are buying the illusion of youth, but at what price? The cost of a face lift, a procedure that lasts about twelve years for women under 50 and sometimes less than half that time for women over 50, typically ranges from $5,000 to $15,000.[23] The process also requires time. A month of recovery is not unusual, especially for patients who have undergone the new "deeper" cutting procedures.

It is a price most women can't afford, yet many insist on paying. A plastic surgery association survey in 1987 found that about half the women who had cosmetic surgery earned less than $25,000 a year, took out second mortgages, and went into debt to cover the expense of surgery.[24]

When we look at the enormous waste of time, money, and energy invested in living up to such unhealthy cultural standards of physical perfection, we're reminded once again why so many women struggle with and fail to resolve Body Image Depression. We can also see why women have trouble focusing energy where it really counts: in changing the political and social systems that devalue us simply because we're female and don't have "perfect," youthful bodies.

The Media

Cultural standards of beauty have, until recently, evolved slowly. Our great-grandmothers weren't nearly as apt to be slaves to fashion, for example, because they weren't exposed to the frequency and volume of changing images that we are today. Their sense of style and fashion was influenced largely by what they saw in the store windows of the towns where they lived or the Sears catalog they received on the farm. But that changed with the advent of modern technology and the development of the media, which brought with it the unprecedented opportunity to create increasingly accessible and instant "perfect beauty" images. The media has played a greater role in creating and changing beauty images than any other force in history. The message, whether it's why you should buy brand A because "blondes have more fun" or brand B "because you're worth it," can now reach millions of women at the same time.

The sources of Body Image Depression we just examined can have such a strong impact because of the mass media, which by association becomes a source in itself. It's a mutually beneficial relationship in which one hand washes the other: the media provides a forum through which the artificial definitions of beauty and sexiness created by the advertisers are perpetuated and exploited, and the money from advertisers, who pay for air time and ad space, keeps the media machine well oiled.

As long as we're exposed to the endless barrage of these images, women are going to experience Body Image Depression and feel bad a good part of the time. Considering the power and influence of these cultural punishers, how can you fight back and what can you do to reclaim some control over your own body and its image?

There are a number of ways to stand up to the cultural punishers. You can become more attuned to how these financial giants play their game. You can learn not to play by their rules, or even not play the game at all. I'm not suggesting that overcoming Body Image Depression is easy for any of us. But it is possible. We need to allow ourselves to feel angry and disgusted enough about how we've been conditioned and manipulated and how hard we can sometimes be on ourselves. Our greatest support comes from understanding the sources of Body Image Depression and mobilizing our ability to act. Get moving and try some or all of the following proven techniques, which have been successful for women of various ages and stages of development. The first three exercises work with childhood and adolescent issues; the last five relate to our experiences as adults.

Action Strategies for Overcoming
Body Image Depression

1. Return to a Time in Your Childhood
When You Appreciated Your Body.

Was there a time in your life when you valued your body and felt much more positive about it than you do today? For most women, returning to that time of innocence means an inner journey all the way back to childhood. Many women find that they remember being most comfortable with their bodies somewhere between the ages 2 and 10. It's not until adolescence that the need to be physically perfect and issues of appearance, competition, and body envy emerge so strongly. Some women search their childhoods and can't find a thing to feel good about, particularly regarding their bodies. If you're one of these women, then imagine a time when your body served you well and left you feeling physically proud of yourself.

After you have identified a positive feeling or experience with your body from childhood, find or make a picture that represents the experience. You might use a childhood photo before cultural body hatred poisoned you. The one I use shows me running down the street at 4 years, pigtails flying in the wind. If your parents still have photos of you at an early age, ask them to send them to you. If you can't locate any actual photographs, find a picture in a magazine, use an image from a greeting card, or draw a picture that reminds you of an earlier time when you truly appreciated your body.

Once you have your positive body picture available, quickly jot down words or phrases this image conjures up for you. Words that may come to mind: impressive, cute, strong, pretty, capable, confident, free, cool, neat, or athletic. If you're at a temporary loss for words, express your feelings in a quick drawing or scribble until the words begin to flow. See if your drawing stirs up any more associations. They often do, and it will allow you to continue until your exploration process feels complete.

When you've run out of words to describe the picture, close your eyes for several minutes and return to the time in your life that your photograph or drawing represents. How did you feel about your body then? Even when you felt proud and confident, did you feel a little anxious and self-conscious? What was your life like? Who was a positive influence for you? Was there a parent, teacher, coach, husband, or friend who valued your strength and encouraged you? Let the thoughts flow freely. Don't analyze or assess them. Try to recapture that positive frame of mind about your body by writing down the positive comments you heard about your body and appearance, as well as the nonverbal feelings communicated to you.

You now have a visual and mental picture of a time when you had a positive body image and could use your body for strength and accomplishment. With that image in mind, mount the picture on construction paper and attach the list of positive associations you wrote earlier. Add any other positive feelings that occur so that your body is finally surrounded again with positive past associations and current positive thinking. You then will be framed by strength and shielded, at least briefly, from the cultural punishers. This can be a first step toward reclaiming a positive body image and protecting yourself against cultural punishment. And that protection is one of the greatest gifts you can give yourself as a modern woman.

2. Identify Your Sources of
Adolescent Body Image Depression.

Now that you have a portable power source for a positive body image and have some experience with positive thinking about your body, the next step is to revisit your adolescence and understand if, how, when, and why your body image began to change.

For most women, self-love as a child deteriorates into self-loathing during adolescence. That's why this next exercise is especially valuable for women who experience Body Image Depression. Use a picture of yourself as an adolescent, find a picture of an adolescent girl from a magazine, or create a drawing to remind yourself of that time when you felt awkward and insecure about your body.

What do you remember about this stage of your life? Does it stir up memories of a time when you thought you were too fat or too thin, when you felt your breasts were either too big or too small? Was your hair stringy and limp? Did you have a clear complexion, or did you have skin problems? Were your clothes attractive, or did you feel they were ugly? And how about your posture—did you stand tall and proud, or did you slouch your way through adolescence, trying to be as inconspicuous as possible?

When you make a list of the feelings that this adolescent picture generates, you'll probably notice a very different set of reactions from those you had to the childhood photo or positive symbol (of appreciating your body) in the first exercise. When college student Joyce did this exercise, she realized for the first time that her need to shop had been rooted in insecurity that went all the way back to her flashy junior high school, where "clothes made the woman."

Kathy couldn't look at her adolescent picture without wincing at how caved in her chest looked to her. Ali devoured chocolate when she saw how awkward and insecure she looked as a teenager. You may find, as Kathy and Ali did, that your reactions to your adolescent picture are uncomfortable. You may feel self-conscious, embarrassed, and ashamed. You may also come to realize that it was at this point in your life that you felt for the first time that how you *looked* was more important than who you *were*.

With a better appreciation for how your Body Image Depression probably began, let's go back to adolescence and undo some of the damage. Take a large sheet of paper and attach your adolescent photo or drawing. Around the body, write the five external sources for Body Image Depression: Diets, Cosmetics, Fashion, Cosmetic Surgery, and the Media. Think back and try to remember how you related to each one of these sources as a teenager and write your thoughts and feelings about your experiences on your source sheet under each category. For Diets, Ali wrote that she was a "diet junkie" and that she was constantly struggling with her weight. For Cosmetics, pragmatic Kathy wrote "I felt I would never learn to use cosmetics well so I never tried." For Fashion and Media, Joyce wrote such comments as "I never felt right in my clothes, but I refused to quit trying," "I always envied the beautiful women on TV," and "If I'm fat, I'm no good."

Doing this exercise can show you how attitudes you adopted as a teenager were a direct result of your cultural conditioning. To see how this punishment continues today, buy copies of young women's magazines such as *Seventeen* and *Sassy*. Count how many ads or images promote excess thinness or unrealistic ideals of beauty. Rip out the most unrealistic ones, the ones that showcase physical perfection as the ideal. Line them up for a clearer view of how pervasive these unhealthy expectations are and then throw them away. This is a particularly effective exercise to do with your daughter or a younger female relative or friend so that you can talk about what she experiences, what she can expect in this area, and what she can do about it to protect herself. In helping her, you help yourself. Although you may not have had much choice to protect yourself from the punishment then, you do have a choice now.

3. Exorcise Your Negative Family Ghosts.

Make your own list of the negative phrases you heard about your appearance while growing up. In addition to writing each down, note who said it and how often. If your little brother made cow or pig noises every time you walked past him for six months when you were 14, write that down. Also write down how those comments made you feel. Did they ever make you cry or make you angry enough to hit him? Take your time with this process. It will very likely provoke memories you haven't thought about for years, and some of them may be uncomfortable. Maintain the courage to let these feelings reemerge.

After you've completed your list, review it carefully and note the vulnerabilities you grew up with. Which ones came from the general culture and which, more specifically, are rooted in your family dynamics? You can now begin healing those body wounds by becoming your own good mother and writing down alternate positive statements next to the negative statements you grew up hearing. It's a wonderful technique for putting negative feedback from your past in its proper perspective. It's also your chance to be the secure, wise, affirming mother you may never have had.

Next to the statement "Why don't you do something with your hair?" which is one many of my clients recall hearing from their mother, you might write "Would you like to go to the hairdresser to try something new? You could look at some magazines for ideas on how you would like to do your hair."

Stifle the echoes of your brother chanting "Fatty, fatty, two by four," by writing another positive statement, such as, "My brother was cruel, but I know he really loved me. I really value the good times we spent together once we grew older." Or, "My brother was cruel. Now I know that the way he treated me revealed a lot more about him than about me. I'll no longer let him influence how I feel about myself. It's just not worth it to give him that kind of power."

Be sure to write a positive affirmation of yourself next to every negative statement from your family. Read them over several times and even memorize the positive affirmations to use when you hear the old voices attempting to put you down again. Learning how to be your own nurturing good mother is a valuable tool in warding off Body Image Depression. Facing the ghosts of the past and reclaiming the power you once gave them is another important step toward resolving Body Image Depression.

4. Shatter Your Cultural Mirror of Perfection.

Moving from the past to the present, let's look more closely at who you are today and how everything that has happened to you over the years has affected the way you see yourself. Most of us still use what I call the cultural Mirror of Perfection. It's a mirror the culture gives to women as a birthday present when we're still quite young to evaluate our progress in achieving perfection. We learn to anxiously examine ourselves in the Mirror of Perfection, not only to see whether anything is out of place, but also to assess whether overnight we've become "the fairest of them all." The mirror tells us that anything less than perfection is failure.

To free yourself from Body Image Depression, you need to shatter your Mirror of Perfection. Forget what you've heard about broken mirrors being bad luck. Ridding yourself of this mirror represents a positive step toward a healthy, realistic self-image. Begin by buying two small pocket mirrors. One represents your Mirror of Perfection; the other, your Mirror of Affirmation, will reflect your new, positive body image.

Take the Mirror of Perfection and use it to help you appraise your body (front and back) in front of a full length mirror. Be as courageous, realistic, and adult as you can. Study your body. Write down what you see in the mirror as honestly and objectively as you can. What are your first impressions? Do you feel comfortable and satisfied with what you see? Are you pleased with your body, or does it disappoint and disgust you? How does it differ from the body you wish you had? What appear to be its physical strengths? What features do you find most attractive?

The last two questions may be difficult for you to answer, at least at first. Many women are much clearer about what they don't like about their appearance than what they do. If you're among them, use this exercise to appreciate how much vulnerability and body hatred our culture has seeded within you.

Make a vow that your body hatred has to stop. Decide that you're no longer willing to live with Body Image Depression just because you live in such an unhealthy culture. When you're ready, shatter your Mirror of Perfection and put the pieces safely in the trash. Commit that you'll not find, look into, or buy another Mirror of Perfection, no matter how much the culture, your husband, boyfriend, girlfriend, mother, sister, or anyone else pressures you to strive for physical perfection.

Pick up your second mirror, your new Mirror of Affirmation. Look at yourself positively now that you are freer to do so. Make a list of five things you like about your body and appearance. Among the features that might appear on your list: your height, your warm smile, the color or style of your hair, your posture, your graceful hands, your strong legs, maybe even your freckles. If your list includes more than five, choose the five qualities you value most highly. If you can't or don't want to find five positive qualities about your appearance, write five positive things your body can do. Some women find that they free themselves of Body Image Depression when they keep reminding themselves of what their body has accomplished rather than how it looks.

When you're finished, put the list on your mirror to remind yourself every morning of your body and/or appearance strengths. Focus on one positive characteristic and really work on using and appreciating that strength as much as possible for that day. It can be as simple as making it a point to share your warm smile or treating those graceful hands to a manicure during lunch or making sure you engage in an activity you love. Carry your Mirror of Affirmation with you as a reminder to build and maintain a positive self image. You may wish to attach a copy of a condensed list of your five body strengths to the back of the mirror to support yourself even more.

Constantly reminding yourself of your body strengths will help neutralize the negative associations you may have about your body image. You'll find that you feel increasingly more comfortable and self-confident with your body, and you'll accept the fact that you can be perfectly good without being "the fairest of them all."

5. Take a Closer Look at the Body Image of the Women You Admire Most.

We all have role models. For some, it's a teacher or mentor who played an important role in our life. One of them may even have been our mother or grandmother. For others, the images that come to mind are of women we've never met. When I ask clients to identify women they most admire, among the names often mentioned are those of such diverse women as Mother Teresa, Margaret Thatcher, Madonna, Jodie Foster, Barbara Bush, and Margaret Mead.

Who are the women you most admire? Take five minutes and make a list of all the women who come to mind. From that list, select the three women you most admire, then write a sentence or two about why each made your list.

Hundreds of women have done this exercise and, with rare exceptions, what most discover is that they admire the women on their lists not for how they look, but rather for who they are—how they live and what they've accomplished and contributed to others. Most of the women who are admired don't conform at all to the conventional standards of beauty and really don't care to. Barbara Bush isn't thin. Mother Teresa isn't young. Pretty was a word rarely used to describe anthropologist Margaret Mead.

Even pop icons like Madonna make the lists for reasons that extend beyond the physical. Although she's worked hard to define her body and is considered sexy by many men and women, most of the women who say they admire Madonna don't talk about her physical attributes. Instead they cite her creativity, the power and control she wields over her life and career, and her unique marketing genius, which enables her to reinvent herself whenever she decides it's time for a change. Madonna clearly sees fashion, style, and image as marketing tools, and she uses them on her own terms and to her own advantage. She plays the game, but she doesn't take the rules too seriously.

Examples of women who have defined their own beauty standards can be found in every culture and in any time. In her book

Hearts on Fire,[25] Muriel James described how gifted poet Elizabeth Barrett Browning was a semi-invalid, a "thin and frail shut-in" who lived in a room "deprived of sunlight and fresh air." Despite her potentially negative body image and her oppressive living and working environment, Barrett married poet Robert Browning when she was 39, had a son, and became a respected and influential poet and an outspoken commentator on Italian politics and U.S. slavery.

Actress Katharine Hepburn was presented a Lifetime Achievement Award by the Council of Fashion Designers for "not giving a damn about clothes" and having enough self-confidence to turn her back on the arbiters of fashion. What was Hepburn's achievement? She long ago opted for black pants and turtlenecks so that she didn't have to be bothered with a garter belt in the pre-pantyhose era.

Gifted artist Frida Kahlo was stricken by polio as a child and grew up under a cloud of ridicule because she had a withered leg. At 17, a streetcar accident broke her spinal column and left her severely crippled. She endured thirty-two operations and eventually had to have her leg amputated. Yet Kahlo went on to enjoy a rich, abundant life. She not only had many lovers, including famous expressionist artist Diego Rivera, she also became Mexico's most famous woman painter.

Think for a minute about the qualities these three women share. All rejected the cultural punishers and cultural conventions of their time and channeled energy that could have gone into hating their bodies into making important, vital contributions to the world. This raises a critical question about your own life that you must ask yourself: "Why am I not important enough to give myself permission to be free of body hatred so that I can live, love, and work as powerfully as possible?"

6. Learn Strength Training and Good Nutrition

Strength training and good nutrition are other important components of healing Body Image Depression and inoculating ourselves against the cultural punishers. Lifting or pushing weights has been shown in various studies to be of enormous value in weight loss and weight management. If we don't use it we lose it, mentally and physically. If we eat junk, we feel like junk, as Ali experienced. And as we lose strength, we lose options. We become increasingly dependent and more prone to Body Image Depression. (We'll explore the value of good nutrition further in the next chapter.)

The value of physical movement and strength training for developing and maintaining a positive body image cannot be underestimated. Strength training can also reduce osteoporosis, the increasing weakness and brittleness of our bones as we age. As we saw in Chapter 6, on Age Rage, osteoporosis is a fact of life for one of every three women after menopause. It's very difficult to maintain a positive body image when your bones feel like toothpicks or you're hobbling through life with a cane or walker. Consuming enough calcium and "pumping iron" to strengthen our muscles are important steps to insure that we don't lose our physical choices as we age. It's also an essential way to use the power of our bodies and remind ourselves that the Traditional Core is wrong when it tells us that weakness is feminine and strength is masculine.

Borrow a book on strength or weight training from the library or check out a video on strength workouts for women. I would also encourage you to invest in a few inexpensive weights. If your money is limited, use cans of food or plastic water jugs filled with varying amounts of water or sand as weights. By doing eight to ten repetitive strength exercises for the hips, legs, chest, and arms at least twenty minutes a day, three times a week, you'll be engaging in a program that's as good for your self-esteem as it is for your body.

Keep a pair of five-pound weights in a desk drawer at work or in a kitchen drawer at home. When you're talking on the phone, lift weights. Use them when you take a break, even if only for five minutes. Not only will you strengthen your muscles, over time you'll strengthen your positive body image and reduce your vulnerability to depression.

8. Develop and Carry Your Portable Power Image.

In the previous action strategies, you have been developing and refining your positive body images from childhood, adolescence, and adult experiences, recovering from your cultural addiction to physical perfection, and converting your body hatred into positive body energy. You can now combine these strategies by developing your own Portable Power Image as a way to summarize and apply what you have learned.

To create your Portable Power Image, begin by examining which of the following images were most meaningful and helpful to you: your positive childhood image, your exorcism of negative family ghosts, a picture or drawing of your Mirror of Affirmation, a picture or quote from the woman you most admire, or a picture or drawing of one of the weights you use for weight training. Take your favorite image or develop another one from what you have learned and make several copies of it. You now have a Portable Power Image to fight Body Image Depression whenever it appears.

Begin to use your Portable Power Image by taping it on your bathroom mirror so you're reminded every morning and evening of your commitment to maintain and develop a positive body image. Your picture can serve as a strong reminder that it's possible to have such a positive image because you've either had one before or can at least imagine having one now. When you experience negative responses to your real image in the mirror, look instead at your Portable Power Image and work on replacing negative associations with positive ones.

In the beginning, you may have to do this over and over, because it's likely you've grown accustomed to negative thinking about your mirror image. With practice, however, you'll find yourself able to convert negative into positive, and to hold on to the positive longer every day. If you have trouble remembering affirming associations, write more positive body thoughts around your Portable Power Image. Among them might be: "I don't have time for the body blues—my life is too full"; "I'm overweight now and that's OK. I'll change it when I'm ready, not because I'm told I should"; "I've earned these circles under my eyes. They come from hard work and loving a lot of people very well!"

Carry your Portable Power Image in your purse, briefcase, knapsack, or appointment book. Take it out any time you feel yourself becoming negative about your body or appearance. The following are some situations where the Portable Power Image can be helpful in warding off Body Image Depression.

- **Dressing Room Terrors.** Prop your Portable Power Image against the dressing room mirror to stay more positive as you try on clothes.

- **Business Meetings.** Keep a copy of your Portable Power Image readily accessible in your appointment book. When you can, look at it to ease your performance anxiety and remind yourself of your physical power.
- **Intimate Moments.** If you're uncomfortable at the thought of your intimate partner seeing your body, look at your Portable Power Image on the bathroom mirror and you'll usually feel less need to hide.
- **Intimidation.** When another woman's, or man's, looks intimidate you, reinforce your positive image by looking at your Portable Power Image. Identifying the negative quality of your thinking and converting it into positive associations represents one of the biggest steps in combating Body Image Depression.

As you do all these exercises, however, it's important to remember a basic truth: there are no quick fixes. Putting on lipstick as you're driving, changing out of your business suit into a cocktail dress, and using a portable curling iron in the ladies' restroom are all quick fixes. But something as significant as confronting your Body Image Depression requires much more than that. It takes patience, determination, and a long-term commitment to change.

Most of us assume that an improved body image will lead to self-acceptance, when in fact the opposite is true—self-acceptance is the first step toward enhancing your body image. Instead of relying on external changes to make us feel good, we must look deep within ourselves and reject the cultural Mirror of Perfection. When you live according to what is right for your body and you treat it with respect, you'll be more able to convert your energy from body hatred to body power and live a life freer of Body Image Depression.

·9·

MIND ↔ BODY DEPRESSION

*Depression is a condition of the mind. It is a physical afflic-
tion. It is environmentally induced. It is a genetic tendency.
It is learned. It is a "biological clock" disorder. It is many
separate biochemical illnesses. . . . No one point of view
represents a complete understanding of this complex and curious condition.*

Mark Gold, M.D.
The Good News About Depression

Even though it happened more than two years ago, Gail remembers that morning in the shower as if it were yesterday. She now
calls it "the first day of the rest of my life," but at the time she
couldn't help but wonder if it was the beginning of the end. She'd
overslept and was in the middle of a hurried shower when she noticed a small lump in her left breast. As she gently ran her finger
across the lump, which was no larger than a kernel of corn, she was
numb with fear.

"My first reaction was that if I just ignored it maybe it would go
away," Gail remembers. "But I knew in my heart that I was fooling
myself. That night I had a nightmare in which both of my breasts
were suddenly missing. I woke up crying and clutching my chest.
I knew if I didn't deal with the matter head-on, my denial could
kill me."

Gail immediately called her internist's office and convinced the
resistant office manager to book an emergency appointment for her
later that afternoon. Gail felt powerful and proud of herself for
taking such an assertive approach but felt sick and powerless a few
days later when a biopsy and a series of tests confirmed the dreaded
diagnosis: breast cancer. That year Gail endured a grueling combi-

nation of traditional medical approaches to treat the cancer, including radiation and chemotherapy.

To cover all her bases, she supplemented traditional therapies with many nontraditional ones, including nutritional therapy, acupuncture, and guided imagery. She read books by other women who had faced cancer. But despite all her efforts, Gail became more and more depressed. Her friends and family noticed her deepening depression, but no one wanted to risk upsetting her further by raising their concerns. Even her doctor was hesitant to suggest any treatment for her depression. He felt depression was a normal reaction to cancer and little could be done to change it.

Finally, Gail's sister, whose best friend had recently undergone treatment for ovarian cancer, told Gail about an outpatient therapy program for cancer patients at a nearby hospital. Gail was skeptical, but her depression had deepened over the past several months and she knew she had better do something. The next morning, Gail reluctantly went with her sister to meet with a counselor at the hospital.

The counselor invited Gail to join the Tuesday night cancer support group. Over the next year, she became an active member of the group. She attended the meetings religiously and thoroughly explored her range of feelings regarding the terror and tragedy she felt about the cancer. Gail felt as if she'd found a second home, a source of hope to challenge the experiment her body had become. She felt supported and understood by the group and developed several close friendships with other cancer patients who knew first-hand what she was going through. She began to feel more in control of her life, became much clearer about her values and what mattered to her, and completely reassessed and reestablished her priorities.

By the end of the year, Gail felt victorious. The combination of traditional and nontraditional approaches was successful. Not only had all signs of her cancer disappeared, she felt as though she had a second lease on life. She now invests more time in her friends and family and less in continuing her struggle up the corporate ladder. Consequently, she is no longer one of her company's superstars, but she's still respected and seen as a capable professional. For Gail, that is now more than enough. She refuses to let her career eclipse the new relationships in her life that mean so much to her.

At 13, Lauren was a star pitcher on a mixed community baseball team. She could throw a fastball that impressed even the boys. In those days, Lauren was very proud of her ability to think and act like "one of the guys."

But later in the season, Lauren was no longer feeling like one of the guys. In fact, she was beginning to feel female, and she didn't like it. One day after practice, she noticed a dark brownish-red stain in her underwear. She also noticed that her jeans fit a little tighter, and she was feeling bloated and uncomfortable. She wished she could accept menstruation as a healthy sign that she was becoming a woman. But instead, she felt anxious about the changes that were occurring in her body.

Over the next several months, as Lauren began to menstruate regularly, she began to lose interest in baseball. She felt extremely self-conscious running the bases with a sanitary pad between her legs and worried that the blood loss affected her strength and focus while out on the pitcher's mound. During her periods, she was lethargic and sometimes found it a challenge to get up in the morning. Finally, during a visit to her family doctor, she asked whether her sporadic symptoms were "normal." After examining Lauren and asking a series of questions, he discovered that she had symptoms of depression, anxiety, irritability, and low energy, and that she often felt physically uncomfortable during the week before each period. He suggested that she might have something called premenstrual syndrome, or PMS. While Lauren was relieved to learn that her symptoms had a name and were something other females experienced, she felt burdened by a physical syndrome generated by hormonal changes over which she seemingly had little or no control.

Eventually, however, Lauren did gain control. Her PMS subsided by late adolescence, once her hormones had stabilized. But ten years later, when Lauren was in her early 20s, she faced a new problem. She began experiencing similar PMS symptoms whenever she was depressed. And thanks to a rocky marriage and the pressures of graduate school, she seemed depressed more often than not.

Frustrated and frightened, Lauren finally decided to take a more active approach to overcoming her bad feelings. She empowered herself by reading as much as she could about depression, PMS, and the female body so that she would have a better idea of what she could do to help herself.

She joined the women's health collective in her college town. The women there helped her understand that PMS can be psychological as well as physical. When she realized she could significantly lessen her physical symptoms by lessening her psychological discomfort, she no longer felt defective. Lauren felt in charge of her body again for the first time in many years. She joined a community softball league and reclaimed the joy of using her body with strength and mastery.

Sugar, on the other hand, enjoyed a charmed childhood and an adolescence void of any real physical or emotional complications. She had a bright, cheery disposition that endeared her to nearly everyone she met and grew up feeling loved and nurtured on a small cattle ranch in southern Texas. Her parents were struggling ranchers but still managed to support her pursuit of a degree in marketing from the University of Texas.

Several weeks before graduation, Sugar accepted a job with a small but fast-growing computer software company in Boston. At 22, she had a wonderful sense of adventure and was delighted to be moving to a part of the country she'd heard much about but had never visited. She found that she loved living in Boston almost as much as she loved her job. Sugar excelled in sales. As the computer company grew over the next several years, Sugar grew with it and became a product development manager.

There was only one problem. After surviving several harsh Boston winters, Sugar began noticing that she became significantly more depressed during the winter months, but she couldn't figure out why. Her feelings and moods didn't seem related to events in her life. They seemed to have a life of their own. Every year as the autumn leaves began to fall, Sugar slowed down, almost as if she were entering a winter hibernation. She felt sad, sluggish, and apathetic and found herself feeling physically exhausted even though she was sleeping at least two hours a night more than she did during the rest of the year. The cold and snow seemed to stoke her appetite for carbohydrates, and Sugar noticed she ate more pasta, bagels, and croissants than in the summer. She gained about ten pounds every winter, but dropped them by mid-June.

Even though she was vaguely aware that her sense of sluggishness lifted and she began feeling happier and more active every year around Easter, she didn't identify a clear pattern for more than three years. One day, Sugar read a magazine article on seasonal affective disorder (SAD) and consulted one of the specialists quoted in the story. Her suspicions were confirmed. Fortunately, there is a very economical and very effective treatment for SAD: phototherapy. Within a week of her first light therapy session her SAD feelings disappeared and she was no longer depressed.

Gail, Lauren, and Sugar are just three of the millions of women in this country who have experienced the black energy of Mind ↔ Body Depressions. There are three kinds of Mind ↔ Body Depressions:

- Mind ↔ Body Depressions are the bad feelings our *bodies* create in our *minds*. In Gail's case, for instance, her depression was a direct result of her cancer.
- Mind ↔ Body Depressions can also result from the physical problems our *minds* create for our *bodies*. Examples include Alice, who developed a rash from her Depletion Depression, and Amy, who experienced a deep fatigue that resulted from her Victimization Depression after being sexually harassed and fired.
- The third kind of Mind ↔ Body Depression is the result of hormonal and biochemical changes that occur naturally in female bodies at various phases of our lives (i.e., menstruation, pregnancy, postpartum fluctuations, menopause, postmenopause, biochemical imbalances, etc.). Sugar's depressed feelings, for example, were the result of seasonal biochemical changes in response to less light in the winter.

As you can see with each of these examples, there is a powerful connection between the mind and the body. This connection has long been discounted and even denied by Western medicine. The attitude is summarized by the common practice of using a slash to permanently divide and disconnect the mind/body. This little line represents a big problem. It suggests we are made up of two separate parts: that what happens in our mind doesn't affect our body and vice versa. It is a dangerous, sometimes fatal, misconception.

Our minds and bodies aren't separated by a slash any more than they're separated by our necks. They're very much interconnected, and how we treat one directly affects the other. If we accept the simplistic and artificial division symbolized by the slash, we're more vulnerable to Mind ↔ Body Depressions because we fail to recognize a crucial reality: that depressions are created and healed by the interaction and integration of all parts of the self.

Too often, health professionals place too great an emphasis on the treatment of either the mind or the body, rather than taking this more balanced approach. Many psychiatrists, for example, see brain chemistry as the sole source of emotional problems. Some have become so enamored with biochemistry that they forget how important expressing feelings and exploring relationships can be in maintaining mental and physical health. They also miss some of the basics, such as how often physical illness causes depression. In one study, it was estimated that psychiatrists missed the diagnosis of physical illness up to 80 percent of the time when illness caused the depression they were seeing.[1]

On the opposite end of the spectrum, many nonphysician therapists focus solely on the mind as the source of our depressions. Most lack training in identifying how feelings are directly related to physical symptoms and how directly body chemistry affects mood. Professionals from both disciplines usually underestimate or ignore the impact of culture in making women depressed.

Because the either/or approaches are incomplete, so are the treatment strategies. These narrow, single-focused approaches can often lead to misdiagnosis and an overreliance on diagnostic labels and medication. Many traditional approaches foster excessive dependence on the therapist by encouraging the patient to believe that he or she can't get well without professional healing, rather than seeing the therapist as a consultant in the healing process.

To help resolve this dangerous, disconnected thinking, rotate the slash that typically divides mind/body forty-five degrees and add a two-way arrow so that it now appears as mind ↔ body. This arrow is a much more accurate visual depiction of the dynamic interaction between our mind and body.

As we've seen, depression can be expressed in physical symptoms rather than as bad feelings, or as bad feelings that stem from physical conditions, whether hormonal and/or biochemical. There are other ways the mind ↔ body connection is linked to depression:

- When the body becomes depleted, ill, or is forced to absorb trauma such as an accident or a wound, the feelings of loss and stress that occur almost always lead to depression.
- Medical interventions such as various prescription drugs, birth control pills, or unnecessary elective surgery, can also cause depression.
- Depression often generates self-destructive behaviors, such as addictions and alcoholism, which wear down and wear out the body.

Mind ↔ Body Depressions are related to all of these factors. Our weakened immune system and depleted brain chemicals are generated in part by negative thoughts and unresolved bad feelings. The same process occurs in reverse: the quality of our thinking and feeling is partly determined by the state of our physical well-being. The following diagram shows how our mind and body work together as a dynamic, powerful circle of energy to create depression and various physical symptoms. The energy in the circle moves clockwise and counterclockwise, showing the dynamic exchange of positive and negative energy between our bodies and our minds. Each element in the circle creates more depression or worsens as a result of depression, as symbolized by the two-way arrows moving in and out of the body.

Mind ↔ Body Depression

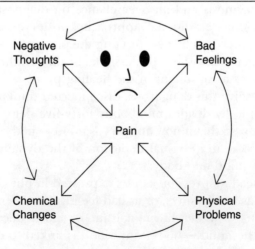

Whether generated by mind, body, or both, these bad feelings are appropriate, natural reactions to biological and psychological processes. Some depressions are normal reactions to painful physical events. Some Mind ↔ Body Depressions create discomfort as necessary warning signs to motivate corrective action to regain health, resolve loss, and balance our system again, such as illnesses, trauma, eating disorders, and seasonal affective disorder. They all become healthy depressions when we convert their pain into gain.

If we deny the warning signs or refuse to accept their purpose, then our pain is in vain. We know we're in physical pain but don't know it's because we're depressed, so it's much harder to heal. Yet if we stay depressed, we're more likely to become seriously ill because, over time, depression weakens our immune system and makes us more vulnerable to germs, viruses, and possibly cancers. We are also more likely to slip further into Unhealthy Depression and risk even more illness and biological imbalance. However, by understanding and expressing these depressed feelings, acknowledging their validity, and learning how to harness their energy toward healing, we can neutralize their negative power and use them constructively to enrich our lives. The first step in this healing process is to become acquainted with the major sources of Mind ↔ Body Depressions.

Sources of Mind ↔ Body Depressions

There are four major sources of Mind ↔ Body Depressions. Some are exclusive to women; others are equal-opportunity depressions that hit both women and men with similar strength. Each source contains a number of specific conditions and experiences that naturally group into four categories: biochemical and hormonal changes, reactions to loss and pain, self-destructive behaviors, and "cures" that depress.

1. Biochemical and Hormonal Changes

Premenstrual Syndrome (PMS)

Menstrual discomfort and the typical symptoms Lauren experienced—depression, irritability, exhaustion, sore breasts, bloating, and crying spells—are usually associated with moody teenagers. We're most vulnerable to PMS, however, in our late 20s and early 30s.[2] Research studies report anywhere from 20 percent and 80 percent of women have some kind of PMS. According to the American Psychological Association National Task Force Report on Women and Depression, however, only 5 percent of women experience significant discomfort and need professional treatment for PMS.[3]

Lauren experienced firsthand the complexity of this syndrome. Her first depression was related to hormonal fluctuations. A few years later, her depression apparently generated physical symptoms. In both cases, her Mind ↔ Body Depression flourished, and no one could provide her with clear answers about how to heal it or even what was wrong. It's not clear how many of the symptoms that pass for PMS are emotional or physical or simply part of what women are expected to experience in a culture that is often sexist and patriarchal in its view of women's biology.

What we do know is that there is often a strong relationship between PMS and depression. A recent study by the University of California, San Diego, shows that some women who are depressed as a result of PMS secrete lower amounts of a brain chemical called melatonin when they sleep. These biochemical changes affect our mood, making us more irritable and depressed, which seems to contribute to PMS.[4]

Another study showed that two-thirds of the women with a lifetime history of major depression had more PMS than women who were not chronically depressed.[5] Even after menopause, a number of these women continued to experience symptoms associated with PMS, although they were no longer experiencing the menstrual cycle and hormone fluctuations that supposedly triggered their PMS reactions. What look like PMS symptoms are instead often signs of untreated depression,[6] which remind us again of the power, complexity, and necessity of the mind ↔ body connection.

Postpartum Depression

Most mothers experience healthy postpartum depression. Some experts estimate that figure is as high as 80 percent.[7] I was certainly no exception. My first postpartum depression occurred soon after I gave birth to my oldest son, Joshua. On the spur of the moment, I visited him in the nursery, only to discover that he had been taken for a standard test. I was instantly worried. I returned to my room and burst into tears.

When the woman who came in to clean saw how distraught I was, she dropped to her knees, crossed herself, and said a prayer. She assumed I had lost my baby. I felt as though I had, even though he was just down the hall. That incident was an important lesson for me in the power of Mind ↔ Body Depressions. There I was, a professional in psychology, fully aware of what to expect but powerless to do anything about the hormonal current that was sweeping me away. Intellectually, I knew it was a Mind ↔ Body Depression, but emotionally it felt like a life-threatening catastrophe.

For most women, these kinds of postpartum depressions usually occur on the third or fourth day after delivery and typically last anywhere from one to fourteen days.[8] They are Healthy Depressions and come from the normal fluctuations in hormones that occur for women during that time. If they last longer or make the woman feel destructive to herself or her baby, they have become Unhealthy Depressions.

Postmenopausal Depressions

The Mind ↔ Body Depressions that occur after menopause do not result from the end of menstruation, but rather from the accumulated losses resulting from the reduction of estrogen. Three of the greatest problems are thinning of the bones (osteoporosis), dryness and thinning of the vaginal walls, and greatly increased risk of heart disease. Women are much more likely to get depressed about these experiences than over losing the capacity to menstruate.

We also confront the massive confusion over hormone replacement therapy, which is depressing in itself. According to current medical thinking, if we replace estrogen, we risk cancer; if we don't replace estrogen, we risk heart disease. New techniques and hormone combinations have made estrogen replacement therapy more promising for many women, however. And recent research has shown that estrogen after menopause cuts a woman's heart disease risk by half.[9] Clearly, women must carefully weigh the risks and benefits and their history of cancer and heart disease to make a difficult choice with inadequate information. Gail Sheehy's book on menopause, *The Silent Passage*, provides a helpful discussion of the subject.

Seasonal Affective Disorder

Seasonal affective disorder, which bears the appropriate acronym SAD, is a cyclical depression. Among the symptoms of SAD are feelings of significant depression, fatigue, weight gain, loss of energy, and diminished sexual appetite. Symptoms tend to peak during the fall and winter and usually disappear in the spring and summer, although for a small percentage, the reverse pattern can be true.

It is estimated that 12 million Americans suffer from SAD and that up to 35 million others experience milder versions of this disorder.[10] It is at least four times more common among women than among men. SAD usually begins in our 20s and early 30s, although it has been reported in some children and teenagers. Some estimates suggest that up to half of all women living in the northern United States experience noticeable winter depressions. Very few of them will receive the treatment they need, however, because they and their health professionals don't know how to distinguish typical depressive symptoms from SAD.[11]

The treatment for SAD is phototherapy. It's effective, inexpensive, and requires less time with a professional than any other depression treatment. Phototherapy simply requires the right diagnosis and the right kind of light box to provide enough high-intensity light for a certain amount of time each day. The extra light seems to increase the secretion of the hormonal chemical melatonin in the brain and regulates the body's natural circadian rhythm so the patient doesn't get out of sync and feel depressed.

Migraine Headaches

Migraines are headaches so severe that those who have them often report experiences of nausea, diarrhea, blurred vision, and other visual disturbances, such as seeing flashing bright lights. An estimated 8 million Americans currently suffer from migraines; 75 percent of them are women.[12]

Changes in the brain chemical serotonin and changes in estrogen levels are suspected to trigger migraines, which may explain why women are three times more susceptible to migraines than men.[13] Depression and stress also contribute to migraines. Depression is also one of the most common consequences of migraines, particularly when no painkiller alleviates the problem.

2. Reactions to Loss and Pain

Cesarean Sections

One of every four expectant mothers who check in to the hospital for delivery leaves with a baby in her arms and a scar beneath her stomach. In his recent book *So Your Doctor Recommended Surgery*, Dr. John Lewis calls the incidence of cesarean sections in America a "shocking surgical excess" and suggests that half the cesareans done may be unnecessary.[14] If the general trend continues, however, some researchers predict that by the year 2000, 40 percent of all births in the United States will be cesarean sections.[15]

Mind ↔ Body Depressions often occur after a cesarean delivery because many women listen to their Traditional Core and accept the notion that they've "failed" by not having natural childbirth and a vaginal delivery. Many women are unprepared for the possibilities of a cesarean delivery and consequently experience a depressing surprise afterward. They encounter pain, restriction of activity, and often feel powerless and angry that the decision to operate was taken out of their hands. If they believe the surgery was unnecessary in the first place, they typically feel much worse. Fortunately, these Mind ↔ Body Depressions are usually healthy, temporary, and forgotten once the mother returns home with her baby and begins the adventure of raising the child.

Miscarriages

With one of every three pregnancies ending before childbirth, miscarriage ranks as one of the most common medical losses experienced by women. It is also one of the most devastating emotional losses a woman can face. Considering the frequency with which miscarriages occur, one might assume that significant research has been done to find out why and how they can be prevented. Unfortunately, that's not the case. As with breast cancer and other health issues exclusive to women, precious little has been done to solve the mystery of miscarriages.

What we do know is that about half of all miscarriages can be explained by hormonal, chromosomal, or biological abnormalities. The other half can't be medically explained.[16] It's virtually impossible for a woman to trigger a miscarriage intentionally, but that doesn't stop most women from riding an emotional rollercoaster that leaves them feeling guilty or defective after they have one. The Traditional Core is quick to blame us for being inadequate as women if we "lose our babies." Mind ↔ Body Depression from miscarriages is not only a reaction to physical loss and stress, but from the more primary assault on our very worth as women.

Hysterectomies

We have a one-in-three chance of losing our uterus before we reach 60 and are most at risk of undergoing this surgery in our late 40s.[17] Hysterectomies are the second most common surgery for women in the United States, where the rate of hysterectomies is nearly double that of most European countries. In fact, only 10 percent of the hysterectomies performed in the United States are done in response to cancerous growth.[18] According to *Women's Health Alert*, at least one in four hysterectomies performed in the U.S. is "extremely questionable, if not clearly unnecessary."[19]

The usual justification for performing the operation is that it's a precautionary measure. The problem is that the uterus acts as a receptor site for estrogen and progesterone. When it is removed and the level of hormones drops, it can create depression and also have a profound effect on a woman's sexuality. Although there has been some controversy over these findings, one study showed that between 33 percent and 46 percent of women who had undergone total hysterectomies complained of reduced sexual responsiveness when their ovaries were removed.[20] The reduction of hormones also puts women at twice the risk for developing coronary heart disease.

While most women initially feel relieved after a hysterectomy,[21] the longer-term consequences often create depression. Indeed, the research has shown that women who have had hysterectomies are twice as likely to be depressed over time.[22] So before you allow your uterus to be removed, make sure it's a medical necessity, not just a convenient precaution.

Abortion

The odds of a woman in America ending her pregnancy through abortion are one in three.[23] There is a prevailing misconception that guilt and anxiety occur in women who elect to have an abortion and that their decision often leads to an Unhealthy Depression. In fact, the opposite is true. Healthy Depression over the stress and loss does occur in the short run,[24] but the typical long-term emotional result from abortion isn't depression but relief.

In one study, 44 percent of the women surveyed had abortions because they were single, while 32 percent aborted because they couldn't afford a child.[25] Considering that these are the typical reasons that motivate women to have an abortion, it's not surprising that research indicates that after recovering from the procedure, women often feel more self-confident, in charge of their lives, and better able to accomplish their goals.[26] In a survey of the research on abortion, Drs. Joy and Howard Osofsky reported that "almost regardless of the source, the objective data reveal a surprisingly low incidence of psychological complications" for those women having an abortion.[27]

Infertility

It's a common misconception that pregnancy is a source of depression. While expectant women do experience hormonal changes that can lead to temporary depressions, a woman's mental health tends to be strongest when she's pregnant. It's women who are unable to become pregnant who are among the most vulnerable to Mind ↔ Body Depression. Prime candidates for this depression are childless women in their late 30s and early 40s who want to become pregnant and cannot, or who do so at greatly increased risk.

According to the American Fertility Society, one in seven women has problems conceiving. Forty percent of these are due to physical problems over which the woman has no control, a classic source of Mind ↔ Body Depression. The reasons the other 60 percent have trouble conceiving remains a mystery and an enormous source of stress and depression.[28] Research has shown that infertility patients often feel defective, damaged, guilty of causing the infertility, and "bad" about who they are and what they do in life.[29] In another study, 40 percent of women at an infertility clinic called infertility "the most upsetting experience" of their lives.[30] Research shows that this depression increases even more if it is their partner who is diagnosed as infertile.[31]

Victimization or Accident Damage

Female victims of assault are highly likely to develop Mind ↔ Body Depressions as a result of their trauma. Dr. Mary Koss, a psychologist at the University of Arizona, has reported that crime victims experience significantly increased health problems. Assault victims are so vulnerable to Mind ↔ Body Depression that they see themselves as less healthy and are more likely to assume less personal responsibility for their health. During the first two years after an assault, those studied visited their doctors 41 percent more often.[32] Another study in the *American Journal of Psychiatry* reported similar findings. They found that women who were molested as children were more likely to experience depression and physical problems than women who had not been sexually abused.[33]

According to Dr. Dean Kilpatrick of the Medical University of South Carolina, victimization is even more important than family history in predicting substance abuse and consequent depression. Crime victims were nearly seven times as likely as nonvictims to have two or more major alcohol-related problems and seventeen times more likely to have a major drug abuse problem, often as a result of a desperate attempt to medicate the underlying depression.[34] These victimization experiences build and deepen Mind ↔ Body

Depressions because they reinforce feelings of ongoing physical vulnerability, helplessness, and unresolved rage.

An experience that produces similar reactions to victimization is accident damage. This tends to occur whether or not the accident (car accident, personal injury, etc.) was our responsibility or whether we feel like a victim because of it. Accidents create enough trauma for our mind and body that most of us become depressed in response.

Serious Illness

The four top killers of women in America today—heart disease, AIDS, cancer, and strokes—leave women who experience them extremely susceptible to Mind ↔ Body Depressions. Up to 80 percent of patients who have physical problems develop emotional problems and depression that interfere with their ability to get well.[35] This is especially true for people with life-threatening diseases such as AIDS, cancer, and Alzheimer's disease.

Many who are diagnosed with AIDS or cancer, for example, immediately enter a deep depression and experience suicidal thoughts. AIDS patients are 36 percent more at risk for suicide than others in their same age groups.[36] One-third of Alzheimer's patients become clinically depressed during their illness and need professional attention. Up to 80 percent of the Alzheimer patient's family members also become significantly depressed in trying to respond to such a demanding illness.[37]

Although doctors are trained to deal with the illness itself, many discount or even overlook the resulting Mind ↔ Body Depression. Some doctors are fatalists and assume the depression is natural and/or untreatable, such as the physician who treated Gail for her breast cancer but failed to suggest treatment for her depression. Others simply don't know how to distinguish depression from the disease itself. One study showed that physicians misdiagnosed or completely overlooked more than 40 percent of the emotional problems that accompanied the physical illness.[38]

The result of an untreated Mind ↔ Body Depression can be devastating. In fact, a study reported in the *Journal of the American Medical Association* in 1989 found that depression is more disabling than many physical diseases, including arthritis, diabetes, high blood pressure, back problems, and digestive disorders. Only advanced coronary disease kept more patients in bed than depression. It was also found that depression made people more socially ineffective than any of the other physical diseases.[39] The bottom line is that depression can take more of a toll than most of the physical illnesses ever do.

3. Self-destructive Behaviors

Eating Disorders

Eating disorders—anorexia nervosa, bulimia, or simply using food as a way to manage stress—are most likely to begin in teenage years, as they did for bulimic Joyce or food junkie Ali, whom we met in Chapter 8. Eating disorders are related to depression as either a cause or consequence of our difficulties in managing food. There are similarities in the biochemistry of women who are seriously depressed and those who have eating disorders. In fact, a number of bulimic women like Joyce who have been given antidepressants experience positive results, so the Mind ↔ Body Depression connection is very important in understanding and treating this disorder.

Smoking

Recent studies have proven an undeniable connection between smoking and depression. One study conducted by the New York State Psychiatric Institute showed that smokers were more than twice as likely as nonsmokers to experience depression.[40] Ironically, the study also suggests one of the reasons people continue to smoke is that nicotine seems to have some antidepressant effects.

How, you might be wondering, can a habit that makes us more susceptible to depression also have antidepressive effects? According to Dr. Alexander Glassman, author of major studies in this field,[41] nicotine calms and stimulates at the same time. The effects of nicotine are immediate. As the chemical enters the lungs, it reaches the brain within seven seconds. While depression is likely to lift somewhat immediately after a nicotine rush, the overall effects of nicotine are clearly negative. Smokers are also vulnerable to an ongoing erosion of self-esteem and consequent depression. They know they're doing something that's damaging to their health and often feel helpless to stop themselves.

Quitting smoking seems to be biologically more difficult for women, because men tend to excrete nicotine from their systems more quickly. It also provides a unique physical challenge. When a smoker quits smoking, levels of certain chemicals, such as serotonin, decrease. Low levels of serotonin are related to increases in depression. These chemical changes often result in depressed feelings and carbohydrate cravings, which can lead to overeating and weight gain. Many women who stop smoking and then gain weight panic and choose to return to the cigarettes rather than put on more weight and feel more depressed.[42]

Substance Abuse

Abuse of drugs and alcohol is often a symptom of an underlying depression, especially among young adults. Conventional wisdom says that people become depressed because they use substances in an abusive way, but recent research is showing the opposite to be true. The *New York Times* cited a study in which Dr. Edward Nunes, of the New York State Psychiatric Institute, reported that more than 1 million Americans are abusing alcohol and drugs because they are suffering from serious underlying depressions.[43]

Another study has found that at least 25 percent of alcoholics may be suffering from depression, and that their depression lingers even after they stop drinking.[44] And the drugs themselves create depression. Marijuana, cocaine, heroin, methadone, and alcohol have all been shown clinically and in the research to produce depression.[45]

4. *"Cures" That Depress*

Prescription Drugs

Women receive about two-thirds of the prescriptions written in the United States for antidepressants, tranquilizers, and sleeping pills. A large proportion of those who use tranquilizers or sleeping pills for more than two months become addicted.[46] In some women, tranquilizers interact biochemically and emotionally to create the opposite effect they were intended to have. Some commonly prescribed drugs, such as Valium, Adavan, and Halcion, are supposed to help you sleep and calm you down, but they can actually stimulate hostility, aggression, and/or depression.[47] Diet pills, over-the-counter cough and cold medicines, and certain drugs prescribed for muscle pain, ulcers, seizures, arthritis, hypertension, and Parkinson's disease can also produce significant feelings of depression.[48]

Author William Styron described this process well in his book *Darkness Visible: A Memoir of Madness.* Styron's depression was so severe that he was able to get only two to three hours of sleep a night, and those only with the help of sleeping pills. He was prescribed the sleeping pill Halcion and unknowingly consumed doses that were much too large, which seemed to broaden and deepen his depression.

Writes Styron: "It seems reasonable to think that this was still another contributory factor to the trouble that has come upon me. Certainly, it should be a caution to others. One cringes when thinking about the damage such promiscuous prescribing of these potentially dangerous tranquilizers may be creating in patients everywhere. In my case, Halcion, of course, was not an independent villain—I was headed for the abyss—but I believe that without it I might not have been brought so low."[49]

Birth-Control Pills

Birth-control pills have been found to create depression in approximately 25 percent of the women who use them.[50] Pills with higher amounts of hormones created depression in 30 percent to 50 percent of the women surveyed.[51] One of the many explanations for this resulting depression is that a vitamin B-6 deficiency, which can be directly related to changes in mood and possible increases in depression, occurs in one of every five women taking the pill.[52] Depression resulting from the use of birth-control pills usually occurs within two to three months of first taking them. The depressions are strong enough that 40 percent of women who start taking the pill stop because of bad feelings.[53]

Action Strategies for Resolving Mind ↔ Body Depressions

The first three action strategies apply to managing all of our Mind ↔ Body Depressions and are essential to our physical and emotional well-being. The rest of the strategies apply more to some of the Mind ↔ Body Depressions than to others, so feel free to pick and choose what is applicable to your own experience.

In using these strategies, the most difficult challenge of all may be letting go of the cultural prejudice most of us maintain that mind ↔ body problems are signs of weakness. Many of us think that if our physical problems are in any way caused by our minds, we're weak and inadequate. As a result we then often overlook the social and psychological factors that cause and contribute to our physical distress. When that happens, the physical problems won't go away no matter how much we treat them because we haven't addressed the reasons they appeared in the first place.

Therefore, one of the most important steps you can take is to overcome the fear and shame associated with psychosomatic illness so that you can be free to appreciate what wonderfully integrated organisms we are. Once and for all, move the slash that separates mind/body to a two-way arrow to unite your mind and body. You will then feel stronger, more integrated, and significantly healthier.

1. Develop Partnerships with All Your Health Specialists.

To cope with and resolve Mind ↔ Body Depressions, you must see your doctor as a health partner rather than an authority figure or someone to be avoided. When your doctor is "the expert" whose orders you must obey, you are much more likely to become passive, dependent, and totally reliant on his or her recommendations and on prescription drugs. When you see your doctor as a partner whose experience and guidance can help you stay or become well, you're far more likely to work effectively with him or her, taking more responsibility for your health, having a more positive attitude, and remaining healthier.

How do you find a health partner you can trust? Here are some basic guidelines to use when choosing a doctor. (These guidelines are equally useful when looking for a therapist.) Consider yourself a consumer and not a patient, and remember that you're doing some of the most important shopping of your life.

1. Ask friends, neighbors, and coworkers you trust whether they're happy with their doctor. If they are, meet the doctor for a brief consultation and explain to him or her what you're looking for: a doctor who's willing to be a partner in your health care. Explain that you're looking for an expert who is comfortable treating you as an equal and talking *with* you instead of *at* you.

   You'll be able to learn a lot about the doctor by how he or she responds to your comments and questions. If the doctor appears uncomfortable or unwilling to discuss the matter with you openly, you have learned what you need to know and can quickly move on.

2. Trust your gut instincts. If you don't like your doctor for any reason, find another. All the degrees and certificates on your doctor's wall don't matter if you don't feel comfortable or supported when you're in his or her office. If you feel uncomfortable, devalued, or unimportant to your doctor, especially during or after an appointment, don't waste your time and energy. Instead, invest it in finding a doctor whose sensitivity, sensibility, and style are more appropriate for your needs.

3. Pay attention to how your doctor communicates. Does he or she really listen? Communicate clearly and directly, without using a lot of medical jargon? How well does he or she respond to your requests for additional information or for obtaining a second opinion?

4. Take notes when you're talking with your doctor, especially if you're discussing a specific medical condition. If you're dealing with a serious illness, take along a tape recorder or a loved one. It's easy to forget or misinterpret what the doctor has told you, especially if you're anxious or emotionally distraught. Taping the session or having someone you trust with you to ask questions, take notes, and listen to the information helps to avoid later confusion and misunderstandings.

Don't hesitate to call your doctor if you have questions or concerns. If your doctor doesn't return your calls within a reasonable period of time, you don't have a health partner; strongly consider looking for another doctor who's more responsive. Contrary to popular belief, they do exist. Most of the women I know find them, though often only after an extensive search. It helps to look beyond traditional channels. I found a terrific obstetrician by asking the head of the hospital's midwife program which doctor she thought worked best with women. On the other hand, if you're always looking and never satisfied, then you would be wise to examine whether "specialist shopping" has become an avoidance technique.

5. Notice how healthy your physician seems to be. If your doctor isn't taking good care of himself or herself, there's no reason to believe he or she will be any more effective as your health partner. One reason this is so important is that physicians and therapists rarely recommend health or mental health practices that they themselves don't do. The American College of Physicians found in a recent survey that 50 percent of the physicians surveyed did not have their own personal physician, 20 percent did not exercise regularly, and 11 percent drank alcohol daily. Fifty percent of the female physicians surveyed fail to do a monthly breast self-examination. More than 50 percent of physicians don't advise their patients to exercise and 25 percent fail to encourage patients to stop drinking alcohol, even when the patients are known to have liver disease.[54]

6. Make the idea of health partnerships more real for you by drawing your own Health Management Diagram. This is a management flowchart to give you a clear overview of the people you're currently relying on for your health care needs and a better sense of what needs to be done with each. Begin by drawing a rectangle at the top of a page. Then place yourself in the center, with your title as CEO of your own health management system. This is an important visual reminder, because it reinforces the idea that you, or whoever you designate to be your representative should you become incapacitated, are the ones primarily responsible for managing and directing your health care. By visualizing ourselves in this central position of responsibility, we're less likely to allow our fear

and anxiety to place us in the more traditionally dependent role of patient.

Once you've placed yourself in the center of your Health Management Diagram, add the names of all your current health partners in the boxes below in the order of their importance. The position of various specialists will change depending on the problem. For example, when Gail's cancer was in remission, her support group and her therapist occupied the central position. Her oncologist was in a side box because his role, while still essential, was less primary at that point. Below is the Health Management Diagram Gail used so effectively to show her team in her battles with cancer.

Gail's Health Management Diagram

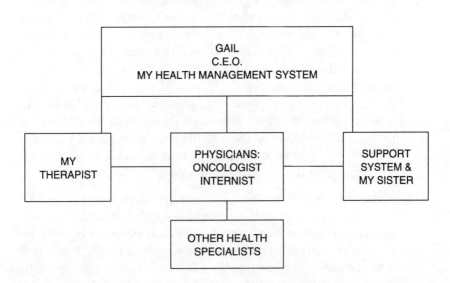

If you're facing a health crisis as Gail did, it's essential for you to request that all of the relevant specialists in your diagram consult with each other about your medical needs and concerns so that they can coordinate their strategies more effectively. It's not typically done but it's the only way you, and your specialists, can each appreciate the overall picture and better understand how the care they're providing relates to the treatments of other professionals.

2. Create Your Own Health Files and Health Journal.

It's not realistic to expect your doctor to stay current on every illness you may experience or to always know exactly what to do. Researchers tell us that only about 10 percent of what doctors do is based on scientific test results. According to a recent article in the *Los Angeles Times,* most of their conclusions are based on intuition and guesswork. Up to a third of medical treatments are unnecessary, not helpful, or even harmful.[55]

This is especially true for women, since most male and even many female physicians don't fully understand the psychology of women or appreciate the gender differences in health needs. Therefore, it's critically important that you make a commitment to stay informed and take the guesswork out of your health care as much as possible by staying updated about your physical vulnerabilities and women's health issues.

One way a number of women have chosen to do this is to become health partners with one or two close friends or relatives. Agree to keep health files for yourself and each other and clip articles from magazines and newspapers about health and mental health. Those related to women's health needs and specific illnesses to which you or your health partner are vulnerable are especially relevant. Trade files every few months so that you can read or copy their articles. Gail learned from a newspaper article her sister had clipped that her high cholesterol was more likely than a man's to be lowered by oat bran, particularly after reaching 50.[56] From that day on, Gail ate an oat-bran muffin every morning. As Gail discovered, health files are particularly important for staying informed of the rapidly changing and critically important information on nutrition and its impact on Mind ↔ Body Depressions.

Commit to staying active and educated about your particular physical vulnerability so that you don't feel victimized by it. Make it a point to watch or listen to TV and radio health programs, instead of automatically switching the channel because those topics are "too boring." Attend the free health lectures offered by many local hospitals. Review nutrition and health books written specifically for women, even if it means just standing around in the health section of the bookstore or taking a lunch hour to visit your local library.

One resource I highly recommend is Dr. Sidney Wolfe's *Women's Health Alert* (Addison-Wesley, 1990), which proved especially valuable in researching this chapter. Also keep an updated, easy-to-read medical reference book at home to help you assess what your symptoms may mean before you decide to see your physician. If you are on medication, you may also find it very useful to buy or borrow a copy of *Physician's Desk Reference* to familiarize yourself with the proper dosages and possible side effects of your medications.

In addition to keeping health files, a number of clients have also found it very helpful to maintain a health journal. Whenever you're having a mind ↔ body problem such as headaches, backaches, dermatitis, diarrhea, stomachaches, ulcers, "bad" skin, constipation, allergic reactions, shortness of breath, chest pains, etc., log it in your health journal and write down all the physical and emotional experiences you're having at that time.

This approach is particularly important if you're experiencing new symptoms or taking new medication, especially birth-control pills or tranquilizers, since the side effects of both can include depression. Among the questions you might consider when assessing new symptoms: What have you been eating? How would you assess your recent stress level? Have you been using any new products—a new brand of shampoo or lipstick or detergent—or had a change in your daily routine? Have you been exposed to pets or pollen that might trigger an allergic reaction? As you answer these kinds of questions, you're likely to gather clues and gain insight that will help you make a more informed self-diagnosis and help you to decide the course of action you need to take. When you collect this kind of data, you're empowering yourself to assume greater control of your own health management. In some cases, the knowledge you gain can save you a great deal of time, money, and worry.

This isn't to suggest that you avoid or delay visiting your doctor when necessary. In fact, as you become more aware of your own health, you'll be more aware when you really should go. And once you're there, you'll be able to provide helpful, specific information, enabling him or her to make a more accurate diagnosis and help correct the problem more quickly.

Gathering and acting on this kind of information is one of the best ways to inoculate yourself against Mind ↔ Body Depression. By taking control and responsibility for your own health, you take a major step forward in improving it.

3. Develop Your Own Symptom Checklist with a Mind ↔ Body Depression Doll.

To fully appreciate the strength of your mind ↔ body connection and how you can use it to your healthy advantage, create your own Mind ↔ Body Depression Doll. To do this exercise, reproduce the doll diagram that follows or draw your own.

The symptoms in the head region of the diagram are those emotional and mental experiences we typically associate with depression. The symptoms listed in the stomach and heart region are the physical experiences we typically don't associate with depression but should. The depression expressway that connects the two is the central nervous system, the body's fast lane of nerve pathways that distribute hormones and chemicals throughout the body and brain.

Making and handling these dolls are direct reminders of our individual vulnerability to Mind ↔ Body Depressions. We see firsthand how necessary both our minds and bodies are to heal our physical and emotional depressions.

Study the diagram, focusing on the head region, and decide which of the mental and emotional stress symptoms listed apply to you. Circle your symptoms if your doll is a copy of the one shown. If you've drawn your own doll, simply list those symptoms that are relevant. In either case, add any other symptoms that are necessary to describe your experiences.

Now close your eyes and focus on the physical symptoms you typically experience when you're feeling depressed or the ones you think could be related to depression. Do the symptoms have a form or a face or a special name? What kind of physical symptoms does your body seem to favor? Open your eyes and focus on the lower area of the Mind ↔ Body Depression Doll.

Circle or list the physical symptoms or illnesses you've had or have. Again add any other symptoms you experience that aren't already listed. Now draw or darken the two-way arrow with ink or connect the dashes on the diagram between your head and your

Diagram of Mind ↔ Body Depression Doll

**Typical
Depressed
Feelings**

empty   hopeless
helpless exhausted sleepy
afraid   ashamed

●   ●

stressed pessimistic depleted guilty
lonely angry confused beaten indecisive

●

hole inside   sad   everything's gray

● ● ● ● ● ● ●

can't concentrate   shy
not worth it

**Depression
Expressway
(Central Nervous
System)**

**Physical
Symptoms
Often
Related to
or Caused by
Depression**

diarrhea
stomachaches   ulcers
rashes   viruses   colds
flu   sore throat   asthma   hay fever
bulimia   blood pressure and/or heart problems
insomnia   loss of sex drive or pleasure
constipation   pressure in the chest or head
breathing problems   irregular menses
soreness and stiffness of muscles,
joints, tendons, ligaments
chronic pain   backaches
fatigue   fibrositis
cramps

body to remind yourself how directly one creates and affects the other. A black or dark blue two-way arrow can stand for the depression expressway of your central nervous system, one of the chief sources for the mind ↔ body connection. Thinking of it as a depression expressway is a helpful way to remind yourself how the negative energy of your mind hurts your body, as well as how your sick body can affect your mind.

To help break up this chain of recycled negative energy, move into action. Start with the three most important wise teachings that you've learned from being sick and from the unavoidable pain of our lives. Gail learned from her cancer that people are more important than success. Lauren learned from her PMS that sometimes only other women can teach us about the mysteries of the female body, and that some symptoms that seem physical in origin are indeed more psychological. And, self-confident Sugar learned to respect how much she doesn't know about what her body really needs, which in her case was something as simple as more light.

Like Gail, Lauren, and Sugar, write out what you've learned from your physical problems and illnesses and attach the list to your Mind ↔ Body Depression Doll as evidence that you can convert Mind ↔ Body Depressions into health and wisdom. To transfer what you've learned into action, select from your Mind ↔ Body Depression Doll one bad feeling you have that is often expressed in a physical symptom. Lauren's was inactivity ↔ cramps, Sugar's was depression ↔ lethargy, and Gail's was stress ↔ diarrhea.

Now develop two specific health strategies to help resolve your Mind ↔ Body Depression symptom during the next two weeks. Write down your goals next to your list of wise teachings. Gail's goals, for example, included a daily ten-minute walk and one imagery exercise per day to reduce her stress. Sugar vowed to maintain her phototherapy and see a doctor to determine the cause of a nagging backache. Lauren went to her university counseling center for three sessions of therapy to learn to cope with her depression so that she could feel better physically.

Keep a copy of your Mind ↔ Body Depression Doll visible so you can be reminded every day of your health goals and how working toward your goals contributes to increased health and wisdom. After the first week, change, renew, or modify the goals for the following

week. After two weeks, return to your Mind ↔ Body Depression
Doll and evaluate the symptoms you've been experiencing. Are they
the same symptoms as when you started? Have they lessened or
weakened? Even if you can't tell, do you simply feel better?

Most people who follow through with this exercise report that
they feel better within a week. Those who commit for a month report fewer physical symptoms of distress and considerably less pain
and depression at the end of four weeks. They feel—and are—more
in control of their emotional and physical health and less vulnerable
to Mind ↔ Body Depressions.

4. Learn New Communication and Control Strategies to Use When You're Ill.

If you're very ill or are recovering from an incapacitating operation
or accident, it's natural to feel helpless, dependent, and out of control. But even if you're physically limited and must rely on the assistance and support of others during recovery, you can use the
following five-step process to regain a sense of control and help
reduce the Mind ↔ Body Depression you'll inevitably feel during
such situations.

Step 1 is readjusting your expectations. Accept the reality that
you're in recovery and have suffered a major physical disruption
and loss. While you can certainly accelerate the healing process by
taking care of yourself, it's important to accept that you can't rush
recovery. The healing process has a timing of its own. Accept that
your body needs time to rebound.

During recovery, it's critical to exercise self-discipline in order to
focus consistently on gains rather than losses. This is necessary because pain drains, both emotionally and physically. Our pain de-
pletes the chemicals in the brain that help us feel good, so positive
thinking is very important for maintaining balance in our biochemistry and aiding our recovery.

Step 2 is to acknowledge that even the tiniest baby steps matter
when moving along the road to recovery. Depending on how ill
you've been or are, progress may be something as simple as sitting
up in bed, taking one shuffling step, or reaching out to touch a
visitor. The commitment to self and to your recovery are what matter, not the size of the steps. By taking enough of them, you'll find
yourself well on the road to recovery. If you can't lift the depression

yourself and suspect it is keeping you ill, consider antidepressants until you've recovered enough to hold your own and stay positive.

Step 3 is to understand how important it is to your recovery to feel connected to other people and to learn to ask for what you need. As Drs. Robert Ornstein and Charles Swencionis observe in their book *The Healing Brain: A Scientific Reader:* "There is no disease that kills people at the rate loneliness does. . . . the single, widowed, and divorced die at rates two to ten times higher than do married people younger than 70. People genuinely need each other."[57] Recent research has shown that pampering and lots of attention do not "spoil" people or encourage them to remain sick. In fact, people who receive lots of visits and attention from family and friends get better faster.

This was further supported in a recent study of heart patients. Those who received the amount of attention they wanted recovered from heart attacks in one month and showed higher self-esteem, less depression, anxiety, confusion, and dependency. Those who didn't get the attention they desired took at least four months to recover and took longer to return to work.[58] Clearly, the support of friends and family is good medicine. This life-saving reality is one we can't afford to forget, whether we're well or ill.

Step 4 is learning how to communicate with those who care for you so that you have greater influence and control over your environment, even when you're quite helpless. This involves communicating your needs clearly and openly and paying attention to the little details that make such a difference when you're sick or in recovery. The idea is to let those around you know what they can do to support you and be very specific and direct about what works and doesn't work for you, without justifying or apologizing for your needs.

Step 5 is learning to use positive visualization techniques such as the one discussed on page 214 in Chapter 7, "Depletion Depression." While their effects are difficult to measure specifically, we do know that visualization reduces depression and seems to trigger healing. In one study men and women volunteers were told to visualize their white blood cells as strong, powerful sharks swimming through their bloodstreams, attacking and destroying the germs that caused colds and the flu. With continued imagery, there was an increase in the effectiveness of the white blood cells among the younger volunteers.[59] Studies also show that placebos are about two-thirds as powerful as the real drugs people think they are taking,[60] reminding us again that the mind ↔ body connection is stronger than previously known. So even if you can't always control your body, you can usually control your mind. Doing so can directly influence your body and help you take another step in recovery.

5. Do a Cost/Benefit Analysis for Your Mind and Body.

Have you ever considered managing your health like you would a business? If some of us applied the same principles we apply to our work to caring for ourselves, we would be much more happy and healthy. Sound management, whether for a business or our bodies, requires attention to detail, a plan, an ability to execute the plan, and follow-through.

If you apply commonly accepted management strategies to your health, you may be surprised at how much easier it will be to justify taking better care of yourself. A cost/benefit analysis, for example, is commonly used in business to determine whether an investment is a sound one. A cost/benefit analysis can also provide an equally valuable understanding of how the positive steps you take toward better health are really making a difference.

A research study reported last year in *Circulation* magazine[61] showed that certain lifestyle and attitude changes can add years to women's lives. Among the reported findings from this and other related studies:

COST/BENEFIT ANALYSIS FOR YOUR MIND ↔ BODY

COST: Effort to lower blood pressure.
BENEFIT: Adds five months to your life.[62]

COST: Effort to lower cholesterol.
BENEFIT: Adds ten months.[63]

COST: Stop smoking.
BENEFIT: Adds four years.[64] One year after stopping, the risk of lung and heart disease is reduced by 50 percent; in ten years, the risk from smoking virtually disappears.[65]

COST: Exercise four to five times a week.

BENEFIT: Lose weight three times faster than those who exercise three times a week; also adds three to four years.[66]

COST: Lose weight; watch your diet.

BENEFIT: Adds two to three years.[67]

COST: Take 300 milligrams a day of vitamin C.

BENEFIT: Adds at least one year.[68]

COST: Reduce heavy drinking.

BENEFIT: Adds four years.[69]

COST: Stop being angry and cynical.

BENEFIT: Calm, trusting people are five times less likely to die by age 50. Hostile, competitive, time-urgent people are typically predisposed to coronary heart disease.[70]

COST: Stop being pessimistic.

BENEFIT: Feel less distress during medical ordeals; get well sooner; less depression and illness throughout life; higher quality of life.[71]

COST: Invest energy and effort in personal growth to elevate your sense of self-esteem.

BENEFIT: High self-esteem is one of the major foundations of good relationships and good health. The lower your self-esteem, the higher your stress hormones and the more likely you are to turn to "quick fix" foods high in salt and sugar content.[72]

COST: Take the time and energy to build and maintain intimate relationships and love and care for yourself.

BENEFIT: There is no greater healer of Mind ↔ Body Depressions.

If you make a conscious effort to take better care of yourself and combine these simple health recommendations, you can add seventeen and a half years to your life![73] It's a priceless gift we can all give ourselves if we're willing to make some basic behavior changes, assume greater responsibility for the quality of our lives, and work to heal our Mind ↔ Body Depressions.

As we've discovered, our minds and bodies are intricately and exquisitely interrelated. We have much more control in preventing both illness and depression than most of us have ever realized. Apply what you've learned in this chapter every day. Next time you indulge in negative or victim thinking, remember that you are increasing your vulnerability to mental and physical illness. And when you are ill, remember that how you deal with your depression directly affects your recovery. By staying aware, informed, and conscious of your mind ↔ body connection, you have much greater power to stay mentally and physically healthy.

PART III

· · · · · · · · ·

Putting It
All Together

·10·

BEYOND SELF-HELP

As a psychologist who's been dealing with both Healthy and Unhealthy Depression for many years, I've often seen how fine the line can be between the two. If you suspect that you or someone you love is vulnerable to Unhealthy Depression, then the information in this chapter is of critical importance to you. If vulnerability to Unhealthy Depression isn't an issue, then skip this chapter and move on to the next one, "Putting It All Together."

It's easier than you might think to migrate from Healthy Depression to various forms of Unhealthy Depression. Among common situations where this tends to happen:

1. When Healthy Depression is an appropriate reaction but a person continues to deny his or her bad feelings.
2. When a person has a Healthy Depression and too much physical and/or emotional stress to cope with it.
3. When a person has a Healthy Depression and too much unresolved pain from his or her past.
4. When a person has a Healthy Depression and is stuck in a pattern of negative thinking.
5. When a person has a Healthy Depression and few or no good relationships.
6. When a person has a Healthy Depression and a significant vulnerability to Inherited Depression.

The more often you experience these conditions and move into Unhealthy Depression, the more likely you are to remain stuck there. When that happens, you've gone beyond self-help. If your depression recurs and self-help techniques such as the ones found in this book don't seem to be helping, it's likely you've moved from a Healthy Depression into an Unhealthy Depression. Or it may be that you have been struggling with an Unhealthy Depression all along and just didn't know what to call it. In any case, self-help techniques are not enough. Professional treatment is essential. Left untreated, Unhealthy Depression can be life-threatening because it kills your joy and energy for living, makes you more vulnerable to serious disease, and can even lead to suicide.

This is a tragic and unnecessary loss. In 1990, the American Psychological Association National Task Force on Women and Depression concluded that in 80 to 90 percent of all cases, symptoms of Unhealthy Depression can be significantly reduced in twelve to fourteen weeks.[1] Unfortunately, however, only one out of five people with Unhealthy Depression pursues help.[2] The rest continue to suffer silently and needlessly, too afraid or uninformed or hopeless to reach out for help that is more available and affordable today than ever before.

Just as with Healthy Depression, the first step in overcoming Unhealthy Depression is realizing there's a problem that won't go away. It's also essential to understand that *it's not your fault*. Unhealthy Depression is not a weakness. It's a progressive illness, a vulnerability that is often passed down in families. Some clients call it a "mood cancer." Cultural, family, and psychological stresses typically trigger this biological vulnerability to depression. The result is an Unhealthy Depression that must be treated psychologically, biologically, socially, and by addressing family dynamics.

The second step in breaking free from Unhealthy Depression is to see a psychologist or psychiatrist who is a depression specialist for an in-depth evaluation. If it is Unhealthy Depression, what kind, and how severe is it? What approach would be most effective to resolve it? Unfortunately, this type of evaluation is easier said than done. Not only are such specialists difficult to locate, but depression is a complex, multifaceted disorder that is too often overlooked or misdiagnosed.

Types of Unhealthy Depression

We have seen that depression diagnosis and treatment is an evolving specialty area. Therefore, it's quite valuable for you to have a basic understanding of the various kinds of Unhealthy Depression and the treatment options available. The more you know and understand, the more you can help the therapist and physician by being an informed partner in your own treatment.

There are five major kinds of Unhealthy Depression: dysthymic depression, atypical depression, major depression, bipolar disorder (also called manic depression), and seasonal affective disorder.

1. Dysthymic Depression

Dysthymic depression used to be called "neurotic depression." It's the kind of Unhealthy Depression most women suffer, and it's more than twice as common in women than in men. Some therapists believe the actual numbers are much greater and maintain that this particular depression is perhaps four to five times more common among women. Dysthymic depression is often experienced as a sense of helplessness about getting what one needs, feeling deprived and sometimes hopeless about the past, present, and future, and feeling sadness and/or anger over real or imagined loss and disappointment. Dysthymic depression can also result from the dysfunctional ways we've learned to interact with other people and think about ourselves. It can also stem from living in an unhealthy culture and constantly blaming ourselves for our culturally defined inadequacies.

With dysthymic depression, bad feelings fluctuate. After weeks of sleeping soundly, a woman may find herself unable to sleep for days at a time. She may also find herself eating too little or too much for more than a few days. Although basically able to function, she feels consistently bad either about herself or those around her. Of all the Unhealthy Depressions, it is easiest to move from Healthy Depression into dysthymic depression.

Healthy Depression fundamentally differs from dysthymic depression, however, because Healthy Depression is based on realistic losses and pain that would make anyone feel depressed. Dysthymic depression is based on a subjective misinterpretation of pain and loss either by exaggerating or denying it, reacting as if losses from the past are still happening now, feeling more hopeless, helpless, and pessimistic than is necessary or appropriate, and having our feelings interfere with our functioning more than necessary.

2. Atypical Depression

Atypical depressions are often disguised as dysfunctional behaviors or other disorders, such as bulimia, anorexia nervosa, compulsive overeating, oversleeping, irritability, impulsivity, and addictions. Some of these symptoms can also occur for major depressions, but with atypical depressions the symptoms don't last as long and aren't as strong. A woman with an atypical depression may report that her physical symptoms, phobias, and hysterical reactions are more disturbing than her depressed feelings. Yet it's her unacknowledged depression that is actually causing or magnifying those symptoms.

No one is certain why many of the symptoms of atypical depression are often opposite to the symptoms typically associated with depression, nor are we sure why atypical depression is more common among women than men. What we do know is that if a woman suddenly finds herself craving too much sleep (hypersomnia), experiencing greatly increased appetite (hyperphagia) or increased sexual drive over a period of two weeks or more, or is developing an addiction, she may have an atypical depression that is likely to worsen without professional help.

3. Major Depression

Major depression is diagnosed when a person experiences an inability to function in one or more major areas of his or her life for more than two weeks. It is often signaled by a person feeling suicidal. Major depression is also more common among women than men, although here the gender differences are not nearly as significant, probably because this is the depression most related to biological and genetic causes.

If a woman is consistently sleeping and/or eating too little or too much for weeks at a time, is having difficulty maintaining or coping with relationships, or finds herself unable to get or keep a job, she is a prime candidate for the diagnosis of major depression.

The major difference between dysthymic depression and major depression is that major depression can be so intense and severe that a person is incapacitated and unable to function. With dysthymic depression, the person can continue to function, although not as well as if she were healthy. What makes major depression so difficult to identify and treat is the fact that it's a recurrent, progressive illness. Like a spontaneous remission in cancer, it can resolve itself—but without treatment, it usually comes back more quickly and with more intensity the next time.

As we saw in Chapter 2, on Inherited Depression, a woman often has a genetic vulnerability to major depression if her close relatives were depressed.[3] Biochemical changes in the brain either cause this depression and/or occur as a result of it. That's why people with major depression usually need medication to help balance their brain chemistry so they can fully utilize therapy to heal.

4. Bipolar Disorder (Also Called Manic Depression)

Manic depression is a disorder in which periods of deep depression alternate with periods of elation and hyperactivity. In the manic phase, those affected feel grandiose and invincible, as though they can conquer the world. They thrive with very little sleep, concoct unrealistic plans for their future, spend money they don't have, convince others to join them in wild business ventures, sometimes become promiscuous, and eat and drink to an excess that most of us can only imagine (and perhaps envy). The adrenaline rush of a manic phase leaves those who experience it feeling that life is terrific, people are wonderful, and no challenge is too great.

But after days or even weeks of feeling on top of the world comes the crash: a debilitating depression that leaves them feeling fatigued, defeated, and doomed. The intense high energy they enjoyed is now eclipsed by a total lack of desire. Their vivid, bright world is suddenly black and bleak.

The rates of manic depression are about the same in women and men. Some evidence suggests creative women and those in leadership positions may have a higher incidence of manic depression than the general female population.[4] Mania may actually help blast through the sexist barriers and fear of success that impede so many women. It may also help generate more creativity and productivity. As long as the mania doesn't become extreme or prolonged, many of these women report that they enjoy being somewhat hyperactive because they get so much done.

Manic depression, like major depression, seems to be the result of a biochemical imbalance in the brain and often requires a combined treatment of medication and therapy. While it's important to recognize one's biological predisposition to manic depression or major depression, it's also vital to understand there are other factors and contributors that trigger its appearance. Just because someone has a genetic or biological vulnerability doesn't automatically mean that depression must follow. In many cases, excessive stress triggers the biological vulnerability.

5. Seasonal Affective Disorder (SAD)

As we saw in Chapter 9 with Sugar, the woman who found herself feeling gloomy and sluggish every winter after moving to Boston, seasonal affective disorder (SAD) can be disruptive. SAD is a cyclical depression. The symptoms usually peak during the fall and winter and usually disappear in the spring and summer, though for a small percentage the opposite pattern can be true. Many people experience a lesser degree of SAD as a case of the "winter blahs," but for those who suffer from the more severe forms, it's far more intense and potentially debilitating.

SAD is one of the most easily treated depressions when diagnosed properly. The problem with seasonal affective disorder is that its symptoms are often misdiagnosed. As a result, the client often ends up in therapy and on medication, when all that's needed is light. Any woman who believes she may be susceptible needs to see a SAD specialist, not a general psychotherapist or psychiatrist, to receive proper diagnosis and treatment. For further information on SAD and how to locate a SAD specialist, write to: Seasonal Studies, National Institutes of Health, Building 10/45-239, 9000 Rockville Pike, Bethesda, MD 20892.

Treatment for Unhealthy Depression

Unhealthy Depression, whether physical, psychological, or a combination of both, is frightening and debilitating, not only for the depressed woman but for those around her. Fortunately, however, treatment technologies have evolved so much in recent years that the great majority of Unhealthy Depressions can be successfully treated. These treatment approaches are more effective, less costly, and require less time to produce results than ever before.

In the pages that follow are brief descriptions of various treatment options and approaches recommended by the APA National Task Force on Women and Depression for the treatment of depressed women. A more in-depth discussion can be found in *Women and Depression: Risk Factors and Treatment Issues,* which summarizes the findings of the Task Force and can be ordered by calling the publications office at APA national headquarters in Washington, D.C., at (202) 336-5500.

Interpersonal Therapy

According to theories in the psychology of women, a woman's sense of self is primarily developed through connection rather than autonomy. Her self-esteem is often heightened or diminished by the quality of her relationships, and depression feeds on relationship failure. Therefore, interpersonal therapy (IPT), which focuses on development and application of relationship skills, would seem a natural treatment choice for many depressed women.

More than any other type of therapy, IPT is based on the health partnership model discussed in the previous chapter. The person seeking help is typically called a "client" instead of a "patient" because she is not regarded as sick or in a dependent position, in need of an "expert" and a "cure." An essential component of IPT is that the therapist helps the client to understand how critical positive relationships are to her well-being, and to assess the quality and quantity of the relationships she currently has. The first several sessions are spent exploring and defining current relationship problems and arriving at goals for treatment.

The client then focuses on developing relationship skills, practicing how she can be more effective in her relationships and developing new ones if that's what she needs. The quality of the relationship with the therapist is critical in this kind of therapy because an important part of the healing occurs as a result of the warmth, support, and validation the client feels from the therapist.

In IPT, the emphasis is on empowering the client in her relationships at home and at work so she can become increasingly independent and able to internalize these skills. The focus is on the "here and now," on the present rather than the past. Homework assignments are mutually developed in a spirit of cooperation between the therapist and client. Outcomes are discussed and strategies are modified until the techniques are effective in helping the client achieve her goals.

There are some problems with IPT. It doesn't work for everyone. It is a short-term behavioral approach, and it is sometimes difficult to know whether clients need longer-term analytic techniques. Until now, it has been used primarily as a research tool so it is difficult to find people teaching and practicing it. But when interpersonal therapy is appropriate—and it often is—it works very well, especially for women. It's the primary focus of the therapy I do, although at various stages of therapy I also use the other techniques discussed in the next few pages. In a major study conducted by the National Institute of Mental Health in 1989 on the treatment of depression, it was found that 57 to 69 percent of clients who completed a sixteen-week course of IPT no longer had their depressive symptoms and were rated more positively by themselves and others.[5] They were more effective at work, in leisure activities, and in interactions with their families.

Cognitive/Behavioral Therapy

Cognitive therapy is based on the assumption that the way people feel is the direct result of the way they think. In other words, if they think negatively, they're going to feel negatively. This therapy defines depression as a distortion in thinking. Many women develop a negative pattern of thinking that automatically causes depressed feelings, and they don't even realize what they're doing to themselves. Negativity becomes a comfortable habit and causes chronic depressed feelings and less effective functioning. One of the best descriptions of this self-destructive process is found in a book called *Learned Optimism*[6] by noted psychologist Dr. Martin Seligman. I would recommend it to anyone who has forgotten or never fully understood why optimistic thinking is so crucial to well-being.

Cognitive therapy helps women and men understand why they think the way they do and how to substitute positive for negative thinking. Negative thinking, or cognitive distortion, falls into clear categories or patterns. An excellent description of these categories can be found in the book *Feeling Good: The New Mood Therapy*, by Dr. David Burns.[7] This book has become a classic in the cognitive therapy field and is one that psychotherapists often recommend to their clients.

Among the more typical distortions cognitive therapists describe are: "personalization," in which one sees himself or herself as the cause of an event they weren't responsible for; "magnification or minimization," in which a person exaggerates the importance of some things and inappropriately diminishes the value of others; and the ever-popular "all-or-nothing thinking," a favorite among women because with this kind of either/or thinking we feel like total failures if we're not totally perfect.

Cognitive therapy trains women to label and understand these typical self-sabotaging distortions and to recognize when they're using them. It is primarily an intellectual rather than an emotional approach. It stresses quality of thinking more than expression of feelings and may appeal more to men on that basis. It's important to understand, however, that despite several shortcomings, cognitive therapy provides vital tools for depressed women. A combination of cognitive therapy and IPT can be a successful recovery strategy for both Healthy and Unhealthy Depression.

Behavioral therapy is similar to cognitive therapy and focuses on changing clients' behavior in addition to changing their thinking patterns. It is based on the idea that the depressed client is not receiving enough positive reinforcement in her life and needs to create more sources of rewards. Therefore, an assessment of the structure of her life and the effectiveness of her functioning skills is conducted. Suggestions and homework in the form of behavioral assignments are then given so that the client can begin to exercise more control over her environment and develop management skills to receive more positive reinforcement. Behavioral therapy is particularly successful in enabling clients to gain control over fears and phobias, as well as for gaining life skills that substantially improve their quality of life.

Interpersonal therapy, behavioral therapy, and cognitive therapy are especially valuable treatments for women with Unhealthy Depression because they emphasize action instead of talk. All encourage the development, through homework and feedback, of practical skills that enable women to function with greater competence and mastery in their relationships and work lives. The client will inevitably feel better about herself because she is more effective and more aware that people are responding more positively to her. She has also learned a new, more positive way of thinking so that she now focuses on what she *has* and what she *can* do, rather than on what she's *lost* and what she *can't* do.

Feminist Therapy

Feminist therapy isn't about politics or rhetoric. It's based on the fundamental belief and acknowledgment that women and men can't fully understand their sources of depression until they appreciate how our society and culture directly contribute to that depression. Each woman has a lifetime of subjective experiences that have helped create or contribute to her depressed feelings. But women also have a collective vulnerability to depression, which results simply from living in a culture in which sexism, discrimination, and violence against women are allowed and sometimes even encouraged.

Feminist approaches in therapy don't encourage blame—that just feeds Victimization Depression—but rather emphasize recognition and acknowledgment of cultural influences on individual experience. Some of women's vulnerabilities to various kinds of Healthy Depressions, such as Depletion Depression and Victimization Depression, clearly come from being cast as second-class members of a society that devalues women. Without understanding this, it's very easy for a woman to assume full responsibility for her depression when other contributing factors need to be acknowledged.

The other key component of feminist therapy is that the client develops a relationship with the therapist in which empowerment and equality are nurtured as much as possible. Rather than promote dependence, feminist therapy encourages women to utilize their own power, to value who they are, and to become as active as possible in the therapy process. Both feminist and interpersonal therapy strengthen the woman with the feeling that she's not alone in the growth process because the therapist is with her for support and serves as a guide when requested.

Group Psychotherapy and Self-help Groups

The longer I teach psychotherapy and continue in private practice, the more strongly I believe in the value of group experiences and group therapy for depressed clients, especially women. Groups can be highly effective for both Healthy and Unhealthy Depression. In fact, with Unhealthy Depression there comes a point where group therapy can become a critical component of the healing process, assuming the therapist running the group is experienced and knowledgeable in depression treatment.

One of the reasons groups work so effectively for most kinds of depression is that many of the special needs of depressed women can be met in a group setting. Women with Unhealthy Depression vitally need to feel a sense of connection, because the depression has often drained their energy and isolated them from others. Groups make it easier for women to explore the sources of their depressed feelings by identifying cultural punishers and the impact of our Traditional Core on our feelings and behavior. Women can formulate and support more effective action strategies together. They can also practice building and maintaining healthy relationships and benefit enormously from the instant relationship feedback available in a group.

In many ways, a good group becomes an intense social laboratory for relationships. It's a safe haven where women can risk new behaviors they may not be ready to try in the outside world. They are encouraged to explore and discover new strengths while challenging old ways of thinking. Groups provide an opportunity to discuss the health and potential of current relationships, learn how to share and effectively help others, and to develop and nurture communication skills that are valuable in every facet of life.

In my private practice, I often encourage clients to use the group as an extension of individual therapy after we have had a number of individual sessions. In time, however, some clients have found that they can cut back individual therapy to an occasional visit and still continue to heal their Unhealthy Depression through the group.

Self-help groups, such as Alcoholics Anonymous, Overeaters Anonymous, Adult Children of Alcoholics, and Gamblers Anonymous, are not designed to do therapy but can provide valuable support for depressed women. In the past ten years, the popularity and availability of such groups have increased, as more people begin to appreciate the value of sharing their pain and feelings with others who understand what they're going through.

Self-help groups based on twelve-step programs can be very helpful to those with Unhealthy Depression because many women are depressed in part because of unresolved addictions. If their addictions are getting in the way of their recovery from depression, a self-help group enables them to go into "recovery" and begin resolving it. Twelve-step approaches can also be more effective in working directly with the addictions than many forms of psychotherapy. They provide an immediate opportunity to connect with others and create healthier relationships. As John Bradshaw observes in his book *Healing the Shame That Binds You:* "In the beginning, just to be feeling our emotions is shame-reducing. Sharing emotions with another is to be vulnerable. It is to externalize and come out of hiding. . . . Only in the life of dialogue and community can we truly live and grow."[8]

Self-help groups can be an excellent introduction to the group process, especially for those who are resistant to any kind of therapy. They teach participants that they are not responsible for their disease but are responsible for corrective behaviors. This can be very helpful in empowering depressed women. The groups are also more supportive than intervention oriented, so many women experience them as less intrusive or demanding. The fact that these groups are free is also important, because many women who need support are economically distressed.

As with group therapy, self-help groups do have their limitations. While they provide an excellent opportunity to express and share feelings, they rarely if ever provide feedback about what to do with the feelings and how to work through the problem. Many women need more individualized information and the structure and support of individual and/or group therapy to guide them toward new levels of growth. Regardless how effective a self-help group may be in working with addictions or other problems, it alone can't provide the support and techniques needed to resolve depression. Women suffering from Unhealthy Depression need a professional evaluation, individual therapy possibly followed by group therapy, and perhaps medication.

Medications for Unhealthy Depression

There are more than thirty different kinds of antidepressant drugs prescribed in this country today. At least 150 others are in development.[9] Americans spend a staggering $700 million a year on antidepressant medication; the use of mind-altering prescription drugs such as Prozac and Xanax is increasing at an alarming rate. According to market analyses conducted by Shearson Lehman Hutton, by 1995 the use of antidepressants in America will nearly triple, making the companies that produce them some of the strongest growth stocks in the pharmaceutical industry.[10]

Is this good or bad news for women? It depends. The good news is that these medications can be very helpful as part of the treatment for Unhealthy Depression. As more money is poured into research and development, these medications will continue to be refined and will ultimately become more effective. The more compelling bad news, however, is that the pressure to prescribe and use these drugs in order to justify their existence and contribute to corporate coffers will continue to intensify for depressed women. Women are—and will continue to be—the group most vulnerable to economic exploitation and physical risk as a result of overprescribed or inaccurately prescribed antidepressants.

Women are currently given far more prescriptions for antidepressants than men. In 1984, 64 percent of the 131 million prescriptions for antidepressants and 72 percent of the prescriptions for tranquilizers were given to women.[11] This disproportionate percentage is alarming enough, but what's truly frightening is the fact that 70 percent of these prescriptions are written by physicians with no specific training in the diagnosis or treatment of depression. Considering this fact, it's not surprising to find that 30 percent to 50 percent of depressions are misdiagnosed.[12] This underscores the very real possibility that perhaps up to half the time, a woman may receive the wrong medication for a misdiagnosed disorder if she works with a professional who isn't a specialist in the diagnosis and treatment of depression.

The biggest problem with most mind-altering medications is that many times they're prescribed without psychotherapy and without proper monitoring for side effects. Unfortunately, doctors sometimes take what seems like a quick and practical solution to stop complaints about vague physical symptoms and "blue moods." They write a prescription and then walk the patient to the door. Even though the patient is bound to return when the medication doesn't work, many physicians feel this approach is better than doing nothing. This "revolving door" approach to depression is also far more profitable.

If medication is to be used in the treatment of depression, it must be done in conjunction with therapy in order to have optimal results. Without therapy, the client is likely to use the medication improperly or to stop using it, which ultimately makes her more vulnerable to feelings of despair and hopelessness. In one study, 67 percent of the patients dropped out of treatment too early to resolve their depression when they took medication but did not undergo therapy.[13]

Another reason a depression specialist is so important is that women need health professionals who are aware of and sensitive to gender differences in depression diagnosis and treatment. A number of studies indicate that women suffer more adverse side effects from medication than men. Older women and women who are overweight are more vulnerable to adverse side effects than comparable men because the extra fat changes how female bodies metabolize antidepressants. While definitive research hasn't been conducted, some research also suggests that dosages may need to be tailored to a woman's menstrual cycle and hormonal fluctuations in order to be most effective. For example, lithium, a natural mineral used quite successfully in treating manic depression, has been found to be more effective at certain times during a woman's menstrual cycle.[14]

As we've seen, drugs can sometimes create more problems than they solve. That's why it's imperative that the client, therapist, and psychiatrist work together carefully to match particular drugs and dosages with the client's changing needs. A depressed client will probably need both a psychotherapist and psychiatrist. Depression treatment has become so specialized that, in many cases, specialists are experts in one area but may not be particularly well versed in other aspects of treatment.

Finding a "good" psychiatrist or psychologist isn't easy, however. It requires time and effort. The guidelines for seeking physicians found on pages 268–271 apply equally well to finding therapists. Referral sources can also be found by calling state psychological associations. The number of your state psychological association can be found by calling the practice directorate of the American Psychological Association at (800) 233-1834.

Once a woman finds a professional she likes and can trust, a victimization history of physical, sexual, and emotional abuse since early childhood should be taken, as well as an extensive drug utilization history that lists all prescription and nonprescription drugs she has taken since adolescence. This often-overlooked drug history is an intrinsic part of developing an effective medication and therapy plan. It's to her advantage not to hide any medical or drug information from those who have been asked to help. Surprisingly, many clients do just that, either because they're embarrassed by their past behavior or they don't think the information is relevant.

While antidepressants are certainly not always the answer to feeling bad, they're essential for those who are suicidal or significantly impaired either psychologically or organically by depression. Antidepressants or other prescription drugs are sometimes the only answer to the biochemical imbalance of certain disorders. They are needed to replenish the chemicals depleted by the depression so that a person can function and begin using therapy to work through the issues that plunged her into the depression in the first place.

Prozac (fluoxetine), for example, has proven to be a generally helpful drug and has become the current antidepressant of choice because it has the fewest side effects. But Prozac has also proven to be a major problem for a small minority of clients, escalating aggressive, agitated, or suicidal feelings to dangerous levels.[15]

Prozac is a prime example of the promise and problems with all such medications. They all have side effects. Most of them are manageable, but for a few the side effects can be dangerous or even deadly. And for nearly one-third of depressed people, these medications don't even work.[16] You can see why these treatment approaches must be carefully monitored by both the psychiatrist and the psychologist and how important it is that they work well together.

Sometimes psychologists, social workers, nurses, and ministers resist or even refuse to refer clients for medical intervention because it might result in successful treatment and reinforce the clients' notion that the solution to their problems can be found in a pill. Female therapists often resent the attempts at intimidation or the condescension they must endure working with some male psychiatrists. Some therapists also fear that referring a patient to a psychiatrist for medication is an admission that medication succeeds where psychotherapy fails. The answer often lies somewhere in the middle, with success dependent on several approaches and professionals at the same time.

In my own practice, I use individual therapy first, unless there are signs of major depression that has made the person either vegetative or suicidal. If there are no significant results in three to four months with individual therapy, I encourage clients to carefully consider medication, and I refer them to a consulting psychiatrist who specializes in the use of antidepressant medication and is knowledgeable about women's issues. This way, the client gains from the expertise and perspective of two professionals, one trained in the medical model and one using a psychological model of mental health and illness. It's a win/win situation. If I've overlooked something, often the other professional will spot it, and vice versa. Between us, we can more thoroughly respond to the mind ↔ body intricacies woven throughout every serious depression.

Medication isn't the panacea many wish it were. But it's essential for the treatment of some types of Unhealthy Depression. The key to successful treatment is for everyone in the partnership—the client, the therapist, the psychiatrist, and any other physicians involved—to communicate so that everyone remains informed and medication is neither under- or overprescribed. By paying attention to these issues, a woman will be much more able to find her way through the maze that occurs "beyond self-help" and emerge with her depression resolved or at least under control.

The main thing to remember is this: If you continue feeling bad, value yourself enough to get help. Depression treatment works for most people most of the time. If you find that the strategies, solutions, and exercises included in this book have only partially helped and you continue battling feelings of depression, don't give in or give up. If one approach or one professional doesn't work, keep searching until you find the right combination. Your challenge is to find the right specialists, ask the right questions, and be prepared to invest time and energy in becoming healthier and happier. You don't have to live with an Unhealthy Depression—and you certainly don't have to die from one.

·11·

PUTTING IT ALL TOGETHER: ACTION STRATEGIES FOR RESOLVING THE HEALTHY DEPRESSIONS

As we've seen from the action strategies described in the previous chapters, the most successful techniques for converting pain into gain and overcoming depression combine two key elements:

- exploring and expressing our deepest feelings and vulnerabilities;
- moving into action to confront and resolve our problems.

Our clinical experience and numerous research studies have found that if either of these two elements is missing, resolution of depression and pain is likely to be incomplete or temporary.[1]

While many women are willing to express and explore their bad feelings, that's often as far as they get. Their problems remain unsolved, and they spend their energy focusing on the bad feelings instead of strategies for action. Impressive research conducted by Dr. Susan Nolen-Hoeksema of Stanford University has found that when depressed, women are inclined to "ruminate"—ponder, over-analyze, and obsess about their bad feelings—far more than men. Since depression can be highly contagious, particularly to other women, many women unwittingly find themselves becoming depressive partners, feeling as bad about the problems and pain of a friend or family member as they do about their own.[2]

An alternative is to take action either before or after exploring the feelings. If you're not too depressed, explore your feelings first in order to gain a better perspective on which action is most appropriate. If you are too depressed and are having difficulty coping, distraction and activity may be more helpful to replenish energy that your depression has drained. Men have been using this strategy for centuries. When depressed, men typically distract themselves through activity such as work, sports, hobbies, gardening, cooking, or other physical exertion. It is helpful for women to do likewise because activity generates energy. Charged with more energy, we are in a better position to explore our feelings without becoming overwhelmed by them. Whatever action you choose to take, you must also make time to explore and experience your feelings. This is a step that men are traditionally trained to avoid. Bad feelings are among our best teachers. When we learn from their meaning, we are less likely to repeat whatever caused them.

The following action strategies combine years of clinical experience with the most promising research in the field of women and depression. They're the most successful strategies to empower women to convert Healthy Depression of any kind into new sources of power and growth.

Action Strategies for Resolving the Healthy Depressions

1. Use Arts and Letters Therapy: Therapy Without the Therapist.

Creative action is what arts and letters therapy is all about. Writing about or drawing our feelings gives us an opportunity not only to creatively identify and communicate what we're feeling, but also helps us view our lives more objectively, with our defense mechanisms less likely to undermine our efforts.

When our feelings have been expressed on paper through words or drawings, they become real and are much more difficult to ignore or avoid. We see them more clearly and therefore have more control over what to do with them. Elusive memories, emotions, and answers inevitably emerge if we just think or talk about them. Let's look at some examples:

Rachele, a media buyer for a small advertising agency, learned to take a five-minute break and draw her feelings when she felt Depletion Depression. One afternoon, she drew two quick sketches: one depicted the anger she felt toward a coworker whose inability to manage her time caused Rachele to have to work late two nights in a row, and the other illustrated how much she missed her children. The drawings helped Rachele identify what she was feeling toward whom, and allowed her to clear her head so that she felt less burdened and victimized.

Amanda, a high-school teacher, learned to use arts and letters therapy as a problem-solving technique. Overwhelmed by multiple demands at school and at home, she took her lunch break and wrote a letter to herself about all the pressures. A quick drawing expressing her stress helped; then she rapidly listed all the possible solutions to the challenges she faced. Amanda finds that her destructive feelings diminish and solutions for problem-solving emerge when she brainstorms and draws on paper rather than simply brooding or complaining to her girlfriends about her problems.

Christy, a purchasing agent for an auto dealership, often woke up in the middle of the night rocked by intense anxiety dreams as she tried to decide whether to end an increasingly unhappy relationship with her boyfriend. She used to forget the dreams by morning, but now she keeps colored markers and paper next to her bed and draws vivid images from her dreams as soon as she wakes up. Then she writes a description of the dream. Christy has learned that her dreams serve as enlightening maps to her subconscious and provide information she could not otherwise know about what she is feeling deep inside. Drawing and writing her feelings helped her decide what to do about the relationship because she understood her feelings better.

With arts and letters therapy, we often gain a much clearer sense of how to resolve our problems or improve our situation. Rather than be overwhelmed by outside events or other people's needs, we stay focused on what our issues, needs, and concerns really are. Learning to integrate arts and letters therapy into your life can save you pain, depression, and therapy expenses, because it is one of our most effective forms of self-therapy.

To give this technique a chance to work for you, you must first resolve any negativity and resistance you may initially feel at the thought of writing or drawing your feelings. Many of us experience the "I Can't Draw" and/or "I Hate to Write" syndromes. Our performance anxiety and resistance is typically rooted in a sense of inadequacy. Most women have been trained to be quite self-critical, especially when it comes to creative endeavors. The need to do it "right" or "perfectly" often gets in the way of doing anything at all.

Many women are also uncomfortable with the notion of dealing with their pain or anger so directly and visibly. Sometimes the fear of the unknown has become a self-imposed barrier; sometimes the discomfort of the Traditional Core makes us withdraw from asserting ourselves emotionally. To break these barriers, commit to being less judgmental and more accepting of yourself so you can begin expressing yourself in more direct, productive ways.

Remember that you're not trying to create great art or write a masterpiece. Your drawings can be stick figures and scribbles; your writing may be grammatically incorrect and riddled with misspelled words. It doesn't matter. What does matter is that it represents how you really feel.

You'll need a large three-ring binder and a supply of unlined, 8½-by-11-inch white paper in which you have punched three holes. Some women find that a zippered three-ring binder that also serves as an appointment book and organizer is more efficient. In one unit, you can carry everything you need for work and for your exercises in self-development and depression management.

Also invest in a set of colored felt-tipped pens. Color is preferable over pencil or pen because colors are more evocative and expressive of emotion. Put the markers in a plastic zippered pencil case that fits through the three rings behind your paper, and you now have a portable kit that you can carry with you anywhere. This will become your Depression Prevention Kit, which includes your feelings journal and any other relevant material from the action strategies in this book.

Carry the kit wherever you go as tangible evidence of your commitment to explore your feelings and resolve your depressions. Rather than carry the actual binder, some women find it more convenient to keep several blank pages and the colored pens in their purse, briefcase, or backpack, and insert their letters or drawings into their binder later.

Before you begin arts and letters therapy, it's important that you remember five key points:

1. It's usually faster and more personal to write or draw by hand than to use a typewriter or computer. You can move back and forth more quickly between writing and drawing.
2. Keep everything you write or draw safely hidden or in a locked drawer whenever you're not using it. To feel uninhibited, and for your feelings to flow freely, be sure that no one will see your work unless you choose to show it to them.
3. If you do want to share your writing or drawing with someone, it's usually a good idea to wait at least several hours. You need time to study and reflect on what you've drawn or written. Sharing it too soon may abort the birth of valuable ideas or feelings. Make sure you share your work only with those you trust to respect your vulnerability and not criticize or judge you.
4. If you've produced something that communicates anger, resist the temptation to send it to the person at whom the anger is directed. After writing a bitterly angry letter to a parent or ex-husband, for example, some women want to drop it in the mail immediately. Don't do it! Such confrontational correspondence typically stirs counteraggression and even more hostility. Instead, use your writing or drawing as a way to understand and express your own feelings. When you are more objective, in control, and can express how you feel assertively rather than aggressively, you can determine whether rewriting and mailing that letter or communicating more directly would be productive or simply a waste of your time and energy.
5. Review your work periodically so that you appreciate the progress you've made and are empowered to make more, perhaps deeper, discoveries. Reviewing journal entries on your birthday, at the beginning of every new year, or on the anniversary of your marriage or a parent's death provides an opportunity to learn new insights from old drawings and letters.

With these guidelines in mind, resolve to do arts and letters therapy for at least one month. By that time, it's likely you'll find the process so valuable that it will become a habit that you'll use often in your life, especially during times of stress, confusion, and depression.

In our art and letters therapy workshops, we start with writing in a Feelings Journal, because most women find it less intimidating than drawing. Poet Adrienne Rich describes the value of writing about our inner experience in her poem "Diving into the Wreck" from the book of the same name:

> *I came to explore the wreck.*
> *The words are purposes,*
> *The words are maps.*
> *I came to see the damage that was done*
> *And the treasures that prevailed.*[3]

To explore your depression "damage" and discover your own unique "treasures," make a point of writing down your feelings *as you experience them.* If you are feeling victimized in a relationship, instead of becoming depressed, write down how you feel about the other person and what you are going to do to improve your situation. If you face Depletion Depression from too many choices, write out the gains and losses for each choice to clarify which choices will really meet your needs. Quickly jot down words that describe how you feel, whether those feelings are positive or negative. Don't analyze your emotions or edit your entries. Simply get them down on paper. Your entries can be a few words or sentences, but they will seldom expand into many paragraphs because too many words often get in the way of genuinely expressing deep feelings.

With each entry, briefly note the time, place, and situation when you experienced the feelings. This factual information is valuable because, over time, it reveals the patterns and context of feelings and the times and days you may be more vulnerable to certain kinds of bad feelings.

Some of your feelings may be associated with a time when you were unable to speak or when your experience was too traumatic for words. If that's the case—or if you just can't think of what to write—draw instead. A quick sketch or even a scribble can unlock your feelings and help you break through your defenses. Says Alice, the pediatrician with Depletion Depression, "Words can get in my way because they support my denial. I often feel stuck. But art is heart. Drawing gets me out of my head, and I need that."

Alice didn't realize how much words blocked her feelings until she worked in her feelings journal. In one of her first entries, done one evening after a particularly exhausting day, she instinctively made the transition from words to drawing:

> February 10, 1992 (12:45 A.M.—in bed—Paul and kids asleep)
> Have begun this journal—probably a stupid idea because it will just take time I don't have—anyway I know what my problems are I just have to find the time to solve them—oh yuk, tired, tired, tired—Paul's no help—drains . . . crummy, lousy, shitty, pissed . . .

Alice then made a scribble representing her tired body with a sad face to show how depressing her exhaustion was. The drawing was simple and primitive, but after several more similar entries, Alice actually felt better as she switched off the light to go to sleep.

Arts and letters therapy is an action strategy that mobilizes energy no matter how lifeless we feel. At first, the difference may be slight, but even a little change is an important step toward creating more positive energy and reducing depression. At first your depression may look like Alice's first drawing—a sad face or a red scribble across the paper. But you'll find that the images come more easily once you start just as they did for her. You're beginning to give your depression an identity. As it becomes more visible to you, you gain more control over it. Alice's drawings progressed until she finally realized the true character of her Depletion Depression: although she kept moving and performing, every step felt like she was slogging through mud because she was so chronically fatigued (Fig. 1).

Since visualizing her Healthy Depression had proved so helpful, and realizing how vulnerable she had become to Unhealthy Depression, Alice decided to give the latter an identity, too. Her drawing frightened her. Her Unhealthy Depression weighed her down with stone boots that restricted and immobilized her (Fig. 2). She hated feeling helpless more than anything, so she renewed her commitment to slow down and recharge whenever she began feeling depleted. The thought of her Depletion Depression moving into

Fig. 1
Alice's Healthy Depression:
Slogging through the mud of Depletion Depression.

Fig. 2
Alice's Unhealthy Depression:
The stone boots weighing her down.

Fig. 3
Gail's Healthy Depression: Reaching for support
to avoid the pit of depression caused by her cancer.

Fig. 4
Joyce's Body Image Depression:
Feeling strangled by her eating disorder necklace.

Fig. 5
Maria's Anger Art: Feeding her ex-husband into the tree shredder.

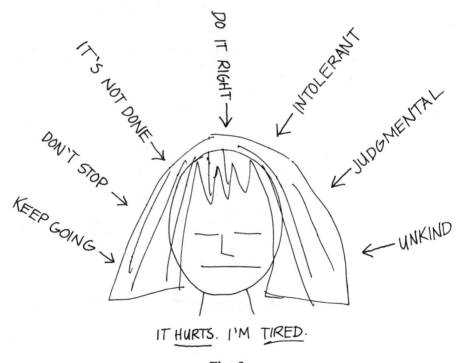

Fig. 6
Dana's Negative Traditional Core: Feeling victimized
and overwhelmed.

Fig. 7
Jack's Role Overload: Controlling too many role demands.

Fig. 8
Maria's Success: Conquering depression
and giving birth to a new self.

Unhealthy Depression became a great motivator to help her set boundaries and frequently say no for the first time in her life.

Arts and letters therapy is particularly helpful in resolving Mind ↔ Body Depressions, since they are often difficult to identify. Gail, the cancer patient, visualized her Healthy Depression as a cry for help. She drew herself as a stick figure perilously close to the edge of a sheer cliff (Fig. 3), calling out to her sister and friends from her support group for help before she plunged over the cliff into the Unhealthy Depression triggered by her cancer.

Joyce, the bulimic college student, drew her Body Image Depression as the tyranny of being strangled by an eating disorder necklace (Fig. 4). Her food abuse necklace weighed her down nearly as much as Alice's stone boots. Joyce became so appalled to see what she was doing to herself that she vowed to dismantle her necklace piece by piece through learning healthy eating. She also made a commitment to go to an eating disorder clinic for an evaluation if she couldn't stop the bulimic behavior on her own.

Many women find that in doing arts and letters therapy, they're able to express anger in ways they never have before. This kind of "Anger Art" can be a little intimidating at first, because the images you draw may be disturbing or even violent. But remember that any feeling you express symbolically on paper is appropriate and healthy, and this kind of expression is often necessary for healing. Communicating the feeling through behavior that hurts yourself, other people, or property is unhealthy.

Expressing anger safely and symbolically is a difficult skill to learn, especially with our Traditional Core constantly whispering that angry behavior is unfeminine. For this reason, many women are tempted at this point to move on to exercises that are more familiar and less scary.

Janet was one of them. When she discovered her Age Rage Depression, she was afraid if she allowed herself to express her anger toward her mother, her blind rage would be uncontrollable. She had no idea how to represent such huge anger on such a small sheet of paper. At first, she refused to do the exercise in the workshop and just watched. An hour later, however, she reluctantly began an anger drawing by slashing her paper with a red marker.

By the end of the all-day workshop, Janet was using the same marker to draw a bright red giant mushroom cloud to show how explosive and devastating her rage would be if she ever let it out. After tapping into the source of her anger and expressing it over and over again, Janet was finally able to mobilize her rage more constructively by demanding independence from her mother and her son.

As Janet discovered, working with Anger Art can be very liberating. Many clinicians believe that depression is often anger turned inward and used against ourselves. If we can get our anger out, even symbolically, and release it toward the external cause, we will be less depressed. Anger Art is particularly helpful in resolving the three most pervasive Healthy Depressions (Victimization, Relationship, and Age Rage) because it gives us a constructive direction to channel anger typically generated by the Healthy Depressions.

If you're angry now or have unresolved anger from the past, make as many anger drawings as you can about what happened to you and who did it. Let your imagination run wild. Hit, smash, splat, cut, and kill—whatever you need to imagine and express your anger on paper. Don't hold back.

The next step is verbalizing your feelings about the target of your anger, out loud if you can. This will help to release them. Challenge yourself to move beyond feeling silly or self-conscious. Scream and curse if you wish. If you're concerned about being overheard, do it while driving alone, playing loud music, or while showering. When you're finished, rip up the drawings and throw them in the trash, or put the drawings in your notebook as long as you're sure no one will find them.

Maria tried Anger Art after Joe hit her for what proved to be the last time. She finally went to a shelter for battered women. A counselor there encouraged her to draw the punishment she would like to see her husband receive for hitting her. Maria found that her seven years of unexpressed rage erupted in surprisingly violent drawings. In her favorite, Joe is strapped to a conveyer belt, being fed into a tree shredder (Fig. 5). Maria did so well expressing her anger that she decided to enter therapy at a community clinic and do more. After creating many similar drawings, and writing and talking a great deal about how and why she had allowed herself to be a victim, she discovered new sources of self-esteem and was finally ready to begin a new life without Joe.

Maria used arts and letters therapy to help break free from a bad relationship. But as Dana discovered, the same techniques work very well to strengthen relationships. Several months after surprising Jack with an Intimate Power getaway, they were having an especially tense Friday night. They'd both had a very stressful work week, and Dana was determined not to let that stress spill over into their weekend. She suggested that rather than vent their frustration through a fight, they agree to draw to release some of their feelings, and discuss their drawings later that evening.

Dana (Fig. 6) and Jack (Fig. 7) each drew pictures that depicted how overloaded, depleted, and pressured they were feeling. They were both surprised to see the amount of stress in the other's drawing. Neither realized how overloaded the other felt. They became closer as they realized how similar their feelings were, and they also appreciated the typical male and female differences in experiencing stress. As they understood each others' vulnerabilities, the seeds of intimacy that had been planted during their Intimate Power getaway sprouted and grew into stronger relationship roots.

Arts and letters therapy can be equally valuable in helping you close a chapter in your life and acknowledge your joys and successes. On the third anniversary of her separation from Joe, Maria drew a picture (Fig. 8) that illustrated how far she had come. It shows her cracking through her shell, finally able to give birth to her new more powerful, independent self. She was so proud of her accomplishment that she framed her drawing and hung it in her bedroom as a reminder of her success, inner strength, and growing self-esteem.

2. Create Your Own Special "Family of Choice."

We inherit our families, but we choose our friends. And often, those we choose can be more nurturing, understanding, loving, and supportive than our family of origin. If we nourish and deepen these friendships, we can develop a Family of Choice.

A Family of Choice is a core group of people who function like members of a healthy family. They are a source of support and encouragement and are available during times of emotional, physical, and financial crisis. They share our deepest vulnerabilities and provide support instead of criticism. They regularly share what's happening in their lives, even if doing so is only a brief phone call during an especially hectic day. In short, they're people in whom we're willing to invest time and energy, people who are really there for us when we need them, just as members of a healthy family are. We can count on them, and they can count on us.

Even if we're lucky enough to have a happy, healthy family that hasn't been fractured by divorce, distance, or differences, we still stand to gain a great deal from creating a Family of Choice. A Family of Choice is especially important for women in transition, those of us who come from dysfunctional families, or whose families of origin are either no longer living or are geographically inaccessible. In other words, Families of Choice are especially valuable when our families of origin just can't, don't, or won't provide what we need and want in our relationships.

Women derive a great deal of self-esteem through love and connection. A Family of Choice provides both. Staying connected with people we care about (and who care about us) increases our emotional health and decreases our vulnerability to depression. Families of Choice provide multiple sources of support and provide a better source of problem solving, as they draw on a wider range of experiences and potential feedback than just one close friend, partner, or relative could ever provide.

Creating a Family of Choice and choosing appropriate people requires a great deal of experimentation, time, and tolerance for disappointment. The goal is to align with people who are loyal, trustworthy, capable of long-term commitment, and somewhat similar to us in personal growth and maturity. They need to be capable of love and emotional intimacy, and be open about their desire to have more of each in their lives.

As you develop friendships, it's important for you to determine what kind of Family of Choice you want to create. For some women, it's essential that their friends relate, get along, and identify as a group. They invite all of their "family members" together to find out whether they're interested in meeting regularly as an informal support group. You might consider meeting once or twice a month at each other's homes and use the time not only to socialize, but to talk about what is really bothering you.

Some women, on the other hand, don't thrive in groups. They prefer more intimate, individual experiences with extended family members. Their Family of Choice includes people who may not even know each other, but who individually provide all the necessary roles of a supportive, nurturing family.

Families of Choice and the experiences we share with the people who are in them are invigorating and empowering. I've created and maintained two extended families, one in New York and one in California. In fact, my children have two sets of godparents, one from each Family of Choice. One family shares my commitment to psychology, personal growth, and intimate family gatherings. The other family doesn't focus much on internal experience and prefers constant activity, excitement, large gatherings, and making things happen in the world. Both families serve different but equally important needs, and their diversity adds an incomparable richness to my life and the lives of my husband and children.

3. Activate the "Mood Boosters" Whenever You Feel Depressed.

A number of the strategies recommended in this book take time and energy. A few require that you spend a little money. But "Mood Boosters" are free, quick, and easy to do. Here are five proven strategies that can rapidly improve your depressed feelings:

1. Act instead of react to your bad feelings and problems.
2. Erase negative thoughts; substitute optimistic thinking.
3. Connect with someone you love by answering machine, phone, fax, or in person for five minutes or less.
4. Be supportive of others who need help.
5. Make the ten-minute energy walk and other exercise a regular part of your life.

The first four mood boosters have been described elsewhere in the book. The last requires further explanation because it is so important.

Make the Ten-Minute Energy Walk and Other Exercise a Regular Part of Your Life

The connection between regular exercise, reduction of depression, and improved quality of life has been well documented.[4] We know that exercise wards off Victimization Depression, Depletion Depression, Age Rage Depression, Body Image Depression, and Mind ↔ Body Depression. Exercise also minimizes Relationship Depression because we feel better about ourselves and therefore more equipped to be open, honest, and intimate.

However, most women who are vulnerable to depression only exercise sporadically, if at all, because when we're depressed, we often feel like we're wearing Alice's stone boots. Depression weighs us down too much to do the one thing that would immediately help: exercise. It is telling, however, that we still somehow find the energy to drag ourselves over to the refrigerator to find something "good" to eat, or we mobilize enough energy to find a vending machine that sells cigarettes.

Dr. Robert Thayer, a psychologist at California State University, Long Beach, has conducted studies that show that although we do feel better immediately after eating a candy bar, we feel even more tired an hour after eating it. Two hours later, the positive effects are simply a memory and we are still tired.[5]

The same is true with smoking. After a cigarette, smokers experience an immediate reduction of tension. But within an hour or two, there is actually an increase in tension and bad feelings. If we factor in the anxiety and depression caused by feeding our body empty calories or toxic smoke, we find that such choices aren't mood boosters; they are mood busters.

We do have a healthier choice. We can trade the stone boots for walking shoes and take a brisk ten-minute walk. That's all it takes to boost our mood more than any candy bar or cigarette ever could. Consider the following energy effects the next time you choose between energy boosters and energy busters:

Candy or Cigarette	After 1 hour:	more tired;
	After 2 hours:	no positive effect/feel worse.
Ten-Minute Walk	After 1 hour:	more energy/better mood;
	After 2 hours:	still positive effect.

Even knowing the value of something as simple as a ten-minute walk doesn't mean we will do it. Walking feels impossible when our depression is literally weighing us down. Many of my clients and students overcome this obstacle by taking baby steps that make the experience less overwhelming. They begin by copying the comparison chart above and keeping it on their refrigerator or desk as a reminder of their choices. They keep reminding themselves they have a choice in how they behave. Instead of saying "I can't do this, I'm just too depressed," they keep the payoffs in mind and turn the thought around to "I can do this, and it'll be worth it. I only have to take a few steps and then I can stop."

Break down your wall of resistance one step at a time. Begin by making a commitment to yourself to walk, even if only for a few minutes. If you can't walk outside due to bad weather or safety considerations, walk around the corridors of your hotel, office building, or a shopping mall. Walk around your house, apartment, or dorm. Once you get started, you're likely to find that the mood boosters have kicked in and you'll find energy to continue. If not, even the change in movement and focus will help your mood. With practice, you'll be able to use mood boosters more easily and more often because you'll like how they make you feel better.

Many people find that listening to music or motivational tapes on a Walkman makes walking easier and more relaxing. To help our clients at the Psychology Center stay focused and energized as they walk, we've made a series of ten-minute walking tapes that feature meditations and tips on how to maintain a positive mood. Get creative and make your own tapes, too. Include several of your favorite high-energy songs or inspirational messages, and listen to the tape whenever you need a little boost to get you started or keep you going on your ten-minute walk.

After the ten-minute walk has become a healthy habit, consider adding some form of regular exercise to your life if you're not doing it already. Even the busiest people I know find the time when they make exercise a priority.

One of the best ways to get motivated and educated about the value of exercise and healthy eating is to treat yourself to a getaway at a health spa. That's how I finally started exercising regularly after avoiding it most of my adult life. Not only can a spa getaway make a profound difference in how you feel about yourself, it can dramatically change how you treat yourself, both physically and emotionally, when you come home.

A spa experience is more affordable than you might imagine. Many offer special weekend packages. Shift your priorities in order to make it happen. Instead of going on a cruise or a regular vacation, for example, make your health spa retreat your vacation for the year. If you can't afford to go, save until you can by sacrificing other less rewarding activities. Tell those close to you how important such an experience is to you and ask that your holiday and birthday gifts from them be contributions toward a stay at a spa.

In addition, you can treat yourself to a gym membership and an occasional facial, massage, or manicure. Make a commitment to attend classes at your local YWCA or get two or three friends together to work out to an exercise video. It's worth the time and effort because the exercise habit is one of the best protections from depression you can find.

4. Chart Your Healthy Depressions to Better Understand How One Leads into Others.

It's important to remember that Healthy Depressions can occur simultaneously or sequentially; one often leads to the development of another. If enough Healthy Depressions accumulate and remain unresolved, we are guaranteed to suffer an Unhealthy Depression.

We have also learned that understanding and accepting the existence and meaning of our Healthy Depressions can lead to new and unparalleled sources of growth and power. Unfortunately, women have had very few role models to demonstrate how this challenging conversion process occurs. The good news, however, is that more positive female role models are emerging. Their numbers are small, but their ranks are growing.

One woman whose personal victories offer invaluable lessons for us all is feminist leader Gloria Steinem. She is an empowering example of how we can convert Healthy Depressions into impressive personal power. Indeed, she has exercised that power so effectively that she has helped positively change the way our culture regards women. Over three decades, she has motivated and influenced millions of women—and men—through her speeches, writing, activities, and by example, culminating in her recent best-seller, *Revolution from Within.*[6]

In her book, Steinem describes her many early experiences with and exposures to depression. She remembers her mother as being bedridden with "nervous breakdowns" and deep depression for much of Steinem's childhood. Her father, a three-hundred-pound foodaholic who separated from her mother when Steinem was only 10, also seemed to suffer from occasional depressions when his impractical dreams and business deals didn't work out. The emotional and physical losses that Steinem describes are likely to have created a vulnerability to depression even before she entered adolescence. And during adolescence she experienced the body image problems that are even more common among today's young women. She describes herself as "a big, plump, vulnerable girl . . . growing up in an isolated family whose food addictions and body image" she absorbed.

Steinem carried these experiences with her when, as a 34-year-old freelance journalist, she became active in the burgeoning women's movement. Feminism offered her a way to help women deal with the lack of support and internal authority that had broken her mother's spirit. It also freed her own energies from the restrictions and biases she continued to face as a woman. As Steinem put it, "Feminism saved my life."

But deep patterns of childhood and societal behavior don't change overnight. Like so many other women, she continued the deeply ingrained habit of taking better care of others than of herself. Instead of subordinating her needs to a husband and children, she made them second to the needs of a movement. Only after spending nearly twenty years in such all-consuming activism did she begin to sense the signs of inner depletion. As she reached the age of 50, she faced the stresses of aging that a youth-worshipping culture bestows primarily on women (see Chapter 6). Combined with the exhaustion of trying to keep *Ms.* magazine and other fledgling, women-run institutions afloat in increasingly tough economic times, she had paid attention neither to her own writing or to her other inner needs.

She hadn't even had time to create a home, which is such a core symbol of the self. As she wrote, "I had less and less time to replenish lost energy—or even pick up my dry cleaning. Pressure is cumulative."[7] Steinem ended up feeling "a burnout and erosion of self so deep that outcroppings of a scared 16-year-old began to show through"[8] (see Chapter 7).

Into this time of denied depression, burnout, and self-depletion came a wealthy and powerful man whose life and values were virtually polar opposites of Steinem's. He had several homes, a hierarchical view of the world, a very organized life, and difficulty in empathizing with others. He was also unhappy and wanted to change. Thus, he appealed not only to her conventional romantic training in completing herself through another person—which is, of course, impossible—but also to her instinct for rescuing others. When he sent his car to pick her up after a particularly exhausting trip, "it's sheltering presence loomed out of all proportion. . . . Remember the scene in *Bus Stop* when Marilyn Monroe, a desperate singer in a poor café, wraps herself in the warm, rescuing sheepskin jacket of her cowboy lover? Well that was the way I felt sinking into that car."

Because his wealth allowed him to play the role of both husband and wife, this man "made every social decision (via his staff), so all I had to do was show up, look appropriate, listen, relax at dinners, dance, laugh at his wonderfully-told jokes—whatever was on his agenda. I found this very restful."[9] Exhausted and vulnerable, Steinem entered into his world far more than he was able to enter into hers. Slowly, she realized she was losing herself further by betraying her values.

At about the same time, she faced a bout with breast cancer; it was detected early and was easily treatable, but still a signal of mortality and, in her case, of inattention to her body's exhaustion. All these events combined to help her admit to the depression that had been brewing beneath the surface. She set aside her past belief that therapy was for other people, that she helped others but never needed help herself and found a wise, "non-Freudian" woman therapist.

She began the process of inner exploration by following the threads of current patterns backward and beginning to uncover and heal the child who had been called upon to play a caretaking role for her invalid mother, thus doubling her vulnerability to the societal pattern of selfless caretaking to which women are heir. She also began to make a home for herself, to save money, and to make an agenda that included her own work—all the things she had been seeking through a romance with someone who possessed these qualities in exaggerated form.

Because she had committed herself to writing a book on self-esteem even while thinking about it for other people—just as so many of us are attracted to what we need, and only later make the long journey from head to heart—she was able to put her experience of Healthy Depression to the service of others. In so doing, she has shown us that feeling bad can be good, provided that we use our bad feelings as a source of learning, growth, and power.

As long as we live in a male-dominant society that denies women a full self, the depression experiences of Gloria Steinem and many other women will continue to exist. But while we make that deepest of changes, listening to our depressions and converting them into positive experiences can help us to reject the cultural punishers and grow free and strong. To become clearer about the impact of your Healthy Depressions and to better understand how they can lead to others, make a chart of the pathways of your own Healthy Depressions. Copy or photocopy the chart found on page 70 in Chapter 3, "The Traditional Core." As you draw the top box, note that the Traditional Core is part of all of us because it is our cultural heritage. Inherited Depression may or may not be present, depending on our genetic makeup. Inherited Depression is the one depression that can lead to Unhealthy Depression without the impact of cultural influences.

Healthy Depressions, on the other hand, result from our cultural heritage and current cultural experience. Every woman has at least one or more in her lifetime, and often we experience several simultaneously. We can't avoid them. But we do have a choice as to how we cope with them. If we use healthy coping mechanisms such as the action strategies in this book, our depressions stay healthy and manageable and even become a source of growth and power. If we use unhealthy coping strategies such as denial, addictions, blame, and feeling victimized, we move into Unhealthy Depression. An accumulation of too many unresolved Healthy Depressions also leads to Unhealthy Depression, such as the one Steinem described in her book.

The Healthy Depressions Pathways diagram can be extremely valuable in two ways. First, the structure enables you to examine the Healthy and Unhealthy Depressions you have experienced in the past. Second, it helps you understand, perhaps for the first time, how interconnected your depressions are and your current degree of vulnerability. To make best use of this diagram, begin by writing down the circumstances of one of your memorable Healthy Depressions, such as a Body Image Depression from a time you felt especially fat and ugly. Highlight the box for that Healthy Depression in red. Write out a few notes as to when and where it developed. What incidents and feelings contributed to the depression? Did this depression lead to any other depressions? Make red arrows to show the pathways to the other relevant depressions and highlight those boxes. Number them in the sequence in which they occurred. Enlarge the boxes or make them smaller depending on the size of their contribution to your feeling bad.

Now move down to the critical choice point. This is where most of us get into trouble. Rather than choose to use our pain for gain and take an active approach to resolve our depression, we often take what at first seems to be the path of least resistance. We use our pain in vain, and often end up engaging in denial, developing addictions, blaming ourselves and others, and feeling like victims.

When you reach the critical choice crossroads, which path have you chosen? Were you active or passive, realistic or in denial? Did your coping mechanisms lead you to Healthy or Unhealthy Depression? Did a combination of Healthy Depressions lead to an Unhealthy Depression? Draw the arrows along the pathways to show the progression of depression you experience.

The chart can also be valuable in helping you assess your current vulnerability to Healthy Depressions. Start at the top of the chart and work your way down, one box at a time. Rate your depressions on a scale of 1 to 10, with 1 being little or no depression and 10 representing strong depression. Your quiz scores from the earlier chapters can be helpful, but it may be even more useful to assign a number based on how you're feeling today. As you assess your own vulnerability, you will see more clearly how your Healthy Depressions can and do grow and evolve into others.

Now draw red lines between the depressions that you find typically lead into each other. Once you begin to experience one of those depressions, you can be more aware of what it is likely to become if you don't take action. This preventive approach helps you anticipate what is likely to happen, and then neutralize it before the next depression grows significant. Once this awareness becomes second nature, you'll be much more equipped to avoid future depression.

5. Develop and Nurture Creativity as Your Lifetime Companion.

Being creative is an approach to life that empowers us to feel a sense of mastery and control. We assert our dignity—and ourselves—by staying or becoming creative. It applies to any activity in which you express yourself while making something that wasn't there before. You can be creative preparing an exquisite double chocolate cheesecake or taking photographs of animals. You can garden, write a family history, or decorate a space. You can do needlework, paint, or draw.

Creativity promotes an intense relationship with ourselves that is as meaningful and satisfying as any relationship we have with another person. It is self-exploration and self-expression of the deepest kind. Make a commitment that you will develop as much creativity in your life as possible now, and plan on making creativity a primary companion for every age and stage of your life. Develop creative skills by focusing on what gives you pleasure. What activity do you enjoy so thoroughly that you lose track of time, forget to eat, or lose sense of where you are? These "optimal experiences" are called "flow" by psychologist Mihaly Csikszentmihalyi. He describes "flow" as:

> a sense that one's skills are adequate to cope with the challenges at hand, in a goal-directed, rule-bounded action system that provides clear clues as to how well one is performing. Concentration is so intense that there is no attention left over to think about anything irrelevant, or to worry about problems. Self-consciousness disappears, and the sense of time becomes distorted. An activity that produces such experiences is so gratifying that people are willing to do it for its own sake, with little concern for what they will get out of it, even when it is difficult or dangerous.[10]

How can you develop "flow"? You do it by choosing activities that focus attention, provide a challenge and require skill, have clear goals, and have some measurable results or method of feedback. In other words, you need to have a way to evaluate what you've done so that you can work on improving it for even greater self-expression.

You learn the basic skills of creativity through books, classes, workshops, educational TV, and trial and error. You learn by staying active, experimenting, and taking chances. But mostly you learn from simply practicing being creative. Creativity is a necessary survival skill and a powerful ally throughout our lives, especially as we grow older. Dr. George Valliant, a psychiatrist at Dartmouth Medical School, found that among a large sample of bright women over 60, those who continue creative activities actually live longer and have fewer health problems and a higher quality of life than those who don't become or stay creative.[11] It also builds our confidence to know that we can create a solution whenever a problem appears. When we possess this confidence and skill, we're considerably less vulnerable to depression. The bottom line is that creativity has become an essential survival skill for women's future.

After you've tried some or all of these techniques, you'll be stronger and more insulated from depression. Remember to keep practicing and readjusting the techniques as your needs change. It takes a great deal of practice to learn how to trade our depressions for growth and power. But if we remain focused and committed to converting our depressions into personal power, we will replace our current dark age of ignorance and discrimination with a future enlightened age of purpose and promise for both women and men.

EPILOGUE

Women have important work to do as we end this millennium and enter another. We must reject the way our experiences are currently categorized—we either have the "everyday blues" (therefore we are "well") or we are "sick" simply because we are depressed more than an hour or a day. This unhealthy dichotomy must be carefully pulled apart to make room for another experience that more accurately reflects the lives of the majority of women: Healthy Depression.

Bolstered by the knowledge and awareness that our bad feelings are often healthy, we can then claim our right to be depressed when appropriate, let go of our victim thinking, and climb the pyramid of relationship skills from a strong foundation of caring for and about ourselves. We can and must change the current negative definition and experience of female aging, refuse to allow ourselves to become depleted no matter how overwhelming the demands are on our time, reject the culturally imposed standards of female physical perfection, and learn how to appreciate and utilize the exquisite, extensive fine wiring between our minds and our bodies.

We cannot choose to avoid the cultural pain of being female because it is simply too pervasive. But the world *has* changed in the past twenty-five years, and this change has produced a unique window of opportunity that women have never seen before—and may never see again. We must seize this opportunity now. Our emerging creative skills will allow us to craft new solutions to old problems, especially the formidable challenge of overcoming our significant vulnerability to depression.

Imagine how dramatically we could improve our relationships and productivity if nearly half the human race wasn't burdened with some type of depression at various ages and stages of our lives. Think about how much positive energy would be released if we weren't so worried about our wrinkles or imperfect bodies, how our hair and clothes look, and how to please everyone but ourselves. If we learned to avoid Unhealthy Depression and convert our Healthy Depressions, women would finally become free to fully contribute our strength and wisdom to an increasingly vulnerable world.

When we do this, a new and exciting experience is ours: we empower ourselves with the capability to convert our depressions into sources of growth and power that we can now only imagine. Being female will then have a fundamentally different meaning in the twenty-first century than it does today. We will be able to unleash phenomenal energy and creativity that is currently imprisoned and paralyzed by our depressions. Our ability to neutralize or resolve depression and use our bad feelings constructively is a gift that we— and our world—need now more than ever.

NOTES

Introduction
1. E. McGrath et al., *Women and Depression: Risk Factors and Treatment Issues* (Washington, D.C.: American Psychological Association, 1990), p. 26.
2. Ibid., p. xi.
3. R. Eichner, "Energy Crisis," *Runner's World* (December 1990), p. 68.

1. "Healthy Depression": A New Model for Women
1. *New York Times*, 11 December 1991, p. C16.
2. E. McGrath et al., *Women and Depression: Risk Factors and Treatment Issues* (Washington, D.C.: American Psychological Association, 1990), p. ix.
3. M. Seligman, *Learned Optimism* (New York: Alfred A. Knopf, 1991), p. 64.
4. McGrath et al., p. 21.
5. *DSM-III: Diagnostic and Statistical Manual of Mental Disorders*, 3rd ed. (Washington, D. C.: American Psychiatric Association, 1980), p. 183.

2. Inherited Depressions: How Vulnerable Are You?
Gertrude Nemerov's quote cited in Patricia Bosworth, *Diane Arbus: A Biography* (New York: Avon Books, 1985).
1. M. Gold, *The Good News About Depression* (New York: Bantam Books, 1986), pp. 195–203.
2. D. F. Papolos and J. Papolos, *Overcoming Depression* (New York: Harper & Row, 1987), p. 47.
3. *USA Today*, 8 October 1991, pp. D 1–2.
4. E. McGrath et al., *Women and Depression: Risk Factors and Treatment Issues* (Washington, D.C.: American Psychological Association, 1990), p. 2.
5. Papolos and Papolos, p. 47.
6. E. McGrath, "The Depressions Past, Present, Future: What You Need to Know," Distinguished Centennial Address, American Psychological Association National Convention, Washington, D.C., August 1992.
7. Papolos and Papolos, p. 45.
8. R. R. Fieve, *Moodswing* (New York: Bantam, 1989), pp. 83–86.
9. Gold, p. 197.

3. The Traditional Core: Our Cultural Conscience

1. *New York Times,* 10 December 1990, p. A22.
2. *New York Times,* 30 January 1991, p. A16.
3. *USA Today,* 27 February 1990, p. A9.
4. "Women: The Road Ahead," *Time* special edition (Fall 1990).
5. K. Dychtwald, *Age Wave* (Los Angeles: Jeremy P. Tarcher, Inc. 1989).
6. J. K. Belsky, *Here Tomorrow* (New York: Ballantine Books, 1988).
7. Aging and Mental Health, Census Bureau, 1986.
8. S. Faludi, *Backlash: The Undeclared War Against American Women* (New York: Crown, 1991), p. 37.
9. Ibid., p. 36.
10. C. A. Emmons et al., "Stress, Support and Coping Among Women Professionals with Preschool Children," in *Stress Between Work and Family,* ed. J. Eckenrode and S. Gore (New York: Plenum Press, 1990), p. 89.

4. Victimization Depression

1. L. E. A. Walker, *The Battered Woman Syndrome* (New York: Springer, 1984).
2. S. Faludi, *Backlash: The Undeclared War Against American Women* (New York: Crown, 1991), pp. 20–23.
3. E. McGrath et al., *Women and Depression: Risk Factors and Treatment Issues* (Washington, D.C.: American Psychological Association, 1990), p. xii.
4. Faludi, pp. xvi, 464.
5. McGrath et al., p. 26.
6. C. L. Mithers, "The War Against Women," *Ladies Home Journal* (October 1989), pp. 137–139, 226–228.
7. *New York Times,* 17 January 1989, p. B1.
8. L. S. Brown, "From Alienation to Connection: Feminist Therapy with Post-Traumatic Stress Disorder," *Women and Therapy,* vol. 5 (1987), pp. 13–26.
9. Mithers, pp. 137–139, 226–228.
10. S. Nolen-Hoeksema, *Sex Differences in Depression* (Stanford, California: Stanford University Press, 1990), p. 92.
11. Mithers, p. 139.
12. *USA Today,* 15 April 1991, p. A13.
13. *USA Today,* 15 November 1990, p. A1.
14. *New York Times,* 5 May 1989, p. A35.
15. McGrath et al., p. xii.
16. *USA Today,* 18 July 1990, p. A2.
17. P. Plagens et al., "Violence In Our Culture," *Newsweek* (1 April 1991), pp. 49–51.
18. "The Invisible Woman," *Adweek* (6 July 1987), p. 4.
19. *Media Watch* 3, no. 1 (Spring 1989).
20. McGrath et al., p. 61.
21. Faludi, p. 338.
22. S. de Beauvoir, *The Second Sex* (New York: Alfred A. Knopf, 1953), p. 331.

5. Relationship Depression

1. I. Gotleband and V. Whiften, "Marital Problems and Treatment Outcome in Depressed Women," *British Journal of Psychiatry* 151 (1987), pp. 652–659.

2. R. Cooper, *The Performance Edge* (Boston: Houghton Mifflin, 1991), p.104.

6. Age Rage Depression

Virginia Satir's quote cited in Laurel King, *Women of Power* (Berkeley, California: Celestial Arts, 1989), p. 36.

1. E. McGrath et al., *Women and Depression: Risk Factors and Treatment Issues* (Washington, D.C.: American Psychological Association, 1990), p. 57.

2. *New York Times*, 14 September 1987, p. B7.

3. D. C. Kimmel, *Adulthood and Aging* (New York: John Wiley, 1990), p. 14.

4. J. Grambs, *Women Over Forty* (New York: Springer, 1989), p. 3.

5. A. Purvis, "A Perilous Gap," *Time* special edition (Fall 1990), p. 67.

6. K. Dychtwald, *Age Wave* (Los Angeles: Jeremy P. Tarcher 1989), p. 269.

7. J. Thornton, "The Cellulite Report," *Self* (June 1992), p. 136.

8. M. Beck, "Going for the Gold," *Newsweek* (23 April 1991), p. 75.

9. U.S. Bureau of the Census, *Projections of the Population*, 1989.

10. McGrath et al., p. xii.

11. Susan Faludi, *Backlash: The Undeclared War Against American Women* (New York: Crown, 1991), p. xiii.

12. P. Uhlenberg and M. A. Meyers, "Divorce and the Elderly," *Gerontologist* 21, no. 3 (1981), pp. 276–282.

13. B. Myerhoff, *Number Our Days* (New York: Dutton, 1979), pp. 250–251.

14. E. H. Erikson, J. M. Erikson, and H. Q. Kivnick, *Vital Involvement in Old Age* (New York: W. W. Norton, 1986), p. 62.

15. *New York Times*, 29 May 1991, p. C10.

16. C. Bowe, "The Up Generation," *Lear's* (December 1990), p. 68.

17. Erikson, Erikson, and Kivnick, p. 62.

18. J. K. Belsky, *Here Tomorrow* (New York: Ballantine Books, 1988), p. 39.

19. *New York Times*, 30 September 1990, sec. 4A, p. 12.

20. P. Hamill, "Losing It at the Fat Farm," *Lear's* (May 1989), p. 139.

21. *New York Times*, 30 September 1990, sec. 4A, p. 12.

22. Belsky, p. 66.

23. *Older American Reports* (12 May 1989), p. 189.

24. J. M. Oldham and R. S. Liebest, *The Middle Years: New Psychoanalytic Perspective* (New Haven: Yale University Press, 1989).

25. *New York Times*, 6 February 1990, pp. C1, C14.

26. Belsky, p. 115.

27. H. Deutsch, *The Psychology of Women, Vol. 2: Motherhood* (New York: Grune and Stratton, 1945).

28. P. King, "The (Meno)pause That Refreshes," *Psychology Today* (December 1988), p. 11.

29. K. Blaker, *Celebrating Fifty* (Chicago: Contemporary Books, 1990), p. 4.

30. Bowe, p. 68.

31. J. Naisbitt and P. Aburdene, *Megatrends 2000* (New York: William Morrow, 1990), p. 225.

32. Ibid., p. 217.

33. Ibid., p. 230.

34. R. Kalish, "The Social Context of Death and Dying," in *Handbook of Aging and the Social Sciences*, 2nd ed., ed. R. H. Binstock and E. Shanas (New York: Van Nostrand Reinhold, 1985), pp. 149–170.

35. M. A. Lieberman and A. S. Coplan, "Distance from Death as a Variable in the Study of Aging," *Developmental Psychology* 2 (1970), p. 82.

36. Kimmel, p. 355.

37. Belsky, p. 47.

38. *USA Today*, 1 April 1991, p. D4.

39. National Institute on Aging, *Special Report* (1988), p. 18.

40. E. Vierck, *Fact Book on Aging* (Santa Barbara, California: ABC-CLIO, 1990), p. 99.

41. S. K. Whitbourne, *The Aging Body: Physiological and Psychological Consequences* (New York: Springer-Verlag, 1985).

42. Vierck, p. 100.

43. Kimmel, p. 354.

44. *Los Angeles Times*, 1 September 1991, pp. E1, E12.

45. U. S. Bureau of the Census, *Statistical Abstracts* 1987–1988, p. 111 (statistics go up to 1985).

46. Vierck, p. 89.

47. Ibid., p. 96.

48. Ibid., p. 97.

49. Vierck, p. 93.

50. L. M. Verbugge, "An Epidemiological Profile of Older Women," in *The Physical and Mental Health of Older Women*, ed. M. R. Haug, A. B. Ford, and M. Sheafor (New York: Springer, 1984), pp. 194–206.

51. Belsky, p. 8.

52. "The Myths of Menopause," *Health* (March 1991), p. 85.

53. National Institute on Aging, *Answers About Aging* 3, Riggs, 1988: vol. 3.

54. Vierck, p. 85.

55. Ibid., pp. 119–121.

56. Kimmel, p. 504.

57. Vierck, p. 85.

58. Belsky, pp. 166–167.

59. U. S. Bureau of the Census, *Statistical Abstracts* 1987–1988, p. 37.

60. E. Shanas, "The Family as a Social Support System in Old Age," *Gerontologist* 19 (1979), pp. 169–174.

61. D. J. Ekerdt, R. Bosse, and S. Levkoff, "An Empirical Test for Phases of Retirement: Findings from the Normative Aging Study," *Journal of Gerontology* 40 (1985), pp. 95–101.

62. J. Liang and E. J.-C. Tu, "Estimating Lifetime Risk of Nursing Home Residency: A Further Note," *Gerontologist* 26 (1986), pp. 560–563.

63. U.S. Bureau of the Census, *Money Income*, October 1989, p. 66.

64. R. May, "Contributions of Existential Psychotherapy," in *Existence: A New Dimension in Psychiatry and Psychology*, ed. R. May, E. Angel, and H. F. Ellenberger (New York: Basic Books, 1958), p. 49.

65. Vierck, p. 48.

66. Belsky, p. 166.

67. Ibid., p. 170.

68. Ibid., p. 169.

69. Ibid., p. 168.

70. Ibid., p. 169.

71. Vierck, p. 141.

72. Kimmel, p. 430.

73. R. Ornstein and C. Swencionis, *The Healing Brain: A Scientific Reader* (New York: Guilford Press, 1990), p. 6.

74. Kimmel, p. 437.

75. M. Miller, "Geriatric Suicide: The Arizona Study," *Gerontologist* 18 (1978), pp. 488–495.

76. W. H. Masters and V. E. Johnson, *Human Sexual Response* (Boston: Little Brown, 1966).

77. S. C. Bakos, "Over-40 Fitness and Health: Endless Desire," *Harper's Bazaar* (August 1990), p. 36.

78. Ibid., p. 36.

79. Ibid.

7. Depletion Depression

Claudia Black's quote cited in Laurel King, *Women of Power* (Berkeley, California: Celestial Arts, 1989), p. 63.

1. *USA Today*, November 13, 1989, p. D3.

2. A. Hochchild, *The Second Shift: Working Parents and the Revolution at Home* (New York: Viking, 1989).

3. M. Levinson, "Living on the Edge," *Newsweek* (4 November 1991), p. 22.

4. *USA Today*, 4 December 1991, p. A8.

5. *New York Times*, 15 February 1990, pp. A1, A22.

6. L. Dotto, *Losing Sleep* (New York: William Morrow, 1990).

7. A. Toufexis, "Drowsy America," *Time* (17 December 1990), p. 78.

8. *USA Today*, 21 November 1991, p. D1.

9. *Los Angeles Times*, 22 October 1991, p. E12.

10. "Some Help for Working Moms," *Time* (9 April 1990), p. 39.

11. Ibid.

12. Ibid.

13. E. McGrath, "The Price of Being a Working Mother," symposium presentation, American Psychological Association National Convention, San Francisco, August 1991.

14. E. McGrath et al., *Women and Depression: Risk Factors and Treatment Issues* (Washington, D.C.: American Psychological Association, 1990), p. 24.

15. V. N. Salgado de Snyder, "Factors Associated with Acculturative Stress and Depressive Symptomotology Among Married Mexican Immigrant Women," *Psychology of Women Quarterly* 11 (1987), pp. 475–488.

16. N. F. Russo and E. L. Olmedo, "Women's Utilization of Outpatient Psychiatric Services: Some Emerging Priorities for Rehabilitation Psychologists," *Rehabilitation Psychology* 28, pp. 141–155.

17. S. Halgesen, *The Female Advantage: Women's Ways of Leadership* (New York: Doubleday Currency, 1990), pp. 71–103.

8. Body Image Depression

1. N. Wolf, *The Beauty Myth* (New York: William Morrow, 1991), p. 12.

2. E. Melamed, quoted in *Meditations for Women Who Do Too Much,* ed. Anne Schaef (New York: HarperCollins, 1991), June 13 entry.

3. *New York Times,* 7 February 1991, p. B15.

4. J. Rodin, "Body Mania," *Psychology Today* (January/February 1992), pp. 56–60.

5. M. Duffy, "The War of the Noses," *Time* (30 September 1991), p. 50.

6. Standard and Poor's *Industry Surveys 1991,* vol. 159, no. 47 (28 November 1991), p. 85.

7. Wolf, p. 17.

8. *USA Today,* 21 January 1991, p. D1.

9. A. Toufexis, "Broader Figures," *Time* (8 July 1991), p. 50.

10. Centers for Disease Control, Youth Behavioral Risk Survey, M.M.W.R., Department of Nutrition, 1991.

11. *USA Today,* 8 January 1990, p. D1.

12. *American Health* (October 1990), p. 52.

13. *USA Today,* 9 January 1990, p. A1.

14. *USA Today,* 7 October 1991, p. A1.

15. *New York Times,* 23 February 1989, p. B10.

16. S. Faludi, *Backlash: The Undeclared War Against American Women* (New York: Crown, 1991), p. 171.

17. *Wall Street Journal,* 27 September 1985, p. B1.

18. *Los Angeles Times,* 22 December 1991, p. A42.

19. J. Rivers, "Rivers Redux," *People* (4 November 1991), p. 125.

20. *Sunday Times* (London), 16 September 1990, Sec. 7, p. 1.

21. *Los Angeles Times,* 22 December 1991, p. A42.

22. Faludi, p. 218.

23. *USA Today,* 26 September 1991, p. D1.

24. S. Wampler, "Mirror: The Changing Face of Beauty," *Indianapolis Business Journal* (February 1990), sec. 3, p. 1.

25. M. James, *Hearts On Fire* (Los Angeles: Jeremy P. Tarcher, 1991), pp. 10–13.

9. Mind ↔ Body Depression

1. M. Gold, *The Good News About Depression* (New York: Bantam Books, 1986), p. 23.

2. S. Gollub, "Menstrual Cycle Symptoms from a Developmental Perspective" in *Sexuality: New Perspectives,* ed. Z. Defries, R. C. Freidman, and R. Corn (Westport, Connecticut: Greenwood, 1992).

3. E. McGrath, et al., *Women and Depression: Risk Factors and Treatment Issues* (Washington, D.C.: American Psychological Association, 1990), p. 9.

4. *New York Times,* 8 January 1991, p. C3.

5. J. Endicott et al., "Premenstrual Changes and Affective Disorders," *Psychosomatic Medicine* 43 (1981), pp. 519–530.

6. P. E. Craig, "Premenstrual Tension and the Menopause," *Medical Times* 81 (1983), p. 485.

7. McGrath et al., p. 10.

8. Ibid.

9. *USA Today*, 12 September 1991, p. D5.

10. E. Goode, "Mind Health: The Winter Blues," *Vogue* (February 1990), p. 230.

11. McGrath et al., p. 61.

12. *USA Today*, 2 July 1991, p. A1.

13. *USA Today*, 3 October 1990, p. A1.

14. J. Lewis, *So Your Doctor Recommended Surgery* (New York: Henry Holt, 1992), p. 72.

15. S. M. Wolfe, *Women's Health Alert* (Reading, Massachusetts: Addison-Wesley, 1991), p. 73.

16. M. Beck and I. Winkelgreen, "Miscarriages," *Newsweek* (15 August 1988), p. 46.

17. Wolfe, p. 40.

18. Ibid., p. 48.

19. Ibid.

20. Zussman et al., "Sexual Response after Hysterectomy-Oophorectomy: Recent Studies and Reconsideration of Psychogenesis," *American Journal of Obstetrics and Gynecology* (1981).

21. *New York Times*, 9 January 1990, p. C1.

22. J. McKinley and S. McKinley, "Depression in Middle-Aged Women: Social Circumstances vs. Estrogen Deficiency," *Harvard Medical School Mental Health Newsletter* 2, no. 10 (1986) pp. 1–2.

23. N. F. Russo, "Adolescent Abortion: The Epidemiological Context," in *Adolescent Abortion: Psychological and Legal Issues*, ed. G. B. Melton (Lincoln: University of Nebraska Press, 1986), pp. 40–73.

24. L. Cohen and S. Roth, *Journal of Human Stress* 10, no. 3 (1984), pp. 140–145.

25. J. Williams, *Psychology of Women* (New York: W. W. Norton, 1983), p. 390.

26. E. W. Freeman, "Influence of Personality Attributes on Abortion Experiences," *American Journal of Orthopsychiatry* 47 (1977), pp. 503–513.

27. Williams, p. 382.

28. "What Causes Infertility?" *American Health* (October 1990), p. 12.

29. M. D. Mazor, "Emotional Reactions to Infertility," in *Infertility: Medical, Emotional and Social Considerations*, ed. M. D. Mazor and H. F. Simmons (New York: Human Sciences Press, 1984), pp. 23–55.

30. S. J. Freeman, M. K. O'Neil, and W. J. Lance, "Sex Differences in Depression in University Students," *Social Psychiatry* 20, no. 4 (1985), pp. 184–190.

31. K. J. Connolly, R. J. Edelman, and I. D. Cooke, "Distress and Marital Problems Associated with Infertility," *Journal of Reproductive and Infant Psychology* 5 (1987), pp. 49–57.

32. K. McCarthy, "Victims of Crimes Incur Rise in Health Problems," *APA Monitor* (November 1990), p. 43.

33. J. Morrison, "Childhood Sexual History of Women with Somatization Disorder," *American Journal of Psychiatry* 146, no. 2 (February 1989), p. 239.

34. McCarthy, p. 43.

35. *New York Times*, 6 September 1990, p. B15.

36. *New York Times*, 15 November 1990, p. B12.

37. Ibid.

38. Gold, p. 23.

39. K. Wells, "The Functioning and Well-being of Depressed Patients," *Journal of the American Medical Association* 262, no. 7 (18 August 1989), p. 914.

40. "Depression and Depressive Symptoms in Smoking Cessation," *Comprehensive Psychiatry* 31 (1990), pp. 350–354.

41. A. Glassman, "New Approaches to Smoking Cessation," *Physician Assistant* (November 1991), pp. 69–77.

42. S. Squires, "Why Women Can't Quit," *Vogue* (April 1991), p. 310.

43. *New York Times*, 15 November 1988, p. C3.

44. "Health and Fitness," *Vogue* (October 1990), p. 286.

45. Gold, p. 104.

46. Wolfe, p. 147.

47. Ibid., p. 151.

48. Gold, p. 118.

49. W. Styron, *Darkness Visible: A Memoir of Madness* (New York: Random House, 1990), p. 71–72.

50. McGrath, et al., p. 69.

51. E. D. Nottelmann et al., "Gonadal and Adrenal Hormone Correlates of Self-concept in Early Adolescence," presented at the meeting of the Society for Pediatric Research, San Francisco, May 1984.

52. Gold, p. 123.

53. J. A. Hamilton, B. L. Parry, and S. J. Blumenthal, "The Menstrual Cycle in Context I: Affective Syndromes Associated with Reproductive Hormonal Changes," *Journal of Clinical Psychiatry* (March 1988), p. 5.

54. "Medical Newsflash," *Self* (May 1991), p. 82.

55. *Los Angeles Times*, 8 December 1991, pp. 1, 40.

56. *USA Today*, 25 November 1991, p. D1.

57. R. Ornstein and C. Swencionis, *The Healing Brain: A Scientific Reader* (New York: Guilford Press, 1990), p. 6.

58. *USA Today*, 12 November 1991, p. D1.

59. Ornstein and Swencionis, p. 72.

60. Ibid., p. 5.

61. *USA Today*, 15 April 1991, p. A1.

62. Ibid.

63. Ibid.

64. *USA Today*, 20 December 1991, p. D1.

65. "Help Yourself To Health" brochure, AMA Women's Health Campaign, American Medical Association, 1991.

66. C. Tarvis, *Every Woman's Well Being* (New York: Prentice Hall, 1990), p. 345.

67. *USA Today*, 20 December 1991, p. D1.

68. *Los Angeles Times*, 8 May 1992, p. A1.

69. *USA Today*, 20 December 1991, p. D1.

70. Ornstein and Swencionis, p. 224.

71. T. Adler, "Optimists' Coping Skills May Help Beat Illness," *APA Monitor* (February 1991), p. 12.

72. R. Laforge, speech given at Rancho LaPuerta, Tecate, Mexico, 9 May 1992.

73. *USA Today*, 24 December 1991, p. D1.

10. Beyond Self-help

1. E. McGrath et al., *Women and Depression: Risk Factors and Treatment Issues* (Washington, D.C.: American Psychological Association, 1990), p. xi.

2. R. Eichner, "Energy Crisis," *Runner's World* (December 1990), p. 68.

3. F. K. Goodwin and D. R. Jamison, *Manic-Depressive Illness* (New York: Oxford University Press, 1990).

4. Ibid.

5. I. Elkin et al., National Institute of Mental Health, Treatment of Depression Collaborative Research Program: General Effectiveness of Treatments, *Archives of General Psychiatry* 42 (1985), pp. 305–316.

6. M. Seligman, *Learned Optimism* (New York: Alfred A. Knopf, 1991), pp. 54–70.

7. D. Burns, *Feeling Good: The New Mood Therapy* (New York: Signet, 1980), pp. 40–41.

8. J. Bradshaw, *Healing the Shame That Binds You* (Deerfield Beach, Florida: Health Communications, 1988).

9. McGrath et al., p. 67.

10. I. Smith, S. Adkins, and J. Walton, "Pharmaceuticals: Theraputic Review," Shearson Lehman Hutton International Research Publication, New York, January 1988.

11. McGrath et al., p. 67.

12. Ibid.

13. M. M. Weissman et al., "The Efficacy of Drugs and Psychotherapy in the Treatment of Acute Depressive Episodes," *American Journal of Psychiatry* 136 (1979), pp. 555–558.

14. Goodwin and Jamison, p. 161.

15. McGrath et al., p. 65.

16. M. Gold, *The Good News About Depression* (New York: Bantam Books, 1986), p. 39.

11. Putting It All Together: Action Strategies for Resolving the Healthy Depressions

1. E. McGrath et al., *Women and Depression: Risk Factors and Treatment Issues* (Washington, D.C.: American Psychological Association, 1990), p. 50.

2. S. Nolen-Hoeksema, *Sex Differences in Depression* (Stanford, California: Stanford University Press, 1990), pp. 162–169, 175.

3. A. Rich, *Diving into the Wreck* (New York: W. W. Norton, 1973), p. 22.

4. McGrath et al., p. 55.

5. R. Thayer, *The Biopsychology of Mood and Arousal* (New York: Oxford University Press, 1989), pp. 171–174.

6. G. Steinem, *Revolution from Within* (Boston: Little, Brown, 1992).

7. Ibid., p. 263.

8. Ibid., p. 265.

9. Ibid., p. 264.

10. M. Csikszentmihalyi, *Flow: The Psychology of Optimal Experience* (New York: Harper & Row, 1990), p. 71.

11. G. Valliant, "Creativity and Achievement Issues for Women," presentation at the National Convention, American Psychiatric Association, New York, May 1990.

INDEX

Dr. Ellen McGrath and Dr. Harry Wexler cofounded The Psychology Center in 1984. It is a national treatment, consultation, and research center for the application of "state of the art" techniques in relationship skills, depression, substance abuse, and media psychology. The Psychology Center offers workshops, individual and group psychotherapy, and training in Action Therapy for mental health and health professionals.

For an information packet and newsletter, please write, fax, or call:

Dr. Ellen McGrath
The Psychology Center
380 Glenneyre—Suite D
Laguna Beach, CA 92651
Phone: (714) 497-2593
Fax: (714) 497-0913

If you have feedback on the effectiveness of the action strategies described in this book or other strategies you have developed, please write to Dr. McGrath at the above address. Thank you.